In the Shadow of Power

SIN THE HADOW OF POWER

INFLUENCE AND SPIN
DOWN THE CENTURIES

Bob Whittington

Whittles Publishing

Published by
Whittles Publishing Ltd.,
Dunbeath,
Caithness, KW6 6EG,
Scotland, UK

www.whittlespublishing.com

ISBN 978-184995-048-0

Printed by Page Bros, Norwich

CONTENTS

Introduction

An éminence grise is a powerful decision-maker or advisor
who operates 'behind the scenes' or in a non-public or
unofficial capacity. (Wikipedia)

A handwritten letter of introduction to diplomatic contacts in Singapore and Malaysia was enough to guarantee me an audience, and spell nervousness and uncertainty, with the people I had come to see. Why was I there? Who had really sent me? As a young BBC journalist simply travelling on holiday in the Far East and wanting to be better informed I was amazed by the impact and influence still exerted by a man in his sixties sitting at home in Kent enjoying semi-retirement.

At the height of his discreet powers Malcolm MacDonald, the son of a former British Labour Prime Minister and a family friend, had been instrumental in guiding the political fortunes of future national leaders and soothing troubled waters in many countries. His diplomatic ability and easy charm as a 'roving ambassador' were acknowledged at the highest levels and yet he refused all honours save that of the Order of Merit which is in the personal gift of the Queen.

From that day I have been intrigued by the role of the *éminence grise*, the fixer behind the throne, the right-hand man who invariably is close by but just out of focus in the group photographs. He usually operates in the shadows only occasionally stepping into the limelight before slipping quietly from view. Sometimes he is the bearer of messages. He is the conduit between warring factions travelling unnoticed across borders, offering the hand of reconciliation which would be condemned outright if it leaked into the public domain before the *moment juste* when the ground had been prepared and the climate for peace judged opportune.

Not all are men of course; the strong woman behind the successful man is commonplace, but among the names below are those who have turned that role into an art form. They have worked for good and ill, guiding or controlling, advising or cajoling. Some have moved from the bedchamber to positions of absolute power; many just like their male counterparts seem to have been energised by their lowly backgrounds with their innate guile and intelligence simply proving too much for their well-born masters.

The position of the *éminence grise* can be a dangerous one. Just like Icarus in Greek mythology, some have overreached themselves and have paid with their lives for their hubris, the jealousy of their competitors or the suspicion of those they served. Today the consequences of failure are less dramatic although the fall from grace can be just as precipitous.

They come in all guises: diplomats of course, concubines and clerics, politicians and today journalists, plucked from their profession precisely because they know the devious methods of the media. The most astute operators outlast their masters going on to serve others who may even have been enemies of their predecessor; they are accomplished at reading the runes both to protect those they serve and save their own skins.

The term fixer is used in my former profession of broadcasting. The fixer will often be the advanced guard establishing the facts of a story, tracking down interviewees until the correspondent or presenter arrives to stand in front of the camera, deliver his piece to camera and receive all the plaudits. I remember the tale of one fixer saying to a junior reporter who had stumbled into a major story, "I can make you or I can break you." To his credit the reporter was wise enough to follow the advice of his more experienced colleague, read the script he was handed with aplomb and went on to become a star in his own right. The fixer has never been mentioned.

The operating style has changed over time from one of absolute discretion to overt spinning, with even a desire in modern times to share in some of the "fame", an idea which would be anathema to the old practitioners of the art. But their presence has always been a constant factor if you look hard enough; standing among the bodyguards who peer anxiously into the crowds, are the shadow men, as one might call them, only having eyes for their charges. They probably have a folio of papers in their hands which might contain the diary for the day, a copy of a speech or some other briefing notes – and of course nowadays the ubiquitous mobile phone. They will have anticipated every question and ensured that their masters' paths are smooth and trouble free.

In the Shadow of Power is merely a selection of these figures down the ages, some of whom will be unknown to many readers although the masters they served will probably all be familiar names. Once you know to look for them, your eyes will always be glancing away from the players in the front row to see who is standing to one side, head slightly bowed to deflect attention but with antennae twitching for the slightest note of alarm. They are consummate performers, polished, suave and debonair or grey and nondescript, but the best of them are utterly adept at protecting the people they serve with unquestioning loyalty.

I remember one who was a highly skilled Russian linguist, fluent in at least four languages and reputed to be KGB, certainly military, trained and much more than an interpreter. At one reception he had to give a contemporaneous translation of a speech his charge was making. Unfortunately his boss had enjoyed too much of the hospitality on offer and was drunk. As he rambled incoherently in Russian, the interpreter simply delivered in English what the speaker should have been saying. Afterwards another Russian linguist in the audience came up to the interpreter and congratulated him on his performance and his discretion.

In an ideal world that is the role of the fixer, the shadow man. He salvages potential disasters and gives an impression of serenity before vanishing from the scene. In that sense he is like the perfect interviewer of old, asking the questions so the interviewee can give his answer without interruption; it's an old fashioned concept in today's world where the cult of personality makes the interviewer the story. But among the names below are some of the ultimate operators treading carefully through difficult territory, gently nursing out agreements to find common ground between bitter enemies. Others of course have their own agenda. They also have a deft touch but it is a Machiavellian one where the main aim is to gain influence, to manipulate and always to survive.

This book neither praises nor criticises these dark arts, it makes no judgement on the cast of characters these men and women served – that is for other books; these pages simply throw a brief spotlight on the people standing in the shadow of the powerful and occasionally moving into the foreground to seize control.

More often than not shadow men and women are the key ingredients in critical moments of history, totally unremarked, moving like ghosts in those famous corridors of power. Those not bent on achieving fame for themselves are instinctively self-effacing but as they often act as the gate keepers to their masters, protecting them from constant approaches for favours or attention, they also attract enemies and therein lies the danger.

Given the very nature of their position conspiracy theories, innuendoes, lies and half truths abound but that is part and parcel of their everyday existence and it can even be part of the armoury they deploy to achieve their own ends.

They are the unsung heroes who make the wheels of diplomacy turn smoothly. They may also be the villains, the malevolent characters, who sometimes abuse their undoubted positions of power to shift the course of events in unhappy directions, like master puppeteers making the marionettes dance to their tune. Whichever role they choose to play, they are always there on the edges of history, standing at the back of a conference hall perhaps with an incipient smile of satisfaction playing on their lips as the production they have choreographed unfolds.

1

Parmenion (c.400–330 BC)

Hero or cautious incompetent, brave general and trusted bodyguard to the young Alexander the Great or a traitor, the story of Parmenion illustrates well the perils facing the close adviser down the centuries. At the peak of his power he is hailed as a great warrior, at his fall his name is besmirched. Parmenion shows all the key attributes of the fixer. He is a survivor, time and again dodging the assassin's real and metaphorical blade and he is acutely attuned to the manoeuvrings of all around him. Then his luck runs out brought down by false rumour and possibly the jealousy of a master he thought he was serving so loyally.

Parmenion (also referred to as Parmenio) was the son of a nobleman, Philotas, from Upper Macedonia, which is roughly modern day north-west Greece. His nobility as we shall see is not an essential qualification for rising to a position of influence but in those turbulent and treacherous times it surely helped him to climb the military ranks and get noticed.

The danger of being the trusted agent of a king or indeed anyone in power is that they can be too obviously associated with one faction or another. The worst situation is to become ensnared in a family row. There was a very real risk of this happening to Parmenion who on more than one occasion found himself serving a family at war with itself as well as its neighbours.

Parmenion is first noted as a young man in the army of King Amyntas II of Macedonia in 380 BC fighting what seemed to be a constant battle with the Illyrian tribesmen to the north.[1] There was also internal familial fighting and an attempted coup d'état instigated by the king's own wife. Parmenion survived the brutal retribution and executions which followed, marking him out as an astute operator in treacherous political waters.

Amyntas was eventually succeeded by Perdicas III but he was not long on the throne dying in 359 BC while invading Illyria. He was succeeded by his infant son, Amyntas. As he was a child Perdicas's brother, Philip was appointed regent. However Philip wasted no time and within a year ousted his young charge and declared himself King Philip II. In the complicated arrangements of the day Philip found no objection to Amyntas later marrying his daughter, Cynane.

No doubt watching the manoeuvrings from his military quarters, Parmenion would have been relieved when Philip set about gathering the army around him to bolster his position by force if necessary, a strategy followed by leaders to this very day. Wherever Parmenion's own loyalties lay he must have declared himself on Philip's side and was soon serving his new master in his various campaigns. Indeed such was Philip's warlike activity that he lent his name to the term "a Philippic" – an oratorical tirade – originating with Demosthenes[2] in his speeches warning the Greeks about Philip's territorial ambitions, warnings which were ignored.

Regardless of how he came to power, Philip is considered by historians to be a successful king determined to unite and modernise his expanding empire. He was a brave fighter leading from the front. In 356 he defeated the Illyrians, the same year that his son, Alexander, was born; this latter event was a development which would be both the making and undoing of Parmenion in subsequent years.

But for now Parmenion was obviously in the thick of the fighting and, as more victories followed, Philip came to trust his loyal general sending him as a delegate to negotiate peace with Athens in 346. It seems Parmenion was no longer just a general, but also developing as a negotiator and a diplomat. Indeed Parmenion was the only general Philip felt he could trust absolutely even though he was well aware that in those days soldiers tended to show loyalty to their immediate military commanders almost more than to their kings. They fought and lived and died together. But in Parmenion Philip believed he had a reliable ally. In the years ahead Philip's son, Alexander, would become convinced that he did not have the same backing.

As it was, Philip kept his favourite general constantly campaigning on his behalf leading thousands of men into battle often as the spearhead of a much larger force. Fighting alongside Parmenion was Attalus, his son-in-law as well as his second in command.

Another family feud broke out when Philip announced that he intended to take a new bride and marry Cleopatra, the daughter of one of Attalus's brothers. During the wedding banquet, according to some accounts, Attalus openly declared that he hoped Cleopatra would one day produce a son to become the next king of Macedonia. If true it must surely have been the most foolhardy declaration anyone could have made. Eyebrows would surely have been raised and at least one regarded it as a threat rather than the drunken exhortations of a happy relative.

Alexander took umbrage at the open assault on what he felt was his rightful position as heir and sought asylum with his mother, Olympias, in Epirus at the court of her brother, King Alexander of Molossis. With Alexander away in a huff, Attalus simply got on with his soldiering duties but it was a perceived slight Alexander would not forget.

For a time relations between Philip and Alexander deteriorated still further when Alexander allied himself to the neighbouring Illyrians and even seemed to be threatening to invade Macedonia. It was too much for Philip who, in a bid to show his people that the family was united again, decided to repair the rift and threw a party welcoming back the prodigal son. As though to prove all was resolved he also invited Alexander of Molossis to marry one of the royal princesses. The wedding took place but at a festival afterwards Philip was assassinated by a man called Pausanias. A lurid account of Pausanias's grievance with the king is retold in *Bibliotheca Historica* ('Historical Library') by Diodorus Siculus the Greek historian writing between 60–30BC.

Pausanias was both Philip's bodyguard and lover. But when the king's roving eye fell on another soldier, Pausanias wanted revenge and apparently was inspired to take the king's life by his teacher who said the only way he would be remembered in history was "by slaying the man whose achievements were the greatest, for the assassin's fame would endure as long as the great man's." While he succeeded in that ambition, at the time he did not get far and was killed by Philip's bodyguards.

When word of the king's death reached Parmenion who was on expedition in Asia, it must have seemed as though everything was going wrong. For once the Macedonian army had lost a battle against the Greeks at Magnesia and, as he led his battered forces away to regroup, Parmenion would have wondered what was to happen next. Presumably he would have discussed these matters with Attalus who would also have been anxious, perhaps even thinking about succession himself.

But Alexander did not delay. He immediately proclaimed himself king and dispatched his men to kill Attalus on the grounds that he and others had been involved in the conspiracy to kill Philip. A wider plot was possible although accounts seem to suggest it was unlikely and a much more plausible explanation was Alexander's desire to remove any potential rivals and claimants to the throne. If it had been just a drunken outburst at a wedding, it had proved to be a fatal one with far reaching consequences.

Parmenion may have had a hand in his son-in-law's murder or just stood by and allowed it to happen, opinions differ. Some suggest proof of Parmenion's guilt can be seen in the rewards which seemed to follow. Apparently recognising his general's loyalty Alexander appointed several of Parmenion's relatives to important positions in the army. Nicanor, Parmenion's younger son was given the command of an infantry regiment – the so-called Shield Bearers, while his son-in-law, Coenus, and a friend called Amyntas were both given key positions. Parmenion himself was confirmed as second in command under Alexander.[3] No matter how deeply he was or was not involved, Parmenion instinctively seemed to know which way to turn and where the new power in the land lay.

By now Parmenion, in his 60s, had survived palace coups, assassinations and regicide not to mention numerous military campaigns; he was a warrior and an astute political operator and he had risen to become one of seven personal bodyguards to the man who would become known as Alexander the Great. Their families were close: Parmenion's son, Philotas, was a childhood friend of Alexander's own son and was recognised by Alexander who appointed him to command a cavalry unit on an expedition to Asia. However while these ties existed it is not clear that Alexander and Parmenion were particularly close personally, although there is nothing to suggest that Parmenion was anything other than absolutely loyal.

As an elderly military man and confidant to kings of Macedonia in the past, Parmenion had a complicated hand to play. He could certainly count on his own troops but such displays of loyalty to a general rather than the king may have rankled with Alexander. At the very least one could imagine Alexander looking on with a tinge of jealousy as Parmenion's troops rallied round their commander. That is speculation of course but human frailties being what they are it seems likely in view of what was to follow.

From 334 to 330 Alexander and Parmenion were involved in numerous battles taking the Macedonians into Persia, central Turkey and Syria. But the king's ambitions attracted the attention of another, King Darius III of Persia who was sitting in Babylon watching the approaching Macedonian forces with concern. He decided to march against them.

At the time Alexander was ill so he dispatched loyal Parmenion to capture the harbour town of Issus and be on the lookout for Darius's advancing army. At the Battle of Issus which followed Alexander deployed innovative tactics and succeeded in routing Darius's troops while Darius himself fled leaving behind great treasures as well as his mother, wife and children who were all taken hostage. They must have feared for their lives but in fact they were treated well, much to Alexander's credit.

As for Parmenion it appears he could do no wrong and even felt emboldened enough to suggest that Alexander take a Persian wife to cement relations between the warring factions. It seems Parmenion had assumed the role of match-maker along with his other functions.

Over the two years following the Battle of Issus, Alexander swept along the Mediterranean coast, occupied Egypt and marched further into Syria threatening the very heart of the Persian Empire.

In 331 he prepared himself to take on Darius once more, this time at Gaugamela near present day Mosul. Again huge numbers, possibly more than 300,000 men although estimates differ, were ranged against each other. Darius, despite his superiority in numbers, still feared another defeat and sent his emissaries to negotiate a truce. He offered an alliance with Alexander, the surrender of vast swathes of territory and the payment of a huge ransom for his relatives. Parmenion, perhaps weary of the fighting or overly cautious as his critics might say, advised his king to accept. This gave rise to the reported quote in *Lives* by the Greek historian Plutarch: "If I were Alexander I would accept the terms" to which Alexander replied: "So would I if I were Parmenion."

There is doubt about the veracity of the quote suggesting it amounts to early day negative spin to show Parmenion's weakness, and some versions of the fighting which followed paint Parmenion in a poor light. Nevertheless it is at this point that Parmenion's star begins to wane.

Accounts of the battle itself make dramatic reading[4] with Alexander demonstrating superior strategy. He divided his Macedonian forces in two – he led one half and Parmenion was given command of the other. Alexander's tactics prevailed tempting Darius into a trap using large wedge shaped formations to drive into the heart of the Persian forces. The Persians were routed once and for all but again it looked as though Darius would escape from Alexander's clutches as he had done at Issus. This is where the disinformation about Parmenion appears to gather momentum.

Alexander knew that if he pursued and killed Darius he could bring the fighting in Persia to end, because the Persian Empire was now in terminal decline. But Parmenion sent urgent messages that he and his men were in trouble. They needed backup in modern parlance. In his account of the battle the Greek historian of the time, Callistenes, a nephew of Aristotle, used this apparent failure of Parmenion to discredit him. The negative spinning against his reputation was thus in full swing.

Alexander was in no doubt where his duty as a soldier lay and he came to Parmenion's rescue allowing Darius to make good his escape. However, having driven off the remnants of the Persian army and saved Parmenion, Alexander was soon in hot pursuit of his prey.

Darius tried in vain to inspire his bedraggled forces, telling them that he would regroup, raise a new army and return to defeat Alexander. It appears few were convinced and he was murdered by Bessus, one of his own commanders who had fought in the Battle of Gaugamela. Alexander felt both cheated and strangely angered by the betrayal of Darius when he came upon his body. He ordered that Darius should be buried showing all due deference that one would accord a king even though he was an enemy. Alexander then hunted down Bessus who was eventually handed over by his own men showing as little loyalty as Bessus had done. His end was brutal. Some say he was crucified, others that he was tortured then killed.

Meanwhile Parmenion, who was then almost seventy, was given one more assignment: the capture of Ecbatana, capital of the Achaemenid Empire. What is important for our story here is that Alexander and Parmenion were apart when Darius was discovered and he did not know of the fate that befell his own son, Philotas, shortly afterwards.

Philotas was everything his father was not: he was arrogant, full of pride with none of the diplomatic airs and graces expected of a loyal courtier. He had been promoted to commander of the Companions, the Macedonian cavalry who literally rode alongside the King and accompanied him into battle. One can presume that he had his eye on even greater power and because of his rank he probably assumed he was untouchable having already seen off previous rumours accusing him of treachery. He would certainly not have been expecting a threat to come from within his own family.

Parmenion (c.400–330 BC)

However in 330 Coenus, Philotas's brother-in-law who had been given military promotion possibly on the strength of his family connections, was among others who denounced Philotas as a traitor for plotting to overthrow the king. He was tortured, forced to reveal the names of other co-conspirators and then either stoned or speared to death.

Alexander now felt that he had no choice. He had to assume that Parmenion himself was also involved in the conspiracy and decided that he had to kill him before news of his son's death reached his encampment. He immediately sent his soldiers to find Parmenion and execute him. In all probability Parmenion was oblivious of what he had supposedly done wrong, right up to the moment the blade struck.

In the end Parmenion paid the price of a family tie and probably not for any false step. His career as a military commander appears to have been exemplary right up to and probably including the Battle of Gaugamela. He evidently commanded the loyalty of his troops which may have ultimately counted against him; Alexander would have been as aware as anyone of the importance of his army's backing.

Nevertheless for a soldier of undoubted bravery Parmenion lived to a good age, and for a loyal courtier, adviser and go-between his survival to 69 years may well have been even more remarkable. This ability to rise to a position of influence and to be able to cling on to that position for so long without being stabbed literally or metaphorically in the back makes Parmenion stand out as an accomplished operator in the shadows of power.

He is also an example of other military men who turned their leadership skills to political activity with mixed success; sometimes their heroic efforts of the past are blighted by a fall at the end of their careers and that is all they are remembered for. In modern times one can think of General Colin Powell who rose to be US Secretary of State under President George Bush. Although regarded as a first class soldier and a moderate Secretary of State preferring negotiation to force, he will always be remembered for his convincing performance at a plenary session of the United Nations Security Council in 2003. There he spoke in favour of military action against Iraq's Saddam Hussein citing first hand information from Iraqi defectors proving conclusively that "there can be no doubt that Saddam Hussein has biological weapons and the capability to rapidly produce more, many more." The following year the Iraq Survey Group concluded that his evidence was inaccurate and based on out of date material and other discrepancies. The invasion of Iraq was launched on a lie. Saddam Hussein was toppled of course but no such weapons were ever found. It put paid to any ambitions Powell may have had in running for the White House.

Powell had been fed the information by his advisers and intelligence experts and he had simply delivered the address in good faith. Parmenion it seems had also acted and served in good faith and there is no credible evidence to the contrary. For the former it had cost him potential greatness as a future leader of the Western World, for the latter it had cost him his life.

The question for all advisers is how far do they go in their chosen role and to a large extent it is something of a performance; they have to persuade the individuals they serve to pursue a particular course of action and they have to convince the supporting cast of courtiers, each anxious to make his or her own mark, that they are right. All advisers know that their time is short and they will eventually be replaced, but while they are in post they have to make the most of all the skills at their disposal. It helps of course to play the part if you are an actor or actress in the first place as the next account illustrates.

2

Empress Theodora (c.500–548 AD)

It would be difficult to make up a story such as the life of Theodora. Rags to riches does not do it justice. How do you combine the virtues of a saint with the morals of a concubine, the antics of a striptease artist with the authority of an Empress? And yet Theodora was all of these things in her short life. She was just as skilful an operator in the world of Byzantine politics and religion as she was able to woo the nobility and royalty with her charms on stage. She may have reached a position of power thanks to her marriage to a future emperor and to that extent she was in the shadow of power, but once there she took command at a critical point in their lives and quite literally saved an empire. What she lacked in education she more than made up in instinctive self-preservation and innate wisdom. She was a role model for feminists, a defender of the abused and, in today's world of self-help gurus, a beacon of what you can achieve if you put your mind to it.

The period of the Early Middle Ages in European history between the 5th and 10th centuries – also known as the Dark Ages – marked a steady decline in literature, culture and trade. However, it should be noted that the term Dark Ages was a concept conceived by the Italian scholar, Petrarch, to register more narrowly what he saw as a lack of Latin literature. Nevertheless in contrast to the evident decline in what was formerly the

Western Roman Empire, in the Eastern or Byzantine Empire life flourished and in 324 Emperor Constantine declared its capital to be Constantinople – the City of Constantine. While the Roman Empire collapsed in the 5th century, Byzantium would survive and prosper for another thousand years.

It was into this thriving environment that Theodora was born. Her father, Acacius, was a humble bear trainer in the city's Hippodrome or circus (a large amphitheatre) which was connected to the emperor's palace – an important juxtaposition as will become apparent. However when Acacius died and the bear act presumably passed to another, Theodora's mother, herself an actress and dancer, had to diversify to support the family. She turned to the only skill she had and quickly trained her three daughters as beguiling dancers to entertain the crowds in the Hippodrome.

Theodora evidently became the star turn with her promiscuous act. According to the historian, Procopius[5], upon whom most accounts about Theodora's life to a greater or lesser extent rely, Theodora supplemented her performances by following her sister, Komito, to work in a brothel; the twin occupations of seductive actress on stage and temptress off were almost the norm. Procopius spares us no detail in his description of her performances as Leda and The Swan with trained geese pecking grains of seed from her all but naked body and off stage she was much sought after for entertainment at banquets for the nobility. But Procopius, to whom we will return a little later, paints two different images of Theodora.

While still only 16, Theodora left home to travel with a Syrian official called Hecebolus, who had been appointed governor to the Eastern coastal region of Libya, Pentapolis, also known as Cyrenaica. But Hecebolus mistreated Theodora, which certainly influenced her in later life, and she eventually left him returning to Constantinople by way of Alexandria in Egypt. It was while she was in Egypt that her lifestyle changed. She may have been inspired by the life of Patriarch Timothy III of Alexandria to convert to his religion, Monophysite Christianity[6].

When she finally returned to Constantinople, still only 22 years old, she was apparently a reformed character and took up wool spinning. Although a far cry from the glamour of dancing before the crowds in the Hippodrome, she still managed to attract the attention of Justinian, nephew of the Emperor Justin 1. Justinian was from humble stock, the son of a farmer, and had been virtually adopted by the Emperor. This lack of noble airs and graces may have played a part in their mutual attraction. It was not long before she moved into his private residence, the Palace of Hormizd on the shores of the Sea of Marmara, as his mistress and was showered with gifts and crucially an upgrading in her status to patrician.

Justinian soon declared his intention to marry Theodora, who was about 20 years his junior, but there was an impediment. As heir to his uncle's throne according to Constantine's law, Justinian could not marry an 'actress'; it would have been the equivalent today of giving him a bad press. But the emperor had a soft spot for Theodora and in due course repealed the law thus allowing the couple to wed in 525. By the time they married Theodora had already given birth to a daughter although it is not clear if Justinian was the father. Nevertheless he evidently accepted the child as his own.

In the latter part of his reign as old age and senility took its toll Justin relied increasingly on his nephew. Finally in 527 Justin died and Justinian was proclaimed emperor with Theodora at his side on the throne. Actress to Empress in little over a decade – it was a tremendous leap in fortune which may have been luck or possibly guile. Her dancing was clearly meant to tempt a noble suitor but finding a home near the palace on her return from Egypt would have been no accident. She may also have benefitted from an introduction from another dancer called Macedonia, who was said to have been an informer to Justinian.

However it came about, it seems clear that this was a definite partnership as Justinian relied heavily on Theodora's advice no doubt putting the noses of the more noble courtiers out of joint.

One of the key moments of his rule was a critical decision on the handling of the so-called Nika riots in 532 at a chariot race in Constantinople. Supporters of the charioteers had their own groups: Reds, Blues, Greens and Whites. The most influential were the Blues and Greens – Justinian supported the Blues. They were much like modern day football fans although as this was the only outlet for complaint in their lives minor riots between the factions were commonplace during and after races. That year the crowds, who were already angry over high taxes and stories of political corruption, turned violent. At the same time two men, a Blue and a Green, who had been arrested for murder, escaped and sought sanctuary in a church which was surrounded by a mob. In an attempt to defuse the situation, Justinian announced that there would be another chariot race in the Hippodrome on 13 January. His ruse didn't work.

The usual chants of 'Blue' or 'Green' to spur on their favoured charioteers turned to 'Nika' which means conquer. The threats united the rival groups who directed their anger at Justinian who was watching on. The racing was soon forgotten and the mobs began attacking the palace overlooking the Hippodrome; for the next five days Justinian and his court were effectively under siege. Fires raged and much of the city was burned down.

This was when Theodora's strength and influence came into play. Justinian was all in favour of fleeing the city and saving his own life, but Theodora had other ideas. She exhorted her husband to stand his ground and said she had no intention of leaving quoting the lines: "Royalty is a fine burial shroud" or as another version has it: "Purple makes a fine shroud." Clearly having pulled herself up from her lowly background to become empress she was not prepared to run away from it all. If she had to die she wanted to die a royal not a fugitive in exile.

Justinian, suitably stirred, conceived of a plan which involved his eunuch going to the Hippodrome and discretely distributing gold among his favoured Blues, effectively causing a split between the rioters. As the Blues drifted away, Justinian sent in his Imperial Guard led by General Belisarius to deal with the remaining protestors. According to Procopius, they killed some 30,000 people in a single day – a terrible casualty list which has probably never been exceeded in putting down a riot.

This marked the turning point of Justinian's reign and clearly cemented Theodora's position as an absolute equal. It also marks a divergence in opinion about the Empress – was she really the saint she is revered as being by some today or the manipulating schemer whose own decisions had also contributed to the Nika riots? She would have backed the assault by the Imperial Guard for the simple reason that if it proved successful she would remain Empress. One thing is certain Theodora saved Justinian's throne that day.

Even Procopius, diligent scribe to General Belisarius, has given us conflicting accounts in the books he wrote about Justinian, his battles and his public works. It was only in his *Secret History* published later that he reveals what he interprets as the unsavoury aspect of the Emperor and Empress's reign.

On the positive side there is little doubt that Justinian's rule witnessed great achievements. Following the devastation of the city in the Nika riots, he set about rebuilding Constantinople's infrastructure along with more than 25 churches. The most famous of these is the Hagia Sophia, one of the architectural wonders of the world. With its mighty dome, it stood as the largest cathedral in the world for more than a thousand years, until Seville

Cathedral was built in the early 16th century. When Constantinople fell to the Ottoman Empire in 1453 Sultan Mehmed II ordered that the building be transformed into a mosque and the four minarets we see now were added. Today it is a museum in modern day Istanbul.

Theodora's influence on religion in her husband's empire is an illustration of the mixed press she has received. On the one hand, although Justinian was a Chalcedonian, she built a Monophysite monastery in Sykae and went so far as to provide sanctuary in the palace when Monophysite followers came under attack from Chalcedonian Christians[7]. On the other hand when Pope Silverius resisted her demands for the dismissal of Agapetus I as Patriarch of Constantinople she thought nothing of dispatching General Belisarius to Rome to remove Silverius and supplant him as Pope with Vigilius, who was papal legate in Constantinople at the time. Vigilius had promised in advance to restore Anthimus to Patriarch in the city. The Chalcedonians inevitably regarded Theodora as nothing short of a heretic.

She was also perfectly happy to outwit her husband on religious matters. When the Coptic Pope in Alexandria, Timothy III, a Monophysite of course, died she arranged for Theodosius to succeed him even though Justinian wanted a Chalcedonian to be enthroned.

The spiritual and legal blur with Theodora is evident when it comes to her efforts to protect women and young girls in their struggle against abuse and exploitation. She is regarded as one of the first feminists and campaigner for women's rights, no doubt as a result of the treatment she received as a young girl at the hands of Hecebolus and others. She arranged for laws to be passed banning prostitution and she had the brothels closed. She built a convent where former prostitutes could support themselves, the death penalty was introduced for rape and women won certain rights to keep charge of their children in the event of a marriage break up. But here again there are contrary stories from Procopius who says that Theodora in fact arranged for about 500 prostitutes to be rounded up and confined to the special convent against their will. In his account some of them committed suicide in their despair.

So what are we to make of Empress Theodora? Was she the most powerful and influential, even saintly woman in the Roman Empire or was she a scheming manipulator? She certainly sat alongside a man under whose reign much was achieved. She may have begun her life in the shadow of power but it is clear that, once close to power, she was able to get results – results she wanted to achieve. She may have been an early beacon in the feminist campaign but she was controlling. She insisted that courtiers prostrated themselves when they came before her throne and fought hard, possibly too hard, to give her own chosen religion an advantage. Can you fight too hard for something you believe in and is it acceptable to work against your husband's own strongly held beliefs to succeed in that endeavour?

Theodora's power was such that when she died, probably of cancer, it continued to exert its influence beyond the grave. She was buried in the Church of The Holy Apostle, one of the churches she had built. Honouring her memory, Justinian sought to reconcile the religious differences between the Monophysites and the Orthodox Christians. He also respected her wish that the followers of her faith who had sought sanctuary in the palace should continue to be protected. In time they were both canonised by the Eastern Orthodox Church.

There is a small caveat raised by some about Theodora's devotion to the Monophysite faith. It is suggested that she was encouraged by Justinian to follow its teaching while he remained a Chalcedonian simply as a way of drawing the two religions and their followers together. There was the other small point that the 'powerbase' of the Monophysites was in Egypt which controlled the grain regions of the Roman Empire. In other words it was good politics to unite them.

In fact Theodora's is a story full of theatrical embellishments as befits her early career. She may never have actually worked in a brothel but instead showed favour to her clients who had come to enjoy her revealing performances in the Hippodrome afterwards behind the scenes. She may never have returned from her travels in North Africa and become a wool spinner, it may just have been a suitably lowly and modest activity created by the writers of the day to paint her in a more positive light and be as far removed as possible from her earlier career. Indeed such is the mythology surrounding Theodora that far from being a seductive dancer one account of her life depicts her as the daughter of a priest and trained in the holy rites of Monophysitism. But this is generally regarded as having been yet another bit of spin by writers trying to improve her image – she was after all a saint of the Monophysite church.

Procopius, of course, heaped praise and damnation in equal measure. Having told the tales of the Emperor's heroic military feats in his work, *Wars of Justinian*, he went equally over the top in his *Secret History* apparently having become disillusioned by what he perceived as the excesses of both the Emperor and Empress. We have seen what he wrote about Theodora but he was equally dismissive of Justinian whom he condemned as cruel and incompetent. But Procopius's vitriol and authority is questioned not least because he saw the Emperor as having demonic powers:

"And some of those who have been with Justinian at the palace late at night, men who were pure of spirit, have thought they saw a strange demoniac form taking his place. One man said that the Emperor suddenly rose from his throne and walked about, and indeed he was never wont to remain sitting for long, and immediately Justinian's head vanished, while the rest of his body seemed to ebb and flow; whereat the beholder stood aghast and fearful, wondering if his eyes were deceiving him. But presently he perceived the vanished head filling out and joining the body again as strangely as it had left it."

Cruel and incompetent as Procopius would sometimes have it or thoughtful and wise as most believe, Justinian surely fell under Theodora's spell. No-one doubts her resolve and even leadership at the time of the Nika riots and she used her position of authority to protect those facing religious persecution. She adopted the cause of women's rights and whether she rounded up prostitutes or not she tried to offer some alternative.

In the end it was not so much being in the shadow of power as being in partnership in power albeit by marriage. Without her strong will and insight Justinian would have fled in fear from his palace and Constantinople, Istanbul today, would have been a different place. Justinian would not have been able to send out his armies under General Belisarius to conquer the Vandal Kingdom in North Africa, defeat the Goths in Italy and establish peace with the Persians to the east; by the end of his reign he would have almost restored the boundaries of the Roman empire at its heights and extended the power of Roman control as far as the Atlantic. Nor would Justinian have been forever remembered as a legislator collecting all the imperial statutes and publishing the *Codex* in 529. This was followed by other treatises and new legislation, in short a complete revision of Roman law which together comprise the *Corpus Juris Civilis*, the Body of Civil Law.

Rightly he became known as Justinian The Great but without the backbone and influence of Theodora, he would have been a short-lived Emperor best known for having run away from his throne in the face of rioting mobs and his marriage to a prostitute.

How will Theodora be remembered? Certainly not as a ghost-like figure on the edges of real power as will be said of some in later chapters. She came from humble origins and used the gifts she possessed, her beauty and her wit, to reach the very centre of power in an empire which could so easily have crumbled. It is surely no exaggeration to say that she played a major part in turning round the fortunes of perhaps a hesitant husband and ruler. But once Theodora had shown Justinian the way and stiffened his resolve he did not look back. What he may initially have lacked in courage he more than made up in his wise judgement of advisers, generals and of course his consort.

Despite the scandals, the allegations and the half truths, the reign of Theodora and Justinian will always be remembered as the greatest in Byzantine history. Together they rebuilt an empire during the 38 years they were in power – it would take just two more years before that empire began to fall apart once again.

3

Sorghaghtani Beki (1190–1252)

When it comes to succession in any dynasty no-one it seems fights harder than a mother for her sons. If the empire in question was one built by the mighty Genghis Khan, it was obviously a prize worth fighting for but along with ambition and fierce family loyalty, patience with a streak of utter ruthlessness was the real quality required in this instance.

Genghis Khan was a ferocious warrior slaughtering some 40 million people and whose razed earth policy eventually led to an empire covering more than 20 per cent of the earth's surface but he had an inauspicious start when his father, Temujin of Borjigin, was murdered and replaced as khan of his small tribe. Genghis, his mother and five siblings were cast out and left to die. So in a sense our story begins again with a family who had nothing.

While Genghis Khan obviously recovered and grew to be a mighty leader he failed, as many great family businesses do, to secure a strong line of succession. On his death in 1227, the so called 'lord of the ocean encircled lands' left four sons by his principal wife, Borte, vying for the position of Great Khan (the usual Anglicised translation of the Mongolian *Yekhe Khagan* that is Grand Emperor or King of Kings). The title of Khan or Khagan was used in China and spread to other countries such as Turkey where the full title of the Caliph of the Ottoman Empire would include the designation Khan of Khans.

However, it seems that Ogodei was Genghis's favourite and he was duly enthroned. He held the post until his death in 1241 when accounts[8] tell us the real battle for succession led by ambitious mothers, wives and widows erupted.

Although illiterate, Sorghaghtani Beki had pedigree, which was important. She was the daughter of Jakha Gambhu, the younger brother of Toghrul, leader of the Kereyid[9] clan which was more powerful[10] than Genghis Khan's at the time. An initial attempt to unite the two clans through marriage was rebuffed by Toghrul who was becoming increasingly concerned about Genghis's growing strength and tried to have him killed at a meeting ostensibly to discuss the marriage proposal. But Genghis got wind of the plot and in an ensuing battle Toghrul was himself killed. Jakha was more amenable than his brother towards Genghis who allowed his son, Tolui, to marry the teenage Sorghaghtani. The families were thus united after all and, critically, a blood line was established.

When Tolui died in 1231 aged 40 probably as a result of excessive drinking or some suggest he might have committed suicide with a poisoned drink[11], he left behind his widow and four sons. By now Ogodei had succeeded Genghis and he gave Sorghaghtani permission to run her late husband's territory which included Eastern Mongolia, parts of Iran and Northern China.

Sorghaghtani was clearly a formidable personality. According to the *Secret History of the Mongols* Ogodei may even have sought her advice. And a scholar wrote at the time: "If I were to see among the race of women another woman like this, I should say that the race of women was far superior to that of men."[12] Ogodei it seems also suggested that she should marry his son, Guyuk – a marriage of aunt and nephew – presumably to unite their families, but she declined deciding instead to focus on her sons' upbringing. In the light of what followed, this was a wise and momentous decision.

The importance and influence of women in Mongol life cannot be underestimated – the mere fact that Ogodei entrusted Tolui's territory to Sorghaghtani to run is not only testament to Sorghaghtani's ability and authority but also to the fact that women were highly regarded and held a position of considerable status if not actual power.

The Mongols led a nomadic existence covering a vast terrain as their conquests continued; from the Central Asian steppes their lands eventually reached out from Eastern Europe to the Sea of Japan and included vast swathes of Siberia into South East Asia and the Middle East. While the men were away fighting and hunting, the women held the domestic structure together tending the herds, making the clothes and rugs, processing the milk, cheese and meat. No sooner had they set up their *yurts* then it would be time to pack up and move on to pastures new.

But it wasn't just a domestic existence. The women were expected to be able to ride and use a bow and arrow. This was the fighting style of the Mongols – lightning fast raiding parties attacking and withdrawing before the enemy had a chance to react. Everyone – men and women – had to be capable of fighting. Acknowledging perhaps their major contribution to the success of a tribe, women were respected and enjoyed a semblance of equality; for instance they could divorce their husbands if the marriage wasn't working.

With this sense of authority, on the death of Ogodei, his widow, Toregene, ruled as regent for five years herself before managing to have her son, Guyuk, installed as the Great Khan at a Mongol congress – a *kurultai*. But Toregene had not counted on the ambition and treachery of her son. No sooner had he been elected as the Great Khan than he set about undermining his own mother's power base. He also turned on Sorghaghtani herself, Alaqai Beki, Genghis Khan's daughter, and Ebuskun, the wife of the regent of the Central Asian Empire. If you are going to take on so much opposition and fight on so many fronts at the same time you need to be an astute operator and it appears that Guyuk was out of his league.

While he was scheming, Sorghaghtani had established her own allies among the other khans and in 1248 as Guyuk was setting out on a campaign – or possibly just a mission to kill another rival and Sorghaghtani ally, Batu Khan, – he himself died in circumstances which can best be described as mysterious. Some suggest that Sorghaghtani took "direct action against Guyuk."[13] There was a great deal at stake and Sorghaghtani had clearly long harboured ambitions for her own sons. The path had to be cleared and if that meant the murder of the emperor himself so be it.

Guyuk's death left another vacuum which his widow, Oghul Qamish, filled as regent because their three sons were still too young. This was the moment Sorghaghtani had been waiting so patiently for over the intervening years. With the leadership still in doubt and only a regency figure holding sway, Sorghaghtani made her move.

She persuaded the other noble families that the Great Khan should be a direct descendant of Genghis himself, in other words from the house of Tolui rather than the house of Guyuk – Genghis's bloodline had to be preserved for the sake of the Mongol nation. She made a convincing argument and so it was that her eldest son, Mongke, succeeded to the Mongol throne in 1251. It didn't come without a fight. Oghul Qamish refused to attend the enthronement but failed to unseat Mongke. It was left to Sorghaghtani to deal with her treachery in brutal style. Guyuk's widow, Oghul Qamish, was brought before her with hands stitched in rawhide. In his book, *Daily Life in the Mongol Empire*, George Lane describes her end: "Though stripped naked before the court, she remained defiant and continued to claim the throne on behalf of the House of Ogodei, and for this she was wrapped in felt and cast to her death in a river."[14] The same fate befell others in the family who were quickly rounded up and drowned. Mongke was then free to lead the entire empire for the next eight years when he was succeeded by the famous Kublai Khan.

Sorghaghtani's four sons were well prepared for the role their mother had always hoped for them. They were groomed for power which demonstrates the extraordinary foresight, planning and patience of Sorghaghtani. She had played the ultimate long game and was dubbed the "directing spirit of the house of Tolui."

Her sons were trained in military skills and horsemanship but, although she was illiterate herself, she ensured that they were all educated, each learning a different language for the regions they were going to govern. They were schooled in administration so they could manage the empires she was obviously certain they would one day inherit. With a keen economic eye, she told her sons that peasants should be looked after because the land they worked ultimately helped pay the taxes and dues they demanded.

Sorghaghtani was also extraordinarily perceptive. She was a Nestorian Christian[15] but made sure that other faiths were shown respect; Kublai Khan received special tuition in Confucianism because he was destined to take his Mongol forces deeper into China. She supported the Muslims, Buddhists as well as Confucianists and took care that her sons treated the people they conquered with mercy. When her son, Hulagu, and his forces swept through Baghdad, his wife Doquez-khatum, who was a Nestorian like Sorghaghtani, begged him to spare the lives of the Christians there. He went further and allowed new churches to be built throughout his territory.

Meanwhile Kublai Khan who was building a powerbase in China helped protect the minority Nestorian community and even recruited Muslims into his administration. The family completely understood the importance of peaceful religious and ethnic integration even before the concept had been devised. Kublai's wife, Chabi, persuaded him to spare the Song Imperial family rather than kill them; evidently Sorghaghtani's sons even chose wisely when it came to selecting their wives.

Crucially their mother had taught them to preserve what they found to be good in the lands they conquered, not destroying everything in sight and then having to rebuild. It is a lesson even modern military powers have failed to grasp. At the time, the Persian historian, Rashid al-Din[16], wrote of Sorghaghtani's ability to manage the potentially hostile and differing religions in this way: "...though she was a follower and devotee of the religion of Jesus she made great efforts to declare the rites of the law of Mustafa and bestow alms and presents on imams and shaikhs. And the proof of this statement is that she gave 1,000 silver *balish* that a *madrasa* might be built in Bukhara, of which the sheikh al-Islam Saif al-Din Bakharz (*may God sanctify his noble spirit!*) was to be administrator and superintendent; and she commanded that villages should be bought, an endowment made, and teachers and students accommodated (in the madrasa). And always she would send alms to all parts and dispense goods to the poor and needy of the Muslims."

Another indicator of Sorghaghtani's influential grip on the reins of power can best be seen in the events which followed her death[17] in 1252 just a few months after Mongke was elected. Mongke ruled for eight years and was the last of the Great Khans to hold sway over the entire empire. While he was governing two of his other brothers, Kublai and Hulagu, were away conquering new lands: Kublai expanding into China, while Hulagu led his forces into Baghdad, conquering Persia and lands towards Palestine; in 1253 he created the Mongol Ilkhanate.

However their absence created an opportunity for the youngest of Sorghaghtani's sons, Ariq Böke, to try to seize the throne of Great Khan when Mongke died in 1259. He had plenty of support: the family of the late Mongke along with other noble families, senior ministers, the royal bodyguards and others related by marriage were on his side. It is highly unlikely that this would have been allowed to happen if his mother had still been alive.

However Kublai and Hulagu had other ideas. They raced back to the capital when they heard the news of Mongke's death and in 1260 Kublai was elected Great Khan by his own supporters. Civil war was inevitable.

Fortunes swung back and forth but in the end Kublai with his superior forces, including Chinese infantry units he had brought back with him, proved decisive. All trade into Mongolia was blocked and without food supplies Ariq had no choice but to surrender in 1264. Kublai pardoned his brother but executed most of his supporters.

Perhaps Kublai was going soft under the civilising influence of all his experiences in China. In 1271 he formerly proclaimed the foundation of the Yuan Dynasty in the Chinese style. He'd 'gone native' while establishing the building blocks of an empire which ruled over the whole of China until 1368. This may have been at the root of the support Ariq had received from senior figures when he tried to seize power. To some Kublai was not warlike enough to be a true Mongol. The scholar, David Morgan, wrote: "Ariq Böke can be seen as representing an influential school of thought among the Mongols, which Kublai through his actions and attitudes after 1260 opposed. Some Mongols felt there was a dangerous drift towards softness, typified in those like Kublai who thought there was something to be said for settled civilization and for the Chinese way of life. In the traditionalist view, the Mongol center ought to remain in Mongolia, and the Mongols' nomadic life be preserved uncontaminated. China ought merely to be exploited. Ariq Böke came to be regarded as this faction's figurehead." [18]

Like all mighty powers the Mongol empire would in time fall, but this in no way diminishes the role of Sorghaghtani Beki whose reputation lived on long after her death. In 1310 she was posthumously declared Empress in a ceremony with a Nestorian mass and a cult in honour of her name developed which continued into the following century. In 1335 her body was enshrined in a Christian church in Ganzhou, today known as Zhangye. It is said that Kublai Khan was born in the Dafo temple there – the site of the longest reclining Buddha in China.

So how do we regard Sorghaghtani Beki in our story? She was never a leader in the official sense of the word so eminently qualifies as being in the shadow of power and she was pivotal in the development of the largest contiguous empire the world has ever seen. She had an innate wisdom that had nothing to do with education or wealth. At some point in her young life it must have dawned on her that her sons had an important destiny to fulfil. Perhaps it was just a mother's pride but she made sure that they were well equipped to stride across the world both as warriors and as merciful and wise leaders.

Sorghaghtani Beki (1190–1252)

In some sense the collapse of the Mongol Empire with the Qing China's conquest in the seventeenth century only emphasises the extraordinary achievements of Sorghaghtani. The important role of women in the Mongolian society has been discussed, tending the herds, maintaining the family structures while the men were away hunting and fighting, but few were given any real rights in the male dominated society. Then when the empire finally collapsed even the special role of the woman in Mongol society quickly diminished.

It would be no exaggeration to say that Sorghaghtani, though uneducated, had an exceptional grasp of the economic realities of life and an insight into the mysteries of diplomacy and tact. Thanks to her common sense, trade links were established across the Mongol Empire, there would have been intellectual, religious and artistic exchanges and sharing of knowledge. It was these values, along with their education far removed from the usual Mongol training ground of war, that she managed to instil in her sons.

If one just considers for a moment the vast expanse of the empire over which her sons held sway, the different cultures, fears, animosity towards invading armies, it makes the almost local domestic squabbles of the 21st century appear trivial by comparison. And yet that is what she achieved.

The last word perhaps should go to the historian, Rashid al-Din, who described her simply as "towering above all the women in the world."

4

SHAGRAT AL-DUR (died, 1259)

If so much of the Mongol dynasty can be traced back to the influence of a woman, it is appropriate perhaps that its advance would eventually be stopped in its tracks by a force galvanised by a woman who rose from being a slave to the self proclaimed Sultana of Egypt.

The Mamluks, meaning 'owned' or slave, were soldiers of slave origin captured from the Asian steppes who rose to become a powerful military caste holding political and military power notably in Egypt. When the slaves were captured they were converted to Islam then went through rigorous training to serve in the army. Standards were high and not every boy was accepted into the military. In 1260 Hulagu, grandson of Genghis Khan was defeated by the Mamluks and the invasion of Syria was brought to an end.

Shagrat al-Dur was of Turkic origin and, together with her guile and survival instincts, it was this native ancestory which would prove critical as she crafted her career from slave girl to Sultana. Her enemies however were not the Mongols but the Crusaders.

Shagrat al-Dur – sometimes written as Shajar al-Durr – and described as a woman of great beauty and intelligence, was bought by Salih Ayyub. He was a descendant of the renowned Salah-al Din, better known as Saladin, leader of the Islamic forces fighting against the Crusaders and the first Sultan of Egypt and Syria. Saladin founded the Ayyubid dynasty in the Levant, a region which includes modern day Lebanon, Syria, Jordan, Palestine, Israel and parts of Turkey and Iraq.

When Salih Ayyub succeeded to the Sultanate in 1240 he brought Shagrat al-Dur with him to Egypt where she gave birth to a son, Khalil, who was called al-Malik al-Mansour. But in April 1249 Salih Ayyub fell gravely ill while in Syria and was forced to return to Egypt only making it as far as Ashmum-Tanah, near Damietta. The timing couldn't have been worse because the Crusader army under King Louis IX of France was massing in Cyprus and preparing an assault on Egypt. Damietta, at the mouth of the River Nile, was to be his launch pad for a planned attack on Jerusalem.

While Salih Ayyub was stretchered away to a better protected palace at Al Mansurah Shagrat knew she had to act. Louis' forces had landed and were rapidly making their way straight to the undefended Damietta. But luck was on her side. Instead of pressing home his advantage, Louis remained in Damietta adding to his defences and allowing his army to enjoy the spoils of war. However he failed to take into account the flooding of the Nile and before long he was bogged down, unable to leave the town where he remained for six months. Nevertheless he was confident of success and issued written threats to Salih Ayyub:

As you know that I am the ruler of the Christian nation I do know you are the ruler of the Muhammadan nation. The people of Andalusia give me money and gifts while we drive them like cattle We kill their men and we make their women widows. We take the boys and the girls as prisoners and we make houses empty. I have told you enough and I have advised you to the end, so now if you make the strongest oath to me and if you go to Christian priests and monks and if you carry kindles before my eyes as a sign of obeying the cross, all these will not persuade me from reaching you and killing you at your dearest spot on earth. If the land will be mine then it is a gift to me. If the land will be yours and you defeat me then you will have the upper hand. I have told you and I have warned you about my soldiers who obey me. They can fill open fields and mountains, their number like pebbles. They will be sent to you with swords of destruction.[19]

However, on 22 November 1249, Salih Ayyub died and it was at this moment that Shagrat stepped forward from the shadows. After consulting with the commander of the Egyptian Army, Emir Fakhr ad-Din Yussuf Ben Shaykh, and Tawashi Jamal ad-Din Muhsin, the chief eunuch who controlled all activity in the Palace, they agreed to keep news of the Sultan's death a secret. Elaborate steps were taken including having the servants deliver food to his room to suggest that while ill, Salih Ayyub was still very much alive. Furthermore before his death the Sultan had signed thousands of blank papers which Shagrat had used to convince government officials and the people that he was still giving orders. Meanwhile his body was taken in great secrecy to his castle on al-Rudah island[20].

The ruse worked for a time but it was inevitable that word would eventually leak out and reach Louis which it did. Emboldened by the news and with the arrival of reinforcements, the crusaders decided to press on with their campaign. First Louis' brother Robert d'Artois attacked the Egyptians in Geideila managing to kill Emir Fakhr before marching on Al Mansurah.

Together with her new commander, Baybars al-Bunduqdari, Shagrat concocted a plan to trap the crusaders in the narrow streets of the town. Robert d'Artois and his men rushed in and, unable to manoeuvre, were slaughtered. Some accounts say Robert fled at the height of the battle and drowned in the River Thanis, a tributary of the Nile, as he tried to make good his escape. In Egypt it is said that Robert was killed by Sultan Qutuz. Baybars distinguished himself and eventually rose to be the first great Mamluk ruler of Egypt.

Events now moved quickly. It was official: Salib Ayyub was dead. In February Al-Muazzam Turanshah, the Sultan's son was enthroned at Al Salhiyah. Turanshah then made straight for Al Mansurah and on 6 April 1250 the crusaders were defeated at the Battle of Fariskurf.

For Shagrat however a new role and new troubles beckoned. The troubles came first as Turanshah realised that as long as Shagrat was around, support-ed by the Mamluks, his position was shaky. Everyone assumed she still held the reins of power. The army commanders all preferred Shagrat, a Turk like themselves, to Turanshah who began throwing his weight about abusing the slave girls when he got drunk and replacing his father's old officials with his own people. To add insult to injury he demanded that Shagrat, now in Jeru-salem, should return the jewels and other wealth that his father had given her.

It was too much for Shagrat who complained bitterly to Faris ad-Din Aktai leader of the Mamluks. He already felt aggrieved because he had not been promoted to commander of the army as he had been promised on the death of Fakhr ad-Din. [21]

On 2 May 1250 Turanshah was assassinated by the Mamluks - it was the beginning of the end of the Ayyubid Sultanate. The military commanders or emirs got together and agreed that the best person to lead them was in fact a woman, Shagrat al-Dur. Unsurprisingly she agreed and was duly declared the new monarch with the official name, al-Malikah Ismat ad-Din Umm-Khalil Shajar al-Durr. She also assumed an assortment of titles including Malikat al-Muslimin (Queen of the Muslims) and Walidat al-Malik al-Mansur Khalil Emir al-Mo'aminin (Mother of al-Malik al-Mansur Khalil Emir of the Faithfuls).

Her new position and authority – a remarkable rise from slave girl – seems from this distance in history to have gone to her head. She was soon being mentioned at the Friday prayers in the mosques dubbed "Umm al-Malik khalil (meaning mother of al-Malik Khalil) and Sahibat al-Malik as Salih (wife of al-Malik as-Salih). The ultimate vanity was having coins minted in her name. Perhaps she just felt a degree of uncertainty about her position; by using both the name of her late husband and her dead son it seems she wanted to imbue her reign with a legitimacy which she probably realised it did not have; after all she had come to power only on the murder of her predecessor, an act of which she undoubtedly approved if not actually ordered.

There was still some unfinished business to deal with relating to the Crusades. King Louis IX was languishing in prison in Al Mansurah. Shagrat agreed to his release along with some 12,000 of his soldiers in return for a ransom of 800,000 bezants. Louis would eventually try to muster another crusading expedition but it too would end in failure. He should have taken the advice of his mother, Blanche of Castile, grand-daughter of Eleanor of Aquitaine, whom he left behind to manage his kingdom in his absence – something she did rather well. Blanche advised him not to go on his first crusade in 1248 and she was proved right.

Shagrat's seizure of power and the killing of Turanshah did not go down well in Syria where the emirs refused to acknowledge her rule in Cairo. Even more importantly at the time Egypt came under the authority of the Caliphate in Baghdad and as far as Abbasid Caliph al-Musta'sim was concerned Shagrat failed to qualify on two counts: they did not like what she had done and she was a woman. The Caliph dispatched messengers to Egypt with the order: "Since no *man* among you is worthy of being Sultan, I will bring you one." The man who was chosen was Izz al-Din Aybak. He was a trusted by his fellow Mamluks and had been made their commander in chief; he was also formerly a *jashnkir*, taster of the Sultan's food and drink. Shagrat must have felt humiliated by Baghdad's refusal to recognise her. There was much jockeying for position and the Mamluks tried to cement Shagrat's position by arresting opponents to her rule, but it seems the thought of a woman ruling Egypt was too difficult a position to sell so in time honoured tradition a marriage was arranged.

Shagrat agreed to marry Aybak. Not only did she agree to the wedding but she also agreed to abdicate allowing Aybak to become the new Sultan. She had reigned for just 80 days.

In order to win back support from Syria and Iraq, the Mamluks also announced that Aybak was merely a representative of the Caliph in Baghdad and they arranged for Salih Ayyub's body to be buried in a tomb in Cairo.

Shagrat must have felt vulnerable. Not only were her erstwhile supporters showing obeisance to the Ayyudbids in Syria but they made 6-year-old al-Malik Sharaf Muzafer al-Din Musa, who was one of the Syrian branch of the Ayyubid family, co-sultan. All the ground she thought she had made appeared to be slipping away from under her and even a child was placed above her. On the other hand it is open to question who was really ruling: Ayback or Shagrat. Accounts written at the time quote one historian, "She dominated him, and he had nothing to say."

The Ayyubids were still not happy and fighting erupted between them and the Mamluks. It took the intervention of the Caliph of Baghdad to bring about peace; in fact the negotiations worked out well for the Mamluks who were given control over southern Palestine encompassing Gaza and Jerusalem. Some semblance of peace having been restored the Caliph was able to focus on the more pressing issue of the Mongol raiding parties striking dangerously close to Baghdad but suspicions continued to swirl around the Sultan's palace.

In 1253 a rebellion in Upper Egypt had been put down by Faris ad-Din Aktai, leader of the Mamluk army. Far from seeing this as a good thing for his authority, Aybak must have regarded it as power shifting increasingly towards the Mamluks and away from him. Aktai was obviously plotting to overthrow him or so probably Aybak thought and as he was convinced Shagrat still commanded the loyalty of the army he decided to have Aktai murdered. This sparked a mass exodus of Mamluks, including Baybars al-Bunduqdari, to Syria leaving Aybak unopposed as the absolute ruler of Egypt. What could possibly go wrong?

The answer was a wife's jealousy. Shagrat would have argued that she had effectively put her husband on the throne by going along with the arranged marriage and agreeing to abdicate – at least officially. She clearly thought that she was still the *de facto* ruler. It was thanks to her strategy and cunning that Egypt had been protected from the Crusaders; without her and her loyal generals Islam might have been brushed aside. She also did her utmost to ensure that key affairs of state were kept from Aybak.

Shagrat was clearly a jealous wife and had persuaded Aybak to divorce his first wife. But in 1257 Aybak decided to marry the daughter of Badr ad-Din Lo'alo'a, the Ayyubid Emir of Mousil to form a closer alliance in the event of retaliation from the Mamluks who had fled to Syria. The Emir warned Aybak that his wife was in touch with the exiled Mamluks and although he must have been suspicious it didn't prevent an inglorious end to his reign. Shagrat arranged to have him murdered by his servants while he took a bath then claimed that her husband had died suddenly during the night. He was about 60 and had ruled Egypt for just seven years.

Shagrat tried to cover her tracks but the Mamluks themselves were divided and one group, the Mu'izi Mamluks led by the loyal Saif ad-Din Qutuz, who had been sold as a slave to Aybak, forced the servants under torture to reveal what they had done. Shagrat was arrested and Aybak's son the 15-year-old al-Mansur Ali was enthroned as the new Sultan.

As for Shagrat al-Dur her end was as ignominious as her late husband's death. Acounts say she was stripped and beaten to death with shoes by the slave girls of al-Mansur Ali and his mother, and her naked body was dumped outside the city. It was eventually recovered and buried in a tomb near the Mosque of Tulun.

Inevitably folklore and romance surrounds these tales of a slave girl who made it to the top. In Egyptian mythology Shagrat al-Dur – or 'Tree of Pearls' so named by her father because he dressed her in a gown made of pearls – was given the gift of Egypt by her father. Salih Ayyub married her in order to stay in power as Egypt was hers already. Aybak is portrayed as a wicked man who wanted to steal Egypt from them. Shagrat slew Aybak with a sword but died when she fell from the roof of the citadel.

Whether fiction or fact, the reality was that upon the deaths of Aybak and Shagrat the Mamluk dynasty was firmly established and dominated the southern Mediterranean for decades until the rise of the Ottoman Empire. The Mongols were driven back under the leadership of Qutuz, who had arrested Shagrat and went on to become the third Mamluk Sultan of Egypt. It was also under Shagrat's direction that the European Crusaders had been expelled from the Holy Land.

If nothing else Shagrat al-Durr's life and rise to power was a tour de force in a world where loyalty was a rare commodity and where men normally dominated. She came from nothing and ruled Egypt both in name and from the shadows. In one sense it was a life of power struggles, mistrust and fear with the military playing a key role – something which has proved to be commonplace in history and right up to modern times in Egypt.

5

THOMAS WOLSEY (c.1473–1530)

*He is very handsome, learned, extremely eloquent, of vast ability
and indefatigable. He alone transacts the business which occupies
all the magistrates and councils of Venice, both civil and criminal;
and all state affairs are managed by him, let their nature be what it
may. He is grave, and has the reputation of being extremely just; he
favours the people exceedingly, and especially the poor, hearing their
suits and seeking to despatch them instantly.*

This description by Sebastian Giustiniani, Venetian ambassador to the court of Henry VIII, gives some indication of the influence Thomas Wolsey had on the fortunes of England, the church and the crown.

It may seem obtuse to talk about Wolsey as being in anyone's shadow and yet that is what he was. He served two kings while at the same time helping himself to every pleasure, perk and preferment available. He was the consummate operator and the last cleric in England to bestride the church and state. He would save one of his monarchs the trouble of ruling his country freeing him to indulge his pleasures, while at the same time climbing the ecclesiastical pole; whether he was striving for the papacy itself is debatable although he might well have been doing so on the king's behalf.

Thomas Wolsey (c.1473–1530)

Wolsey's own start in life is obscured by misinformation. He was born in Ipswich, Suffolk around 1473. It is said he was the son of a butcher but that may have been negative gossip directed against him later in life by nobles whose own power and influence at court Wolsey had neatly sidestepped. His father was certainly a merchant and probably sold other produce as well as meat. He owned property and was regarded sufficiently to become a church warden. Whatever his precise employment he was wealthy enough to be able to send his son, Thomas, to Magdalen College, Oxford from where it seems he graduated with a B.A. aged just 15 although the records are inconclusive.

It was while teaching at Magdalen College School that Wolsey had his first break in what was to be an astounding career. Three of his pupils were the sons of Thomas Grey, first Marquess of Dorset, who may have encouraged him to join the priesthood and then later introduced him to the rectory of Limington in Somerset. He served for a time as the domestic chaplain to Henry Deane, Archbishop of Canterbury, upon whose death in 1503, he became chaplain to Sir Richard Nanfan, deputy of Calais, England's last remaining possession on the continent. Wolsey was now making the connections which would matter later in his career. Through Sir Richard he was recommended to King Henry VII who in due course made him chaplain. But Henry must have seen something more in the young priest than just a man devoted to the church. He dispatched Wolsey on repeated trips across the Channel to help secure the hand of Margaret of Savoy following the death in childbirth of his beloved Elizabeth of York[22], who had born him eight children and by whose marriage the Wars of the Roses had been ended.

Wolsey's diplomatic activity was appreciated and he was duly rewarded by the king with the first of many ecclesiastical appointments, including the deanery of Lincoln, which enabled him to live in grand style.

But Henry died in 1509 before he could remarry and everything was about to change. Out went the slightly dull father and in came the flamboyance and apparently devil may care attitude of the son, Henry VIII, who promptly executed a number of his father's advisers. Like so many individuals in our story it is the ability to survive such purges which often marks out the ablest fixers and advisers. Of course the first thing the young King Henry did was to marry his own brother's widow, Catherine of Aragon[23], thus sowing the seeds of future trouble. On the face of it the marriage seemed a good political move. She was the daughter of Ferdinand

and Isabella thus uniting England with Spain and against their common enemy, France.

On his accession Henry appointed Wolsey as his almoner, officially Keeper of the Privy Purse and distributor of alms to the poor – a small but important step as it placed Wolsey at the heart of the royal household. Two years later in 1511 he was made a privy councillor securing a critical position in deciding the affairs of state. In fact it was Henry VII who had revived the Privy Council whose job it was to cut through red tape and get things done – a perfect tool for Wolsey.

With the young king amusing himself jousting and in the hunting field, Wolsey single-handedly changed the tone and direction of English foreign policy. Some accounts suggest he was much more belligerent than the other advisers surrounding Henry, although this may well have been because he believed that that was what his monarch desired. Wolsey, while often portrayed as the arch-manipulator, may actually have been the ultimate servant, divining what his master wanted – territory in France, influence in Rome – and doing everything in his considerable power to achieve that wish. Wolsey was a pragmatist; he would enable Henry to win power and glory by war or peace – peace was cheaper but he was prepared to fight.

His first major adventure in 1511 was to persuade Henry that England should join the Holy League declared by Pope Julius II against France and supported by Ferdinand II, both King of Aragon and Regent of Castile, and Maximilian I, the Holy Roman Emperor. In November they signed the Treaty of Westminster and Henry sent Lord Dorset with an army to France in 1512. It appears Henry required little persuasion to go to war with France. Academics like Professor Jack Scarisbrick in his definitive book, *Henry VIII*, assert that there were 'moments when the royal urge for war was at least tempered by the minister's quest for peace and there seem to have been moments when the king's belligerence finally broke the cardinal's designs'.

It was a fruitless enterprise which the English said "ended in inglorious failure"[24] although Ferdinand was happy enough. He had effectively used the English forces as a shield against the French allowing him to take control of Navarre. If that was the plan it worked because Louis XII of France did nothing to protect his Navaresse allies.

Whether Wolsey was the warmonger or the peace broker, English troops found themselves campaigning in France again in 1513 led by Henry himself with Wolsey alongside him. However it wasn't popular with his allies who feared Henry secretly wanted to depose Louis and crown himself King of France and with winter approaching Henry returned home.

Wolsey's diplomatic skills however secured a small victory in 1514 by arranging the marriage of Mary Tudor, Henry's 18 year old sister, and the 52 year old Louis XII thus restoring peaceful relations with France albeit briefly as Louis was dead within a year. The proposed match no doubt displeased Henry's wife, Catherine, who saw this as distancing England from Spain and an illustration of Wolsey's growing influence.

Wolsey's personal good fortune continued when in the same year he was appointed Lord Chancellor by Henry; some wondered who was really ruling the country, the King or his most trusted adviser.

While his position in England seemed unassailable Wolsey also had another agenda. With half an eye on Rome he wanted to be seen supporting the Papacy, by now with Leo X, son of Lorenzo di Medici, in the Vatican. Recognising his allegiance, Leo soon made Wolsey Archbishop of York by Papal Bull adding to his collection of other lucrative preferments which included the bishoprics of Lincoln and Tournai, the oldest city in Belgium. In 1515 he was elevated to cardinal.

European troubles flared up again following the death of Louis XII in 1515 and succession of Francis 1 who took up arms against the Old Swiss Confederacy (a collection of Swiss cantons) defeating them at the Battle of Marignano. It was another exchange Wolsey seemed unable to resist and Henry was persuaded by Wolsey that the right course of action was to declare his support for the Emperor Maximilian and Ferdinand II, Henry's father-in-law, and underwrite part of the war effort on behalf of the Swiss and imperial forces against France.

By now Wolsey held sway in all domestic and foreign policy matters, and his grasp of the constantly shifting allegiances in Europe and their impact on England must have required all his attention such that he scarcely had time for his religious duties. But he was a diligent administrator and exceptionally hard working. George Cavendish, his biographer, wrote of him one day rising at dawn and then he "continually wrote his letters with his own hands till four in the afternoon all which season my lord never rose once to piss not yet to eat any meal."[25]

However it wasn't all work and no play. Wolsey liked to party and needed suitable places and palaces to stage his lavish entertainment. With his great wealth he built Hampton Court Palace on the site of a more modest manor house, filling the rooms with the finest tapestries and decoration although always being careful to say he was doing it all for the king. But his ostentation, his gold throne in the audience chamber, his insistence that nobles who regarded him as socially inferior, bowed before him, did not go unremarked. He was accused of "imagining himself the equal of sovereigns" and became the subject of the satirists' wit. John Skelton wrote:

The king's court
Should have the excellence,
But Hampton Court
Hath the pre-eminence

In 1518 Wolsey was appointed *legatus à latere*, literally meaning at the Pope's side which made him the most senior cleric in England, placing him above the Archbishop of Canterbury, and in effect the Pope's man. There was only one place left for him to go, but his pitch for St Peter's chair would have to wait. There was more diplomacy to be done in Europe where Charles V was Emperor and at loggerheads with Francis 1. Wolsey was called upon to use his charms to bring about a "universal peace" and he arranged the summit meeting of all summit meetings forever known and beautifully illustrated in painting as The Field of the Cloth of Gold[26]. For two and a half weeks in June 1520 Henry and Francis met near Calais in a bid to secure lasting friendship between the two countries and secure peace between the Christian nations of Europe. It was a lavish display of wealth and apparent solidarity but Wolsey had already made his mind up that England should side with Charles who had given him assurances that he would back his candidacy as the next Pope. In fact there is evidence that he only wanted the position because Henry thought it might be useful and it was Charles who had prompted him to consider the idea with assurances of his backing[27]. It was a promise Charles would not fulfil. Despite the sumptuous extended picnic, hostilities between the two countries would soon begin again. Encouraged by Charles, Henry was persuaded to attack France in 1522 in support of a rebellion by Charles de Bourbon but the rebellion quickly collapsed and the English forces had to withdraw.

England meanwhile was feeling the economic effects of expensive and increasingly unsuccessful campaigns and parliament resisted Wolsey's demands for more taxation; he had even dissolved some smaller monasteries and stripped them of their valuables partly to fund his foreign adventures and partly to support his lavish lifestyle. With Parliament proving unhelpful,

Wolsey imposed a new tax, called the Amicable Grant, which amounted to a forced loan on the laity and the clergy to fund a new attack on France. It sparked an outcry which fell just short of open rebellion and Wolsey was forced to back down. It was a humiliation from which he would never recover.

Charles meanwhile succeeded in defeating and capturing Francis 1 at Pavia in 1525. It was the decisive battle of the Italian Wars and resulted in Francis being forced to sign the Treaty of Madrid. Charles now felt confident enough to stand alone – he hadn't needed English backing.

Isolated in Europe and facing resentment from all the nobles and senior clerics he had bullied and snubbed, Wolsey found himself with few friends. But he still had support from the king who had another task for his Cardinal. Catherine of Aragon had failed to produce a son and heir and Henry wanted a divorce. He expected Wolsey to be able to use his influence as *legatus à latere* to persuade the Pope to annul the marriage on the grounds that it was invalid[28]. It was a forlorn hope.

In 1527, Charles V and his Hapsburg forces sacked Rome and gained control of Pope Clement VII who had sided with France. Henry was alarmed at the growing power of Charles and had switched allegiance to the French. Wolsey, once the capable mediator between European warring factions, failed to negotiate a peace. His grip on foreign policy was slipping. Furthermore the Pope would never agree to the annulment because he wasn't in control of his own destiny let alone Henry's marital crisis; furthermore Charles, the Pope's 'jailer', was Catherine of Aragon's nephew.

One can only imagine how Wolsey must have felt having been rebuffed by the Pope. This was the one thing Henry would have expected his chief fixer to have accomplished. He had trodden on so many fingers in his climb to the top that there was no-one to put out a helping hand as his fall from grace gathered momentum. In addition a new clique had begun a whispering campaign against him – the friends and supporters of Anne Boleyn who had caught the eye of the King. Wolsey in their view was simply an impediment and her supporters suggested the cardinal may even have been actively encouraging the Pope to delay matters.

Henry immediately dismissed Wolsey as Lord Chancellor and all Wolsey could think of doing to save himself was to throw himself on the mercy of the King. He gave up all his land and his grand houses, and either renounced or was stripped of all his preferments save that of Archbishop of York, a city he had never visited and to where he was now effectively exiled. His letters to the king pleading forgiveness were ignored.

He may also have made one other desperate throw of the dice asking Charles V, Francis I and the Pope himself to intercede on his behalf. The man whose judgement had guided the realm at home and abroad with undisputed authority from 1514 to 1529 was now floundering. His appeals to Henry's enemies, in particular the Pope, only made matters worse. The Papacy and all it meant no longer had the king's favour. Henry used the law against his former chief law officer and charged him with *praemunire,* that is exercising Papal powers against the King or his subjects. It was an old law which the Pope's man in England would have been well aware of but had chosen to ignore as his glittering career expanded. *Hubris* was to be his downfall. With this act of treason against him Wolsey was rearrested in York and brought south to face trial in London. He never made it and died on the way from unspecified causes at Leicester Abbey where he was buried.

Throughout his rapid rise Wolsey had always argued that everything he did was for the king but the power he quickly acquired went to his head.

Lucy Wooding in her book, *Henry VIII*[29], wrote: "That Bluff King Hal suffered from megalomania is beyond dispute; for lesser men had become puffed up with the satanic pride that they could do no wrong. Early in the reign, when the monarch was engrossed in the pleasures of joust, the masque and the hunt, Cardinal Wolsey, the King's alter ego, had fallen prey to the same self-destroying egotism. He started out his career humbly saying His Majesty will do so and so, but subsequently and by imperceptible degrees he developed the habit of announcing "We shall do so and so." Finally, he attained the ultimate conceit of claiming "I shall do so and so."

His extravagance and good living with hundreds of servants at his beck and call must have made an impression on the young king he served particularly when the royal entourage visited Hampton Court which Henry evidently coveted. If a priest could live like this he may have thought, fathering countless illegitimate children, why shouldn't he as monarch? If this was the case, Wolsey taught his own master well. Not only would he have seen the extravagance but he must have witnessed and possibly been attracted by the notion of the control of both church and state in the hands of one man.

The tangled web of European allegiances, marriages of convenience and political intrigue inevitably involved the English crown but pursuit of foreign policy to distract from domestic issues has been a common strategy down the ages. Wolsey, the polished diplomat, was made for the game.

While Henry obviously trusted is astute Chancellor and gave him a long leash, it is probable that the king kept a wary eye on Wolsey's activities and from time to time would firmly slap down his servant, for that is what he was. For instance in 1528 when a new abbess had to be appointed to Wilton Abbey[30] in Wiltshire on the death of Cecily Willoughby, Wolsey disregarded Henry's suggestion that the post would best be filled by Eleanor Carey, who happened to be the sister of Anne Boleyn's brother-in-law. Wolsey instead saw to it that Isabella who was the Prioress at the time got elected by the simple means of imprisoning any of the nuns who objected. Neither candidate seemed entirely without sin; Isabella had had two illegitimate children and, as Henry wrote to Anne: *As touching the matter of Wilton, my lord cardinal has had the nuns before him and examined them, Master Bell being present, who has certified to me that for a truth she has confessed herself to have had two children by sundry priests, and further since has been kept by a servant of Lord Broke that was, and not long ago; wherefore I would not for all the world clog your conscience nor mine to make her ruler of a house who is of such ungodly demeanour, nor I trust, you would not that neither for brother nor sister I should so stain mine honour and conscience.*[31] Henry was furious not only because Wolsey had ignored his wishes, but he had promised Anne that Eleanor would get the post. Anne would remember Wolsey's actions.

It is argued quite simply that Henry allowed Wolsey to accumulate wealth and power because he was no threat to the throne. He was not a nobleman and therefore could not stir up the aristocracy against the crown as they would never allow themselves to be led by a commoner – if he was not the son of a butcher as rumours had it he was certainly not of noble stock. Wolsey no doubt was aware of this snobbery so there was no love lost between him and the nobility which meant he could keep them under control on behalf of the king. It was as they say a win/win situation for Henry, so long as his tame cardinal delivered.

Once again in our story, those who strived to serve a master loyally had their loyalty rejected or blinded by gossip and innuendo combined with false accusation. Wolsey was dismayed and perplexed by the fate that had befallen him. On his final journey to London, as a broken and sick man, Wolsey said to Sir William Kingston, "Had I but served God as diligently as I have served the King, He would not have given me over in my grey hairs."

6

Nur Jahan 1577–1645

One wife or two or dozens were not an issue in the courtly life of a Mughal Emperor and it was in this jewel-encrusted world of abundant wealth that Nur Jahan was to make her name and become one of the most powerful women in Indian history – all from behind the harem's screen.

Jahan was born Mehr-un-Nisaa in 1577 into an aristocratic Persian family. Her father, Mirza Ghiyas al-Din Muhammador, decided to seek his fortune in India which was regarded as a thriving industrial and cultural centre under the rule of Emperor Akbar, known as Akbar the Great for his prowess not only as a soldier but for his wise administrative skills uniting his far flung empire.

However on their way to India the family, including Mirza Ghiyas's pregnant wife and three children, was attacked leaving them virtually destitute. As they struggled on their way they were befriended by a passing caravan led by Malik Masud, a merchant nobleman who took them under their wing. When they reached Kandahar, Mirza Ghiya's wife gave birth but the family were penniless and the last thing they needed was another mouth to feed. Realising their predicament the nobleman arranged for Mirza Ghiya to get a job working for the Emperor as *diwan* or treasurer in the Kabul province. Mirza Ghiya's luck was about to change and he decided his new daughter should be called Mehr-un-Nisaa, meaning Sun of Womanhood to mark the occasion. His skills meant that he received rapid promotion and he was given the title Itimad-ud-Daula or 'Pillar of the State' by the emperor.

Now wealthy once more Mirza Ghiya ensured that his new daughter had the best education that he could provide with lessons in Arabic, Persian, art, literature and dance.[32] It would be money well spent.

Not only was she now highly educated but she was a great beauty. By the time she was 17 she was married to a brave Persian soldier called Ali Quli Istunjuloo who reputedly killed a tigress singlehandedly when the future Emperor Jahangir was attacked earning himself the title, Sher Afkhan or Prince of Lions. It wasn't long before he was promoted to an administrative post in the Mughal Empire about the time Jahangir succeeded to the throne in 1605.

Sher Afkhan's courage however was not matched by his judgement. He was killed in 1607 by Imperial soldiers having refused to obey an order from the Governor of Bengal and for attacking the Governor's troops. In fact his death, or murder, may have been arranged by Jahangir himself who according to some accounts had already noticed the beautiful Jahan – some suggest they may have even met as children when he first coveted her for his wife although that is in question as the Emperor is unlikely to have honoured a rival suitor. Nevertheless what the emperors wanted they generally got.

The Muslim Mughal Emperors were direct descendants of Genghis Khan and their empire at its height, between 1526–1757, stretched over a million square miles of the Indian subcontinent commanding a population of about 150 million. They certainly retained the ruthlessness of the Mongol way. In the first year of coming to the throne Jahangir saw off a rebellion led by his eldest son, Khusraw, and executed some 2,000 of the rebels. As for his son he was dragged before Jahangir in chains and blinded.

While their word was law and sometimes brutal, the Emperors also helped India enjoy a period of economic growth and religious tolerance, and witnessed the golden age of Mughal architecture during the mid-16th century. It was into this environment that Nur Jahan found herself drawn.

Now alone with a daughter, Ladli, she was brought to court in Agra as a lady in waiting in the royal harem. Her own family's fortunes appear to have taken a turn for the worse: her father was accused of embezzlement and was out of favour, and one of her brothers and her mother's cousin were accused of involvement in an assassination attempt on the emperor and were executed. But Jahan's beauty and refinement were to save her.

She was noticed again by Jahangir at the palace *meena bazaar* in March 1611, a gathering where the women of the court could meet, buy jewellery and probably most important of all flirt with likely suitors. This was a mock fair where the wives and daughters of nobles pretended to be traders and 'bargained' with the Emperor and his entourage mimicking the traders' banter. Within two months they were married – Jahan becoming the emperor's twentieth wife. Some accounts suggest that Jahan played hard to get from the time she was first brought to court until their marriage. It seems reasonable, after all the Emperor had probably arranged for Jahan's first husband to be killed. But Jahangir persevered and eventually Jahan gave in to his devoted courting.

By now in her thirties, Jahan would have been considered middle-aged and passed marrying age but to Jahangir she was perfection. He gave her the title Nur Mahal, meaning "light of the palace", and then in 1616 bestowed on her the new name of Nur Jahan, or "light of the world" as well as making her his principal queen over all the others in his harem or *zanana*.

It was from this point that Jahan's power and influence over the entire empire began to grow aided and abetted by her husband who had no interest in ruling as emperor preferring instead to indulge in drinking, eating and enjoying copious quantities of opium. But there was still court protocol to observe so from behind the screens of the *zanana*, Jahan set to work at first carrying out small duties within the harem and gradually affairs of state, all instructions being carefully channelled through trusted men. In Jahangir's own memoirs quoted in *A History of India* he writes, "Nur Jahan was wise enough to conduct the business of State... (while I) only wanted a bottle of wine and a piece of meat to make merry." The author Vidya Dhar Mahajan, also observed that: Nur Jahan had a piercing intelligence, a versatile temper and sound common sense. [33]

It is worth noting the importance of the royal harem which would have run to thousands of women, their children, slaves and eunuchs. These were hierarchical structures with a strict pecking order. Jahan's 'promotion' to the emperor's principal queen would have been a considerable appointment and, in a world riven with jealousies and closely monitored allegiances, it says much about Jahan's diplomatic skills to able to control life both inside and outside the *zanana*.

In time Jahan became the absolute authority in the land, conducting all business without apparently breaking her *purdah* or showing her face in public. The first British ambassador to the Mughal Court, Sir Thomas Roe, is quoted as saying: "He hath one Wife, or Queen, whom he esteems and favours above all other Women; and his whole Empire is govern'd at this day by her counsel." [34]

This was also a time to build her family's position. Her father was restored to favour and was appointed the emperor's chief minister. Her brother, Asaf Khan, was given the second highest rank in court – grand *wazir* to the emperor – and two critical marriages were arranged. Her daughter, Ladli, was married to Prince Shahriyar, the fourth son of Jahangir by one of his numerous concubines, and she arranged for her niece, Mumtaz Mahal, to marry Prince Khurram (the future Shah Jahan) thus binding their two families more closely together.[35] These marriages also ensured that Jahan's family would remain an influential power regardless of who succeeded Jahangir when he died. As so often, succession would be an issue because Khurram had already rebelled against his father taking up arms against him in 1622 when he feared that he was going to be overlooked when it came to succession. It would take until 1626 before Khurram finally unconditionally surrendered.

Meanwhile Jahangir was ever more gripped by alcoholism and opium addiction which had claimed the lives of his two brothers and had enfeebled his second son, Parviz. Every order, every decision was now completely under Jahan's control. She held court in the seclusion of her palace from where she conducted the affairs of state. No-one was in any doubt where the real authority in the land lay. As though to confirm her power she had coins struck with her name, a privilege normally reserved for a monarch.

But aside from this vanity, occasional bouts of nepotism and some bending of the laws to suit her ends, Jahan was clearly a formidable administrator. Senior appointments and positions of influence were all in her gift, as was the freedom to travel through the land. Taxes were demanded from merchants which all contributed to the vast wealth she accumulated. In time Agra grew into the focal point of commercial activity. It was the capital of the Mughal Empire from 1556 to 1658.

However, it wasn't all greed. Jahan appreciated the fineries and other luxuries from European countries and she was in large part responsible for opening up trade links. Her own fleet of ships criss-crossed the seas importing and exporting goods as well as providing transport for the pilgrims making their way to Mecca. She was evidently caring and generous giving alms to the poor and providing dowries for orphan girls so they could marry well.

She was instrumental in designing new fashions influenced by her Persian background, developed for the ladies of the harem and then carried into the outside world. The finest jewellery was created and, as she was something of a poet, she organised poetry contests. Her beauty inspired artists to paint many portraits of her and the emperor. This was not just a woman bent on gathering wealth for wealth's sake nor an aesthete obsessed with the beautiful things in life. She was also a woman of action, capable of hunting and killing tigers firing from behind the screens of her enclosed *howdah* mounted on the back of an elephant.

Above all, architecture was a passion and one which she obviously shared with her immediate family; her son-in-law, Jummar as Shah Jahan, would one day build the incomparable Taj Mahal in Agra in memory of his wife, Mumtaz Mahal.

It was inevitable that rivalries within the extended family would boil over. When Persian forces threatened to overrun Kandahar, it was Jahan who order Jahangor's third son, Jummar, to lead the defence but he refused fearing that in his absence Jahan would plot against him. As a result of his refusal after a forty-five day siege. Kandahar fell to the Persians. In 1626, still worrying that he was going to be passed over in the line of succession, Jummar raised an army to try and overthrow his father and more particularly the influential, Jahan. It failed but while he was forgiven the resentment continued.

In 1626 while travelling to Kashmir, Jahangir was captured by rebels. Of course it was Nur Jahan who parlayed his release but the emperor's health was failing him and Jahan, whose all-encompassing power was not universally popular, now had to decide who she was going to back as the next Emperor.

Throughout Jahangir's reign she had been a staunch supporter of Jummar but in the end, as a result possibly of his rebellious attitude towards his father, she switched allegiance to Prince Shahriyar who was married to her daughter, Ladli. She made the wrong choice.

Jummar won important allies to his cause including key military figures like the loyal general, Mahabat Khan, who had grown to loathe the power Jahan had exercised over the emperor, "Never has there been a king so subject to the will of his wife," he said.

The death of Jahangir on 28 October 1627 triggered an immediate war of succession. His eldest son, Khusraw, who had already rebelled against his father and had been blinded for his treachery was killed during an uprising in Deccan. The second son, Parviz, was an alcoholic which just left Jummar. To begin with Jahan and Khusraw's campaign looked like prevailing but family disloyalty once again played its part when Jahan's own brother, Asaf

Khan, jealous of his sister's power, sided with Jummar and the battle was lost. Jummar ordered the execution of his brother, Khusraw while Jahan herself must have wondered what fate would befall her when Jummar declared himself the new Mughal emperor, Shah Jahan in 1628.[36]

In fact such was the level of political stability, religious tolerance and cultural sophistication which had been built up during Jahangir's rule that Jahan was fortunate to survive in some comfort. Revenge was not an issue at least at this time. In particular Jahangir, a Muslim, insisted that his nobles should not impose Islam on his people; the Jesuits were allowed to preach and convert their followers to Christianity. Today of course India is a secular nation while also rejoicing in a multitude of different and tolerant religions.

Under Jahangir the imperial boundaries had expanded. Agreement was reached with the Hindu rulers of Rajputana – 18 princely states in an area comprising roughly present day Rajasthan. The Mughal authority was accepted and in return the Hindu rulers were rewarded with positions of rank within the Mughal aristocracy. But it was the cultural and artistic legacy of the period which is remembered by scholars today.

As a young man Jahangir was fascinated by painting and even had his own studio. Mughal painting during his reign is regarded as exceptional ranging from portraiture to the documentation of plants and animals; with scientific precision records were kept of all the plants and creatures in his aviary and zoo. Under the influence of Jahan, he promoted Persian culture throughout his lands.

Mughal architecture and exquisite gardens stand as a lasting legacy of Jahangir's reign including the Shalimar Gardens in Kashmir built for Nur Jahan in 1619 and later extended by Shah Jahan.

But upon Shah Jahan's succession Nur Jahan's power in court came to an abrupt end and she was exiled to luxurious imprisonment – or house arrest as it might be called today – in Lahore with her daughter. Jahan spent her remaining days designing and overseeing construction of the tomb and gardens of Itmad-Ud-Daulah in Agra for her father, Mirza Ghiyas Beg. The walls are made of white marble from Rajasthan and encrusted with semi-precious stones. It has been dubbed the mini Taj Mahal. Jahan then drew up plans for the mausoleum at Shahdara in Lahore where the body of her husband, Jahanghir, lies. Alongside his tomb is a more modest one for Jahan herself.

Until her death on 17 December 1645 at the age of 68, Jahan confined herself to her Persian poetry and the traditional Persian pastime of perfume-making as well as architectural design. It seemed like a genteel and peaceful 'retirement' for one of India's most powerful people – man or woman. Together with her husband she will always be remembered not only as the effective ruler of her husband's empire but also as a woman of culture and refinement, and a great patron of the arts.

To this day the stunning architectural legacy of their reign remains, including buildings such as the NurMahal Sarai in Jalandhar. NurMahal itself is named after Nur Jahan as this is where it is thought she spent part of her childhood.

Nur Jahan was one of history's most powerful female figures while never actually formally holding a position of power. She influenced, teased and possibly bullied all the men who crossed her path for the most part because she saw weakness in them. She knew she had to fight her own corner using the considerable talents at her disposal. In a world where retribution and revenge could be savage, she managed to control a mighty empire and introduce a degree of culture and sophistication. She was charitable and kind to the poor and supported tolerance among religions. When her moment as an unofficial leader of a great nation was over she devoted her final days to works of art and architecture. Nur Jahan was an atypical shadow player but she was a survivor in a world when men dominated affairs of state and where women were confined behind screens. But when the time came for her to sit alongside her husband millions of people knew who was really giving the orders.

7

François Leclerc du Tremblay (1577–1638)

France in the 16th century was a nation in turmoil wracked in particular by the Wars of Religion (1562–98) pitting the Catholic League against the Protestant Huguenots. It was also a struggle between the nobility and the monarchy whose chief protagonists seemed to switch readily between religions to suit prevailing circumstances. When Henry, King of  Navarre, made his final assault on Paris he adopted Roman Catholicism for a second time in order to win the favour of the city and its citizens reputedly saying: "Paris is worth a mass." He was duly proclaimed king as Henry IV of France in 1589, the first Bourbon king.

Henry was a popular and tolerant monarch and guaranteed religious freedom for all, including the Protestants, when he enacted the Edict of Nantes in 1598. Such tolerance would cost him his life when a fanatical Catholic, François Ravaillac, later assassinated him.

It was into the midst of this unrest that François Leclerc was born on 4th November 1577, the eldest son of Jean Leclerc, Chancellor of the Duc d'Alençon, and Marie de La Fayette. His mother was from minor nobility. Her father Claude de La Fayette held four baronies one of which, Baron de Maffliers, was bequeathed to François.

The young François very quickly showed two distinct characteristics: he was exceptionally bright mastering Latin and Greek fluently by the age of ten, and he was strangely introverted although always active. He even asked to be sent to boarding school for fear of becoming too much of a mother's boy – a sign of the ascetic life which beckoned. During his early manhood he was confused, attracted by parties and beautiful girls on the one hand and the intensely powerful pull of religious life on the other.

Like other young men from well-to-do families in 1595 he went on the Grand Tour of Europe with his noble friends but unlike them instead of pursuing a life of fun he took the opportunity to expand his studies in Florence, Rome and Venice. He was soon back in Paris where his intelligence, manners and good looks attracted considerable attention. The king's mistress, Gabrielle d'Estrées called him "The Cicero of France and of his age."[37] But while he may have been turning heads François always maintained a curious reserve – it was as though he was afraid of having too much fun lest it distracted him from his religious studies which were becoming more intense.

He served briefly in the military participating in the Siege of Amiens in 1597. He also made a short visit to London but returned appalled convinced it was a land of heretics condemned to everlasting damnation in hell. Two years later on 2nd February 1599 he joined the Capuchin monastery in Orléans and put on the grey habit of a Franciscan friar. His mother was at first horrified having hoped for greater things in public life for her talented son but in the end she accepted his vocation little knowing that his chosen path would far exceed anything that he might have achieved in his former life. Achievement may not be the right word because this highly religious man was to become confused in his priorities and his actions would lead directly to untold suffering for hundreds of thousands and yet, while well aware of what was happening, he would justify everything because he believed with a fervour which commanded admiration from the highest in the land that it was God's will.

The new novitiate immediately stood out. He was sent to the Capuchin seminary in Rouen where he was allowed to skip two of the four years of study because he was already so advanced. His devotions, long hours of prayer greatly in excess of what was required, marked him out as exceptional, a potential saint even, because what his superiors in the seminary noticed was his gift for orison. He was obsessed with the image and suffering of the crucified Christ and his extended prayer time and contemplation (more than the two usual for the order) led him to episodes of ecstasy and the seeing of visions.

François Leclerc du Tremblay (1577–1638)

In 1604 he was ordained, Father Joseph, and appointed to the Capuchin house of Meudon to teach the novices there. But not content with that role he also began converting those in the surrounding the countryside who had suffered during the Wars of Religion. Such was his eloquence and talent for preaching that his congregations would groan aloud at their sins and wrongdoings. But the young priest was already showing signs of the enormous workload he would come to impose upon himself, retiring to his spartan cell for more time in prayer, meditation and self-annihilation before rising early after a few hours sleep to return to his work of evangelisation. His emphasis in his sermons which could last two hours was often the importance of mental prayer. "A man who neglects his duty of orison is blind indeed, not knowing his friends from his enemies," he wrote at the time.

The turning point in Fr Joseph's career from cleric to politician can be marked by his appointment to preach in the city of Saumur which under the terms of the Edict of Nantes had been given to the Protestant Huguenots under its governor, Du Plessis-Mornay. Dissatisfied with merely preaching, Fr Joseph won agreement to establish a house for his Capuchin friars in the city.

His success had come as a direct result of the intervention of Eléonore du Bourbon, Abbess of Fontevrault, not far from Saumur. The abbess, one of Henry IV's aunts, had been impressed by the young friar, despite his unkempt appearance and ragged grey friar's habit; beneath it all she reasoned he was after all nobility – Baron de Maffliers. Du Plessis-Mornay had only given his grudging agreement because he had no wish to offend the crown. The key here is the importance of the noble status of the abbesses in the convents – positions which were in the gift of the royal family. These were not just matters of religion.

Fr Joseph was encouraged to help establish a new convent for genuine contemplatives under Madame Antoinette d'Orléans and to do what he could to inject some piety into the way of life of the well-to-do nuns of Fontevrault. Despite his best efforts Fr Joseph conceded that he needed help and sought the advice of the twenty year old bishop of Luçon, one Armand du Plessis de Richlieu. An unbreakable but terrible lifelong friendship was immediately forged as Fr Joseph would assume the role of secretary to Richelieu in 1611.

In due time in 1617 Madame d'Orleans's convent was established as an independent order from that of Fontevrault and called the Congregation of Our Lady of Calvary. Throughout his future career Fr Joseph would continue to spend time guiding and preaching and writing (a manual of devotion) to his Calvarians.

However, two years earlier France found herself gripped by civil war following the murder of Henry IV and the calamitous regency of his widow, Marie de Medicis, while the new king, Louis XIII, was still a minor. Not only did Louis hate his mother who insisted that he receive daily birchings even when he was actually king, but more worryingly the nobility were once again flexing their muscles angered by the corruption they saw being exercised by Marie de Medicis who tried to buy them off with lavish gifts. These only served to strengthen their resolve and further angered the people.

One of the leading nobles was the Prince of Condé. Fr Joseph took it upon himself to meet the Prince and his allies in order to persuade them to spare the people more bloodshed. By all accounts he bewitched them with a combination of appealing to the better side of their natures and then switching to threats of what their actions might mean for them in the afterlife. This was a tactic, albeit an unwitting one, which the friar would use time and again. It must have been convincing because he was asked to act as an envoy on their behalf with the Queen Mother and her own now close adviser, Richelieu. He drove out in his carriage to meet the approaching friar who travelled everywhere on foot as he never allowed himself the indulgence of riding a horse or in a carriage. But Richelieu being a bishop was able to order him to break that rule and once more the two men were able to discuss at length what was happening to the country and the direction they believed it should take. They resolved quite simply that the power of the nobles and the Huguenots in particular should be broken allowing central government to rule supreme. To achieve this, in the name of God, Fr Joseph believed it required the collaboration of the most powerful Catholic powers against the heretics – in short a united Christendom. Already the two driving forces of the rest of Fr Joseph's life were being refined. Everything he now did could be justified because it would be God's work.

Richelieu was more concerned with Spain and Austria but despite their differences on tactics Fr Joseph was now in awe of the intellect of his friend, seemingly the only man in court capable of achieving their mutual ends. The all powerful Richelieu for his part would come to rely on the humble Fr Joseph for spiritual and moral guidance. He would call him *mon appui* – my support. Their two driving ambitions fell into unhappy alignment –

Richelieu wanted French domination in Europe and his secretary wanted nothing less than the conversion of all European Protestants to Roman Catholicism.

Fr Joseph's diplomatic reputation was further enhanced thanks to his negotiations which led to the Treaty of Loudon signed on 3 May 1616 bringing a temporary end to the fighting between the nobles and Marie de Medicis's rule. One of the chief protagonists was the Duke of Bouillon who said of Fr Joseph: "This man penetrates my most secret thoughts; he knows things that I have communicated only to a few people of tried discretion; and he goes to Tours and returns, on foot, in the rain, the snow and the ice, in the most frightful weather, without anybody being able to observe him. I swear, the devil must be in this friar's body."[38] Henceforth Fr Joseph would find himself wheeling and dealing in political circles albeit for the good of God's work on earth.

1616 also marked a significant change in the powerbase of France. Louis XIII, no longer a minor, finally snapped after a lifetime of abuse by his mother and ordered the arrest and execution of her closest supporter and chief minister, the Italian nobleman Concino Concini. This was a setback for Richelieu who enjoyed Concini's backing and he escaped into exile for the next four years along with the Queen Mother while Louis relied on Charles d'Albert, Duke of Luynes, who had plotted to assassinate Concini, to run France.

There was another concern which had exercised Fr Joseph since his childhood spent reading about St Francis and in particular about his desire to recover the Holy Places from the Turkish infidel. Now in adulthood Fr Joseph was convinced that a crusade was required which of course France would lead. The only sticking point was that Spain quickly realised if they supported such a military adventure the real beneficiary would be France and as a result Spain failed to give her backing.

However Fr Joseph's desire for a crusade had to be put on hold as Central Europe was plunged into what would develop into the Thirty Years' War, essentially a religious conflict between Protestants and Catholics of the Holy Roman Empire. It would lay waste the region leaving it wracked by starvation and untold brutality with atrocities perpetrated on the hapless people by the mercenary style armies who sustained themselves on wanton looting and pillaging. If Fr Joseph could not have his crusade (he even wrote an epic poem on the subject, *La Turciade*) then he would do the next best thing – focus on the destruction of the Hapsburgs.

In 1619 however there was an important development in the rehabilitation of Richelieu. The Queen Mother had escaped from the castle in Blois to where she had been exiled and there was a threat of potential rebellion against the king who turned to Fr Joseph for advice. His friar recommended sending Sébastien Bouthillier, the dean of Luçon, who happened to be one of Richelieu's closest supporters to sue for peace. As part of the negotiations the Queen Mother insisted that Richelieu should be allowed to return to Paris. The King agreed and in fact Richelieu proved to be a moderating influence in bringing some temporary harmony between Louis and his mother. In return he demanded that Luynes should send a request to Pope Urban VIII in Rome that he be made a cardinal. Luynes reluctantly agreed although Richelieu did not receive his hat until 1622.

Nevertheless Richelieu was now unstoppable. While the king positively disliked Richelieu he also acknowledged that he was the ablest man in the kingdom and in 1624 admitted him to the council of state and shortly after appointed him prime minister. Richelieu's first act was to summon Fr Joseph from his friar's duties to Paris where in effect he became the unofficial head of foreign affairs and together, until Fr Joseph's death in 1638, they would lead France into turmoil.

The two men were so different and yet with the same ambition: Richelieu accumulated great wealth through his multitude of benefices as he sought to strengthen France's position. Fr Joseph however refused all offers of reward, constantly denied himself any comforts and yet permitted himself the vanity of doing everything for the greater good of France and his king no matter what the cost and no matter how high a price the population had to pay because it was the will of God. The historian, Gabriel Hanotaux, in his biography of Richelieu said of Fr Joseph: "...he gave himself to two high causes, which absorbed his life, God and France, always ready to work and fight for either cause, but never separating one from the other, always responding to the call of an inner conviction, namely that France is the instrument of Providence and French greatness is a providential thing."[39] The united aim was to destroy the Hapsburgs, defeat Spain and Austria and of course to create one unified France under King Louis. To achieve that ambition anything was justified including prolonging the rape of the rest of Europe by marauding armies now well into the Thirty Years' War. Nor was Fr Joseph averse to working with his 'enemies' using the Protestant forces to attack Austria and at the same time use the House of Austria fatally to weaken the Protestants.

Meanwhile Fr Joseph had been appointed Apostolic Commissary of Missions which in effect enabled him to establish foreign missions wherever his tired, bare feet carried him. Importantly, in so doing, he developed a network of his friars and other informants who reported back to him on matters both religious and political. His critics accused him of creating his own spy network and to maintain his secret service he thought nothing of bribing his agents to betray their loyalties as he listened to their whispered information in secret late night meetings. Come the dawn he was on his knees again devoting his political manoeuvrings to God. His evangelisation knew no bounds eventually establishing missions as far afield as Greece, Asia Minor, Egypt and Abyssinia.

The breaking of the Huguenots' political power was achieved with the end of a long siege of La Rochelle which cost the lives of twenty thousand of the twenty five thousand inhabitants. Fr Joseph fervently hoped this was an opportunity to launch a crusade against the Turks in the Holy Land but the war in Europe persisted and in time Fr Joseph's own reputation began to suffer as he was being openly criticised for apparently turning his back on his clerical duties in favour of political power albeit in the service of Richelieu. Pamphlets were circulated attacking both Richelieu and his friar and one man openly said to Fr Joseph's face that he should be ashamed as a priest for starting "a bloody war between the Catholic sovereigns – between the Emperor, the King of Spain and the King of France." For his part the cardinal was using a cleric to achieve his aims in Europe and hide behind the friar to carry out his crimes.

Richelieu's, and by association, Fr Joseph's position in court for a moment looked in jeopardy when Louis fell ill and seemed about to die. Immediately political manoeuvring got underway led by the king's mother, Marie de Medicis, and it was agreed among the plotters that on his death Richelieu would suffer the same fate as Concini. In the event the king recovered and on what became known as the Day of Dupes, 10 November 1630, Richelieu's position was guaranteed and Fr Joseph was naturally assumed to be his successor on the cardinal's death. Marie de Medicis was exiled from court once again to Compiègne in northern France never to return.

Fr Joseph meanwhile moved between his Capuchin cell in the convent on the Rue Saint-Honoré and an apartment in the cardinal's palace, although the accommodation was as spartan as his cell. The question remained – who was influencing whom? Was Fr Joseph, the éminence grise in his shabby friar's habit, the menacing figure moving secretively through Paris the real power or was Richelieu contrasting in his cardinal's scarlet robes – the éminence rouge – simply using his devout and malleable secretary to do his bidding. No matter, together the two men plotted the foreign policy of France which inevitably meant more fighting which in turn meant an even greater tax burden on the population rising by more than four times the level they had had to endure under Henry IV. The heavy burden provoked revolts throughout the country which were duly put down without mercy and always justified by Richelieu, "...extortions which are intolerable in their nature, become excusable from the necessities of war."

This is not the place to detail every battle during this period, the manoeuvrings, the changing allegiances all of which Fr Joseph artfully controlled but towards the end of his life his influence over Richelieu can best be illustrated in one incident when Cardinal-Infante Ferdinand and his Spanish forces were on the verge of besieging Paris itself. Richelieu was contemplating resignation and even fearful of Parisian people who were at their wit's end following the years of his tyrannical rule. Fr Joseph exhorted him not to be a coward but to go out in his carriage, unguarded, and to tell the people to have courage. The tactic worked and he was cheered by one and all. In the end the Spanish forces delayed any possible attack which allowed the French to regroup and the threat receded when the Cardinal-Infante led his troops northwards.

As it had always been assumed that Fr Joseph would succeed Richelieu, all that remained was for him to be elevated to cardinal and Louis made numerous requests to the Vatican. But Pope Urban was reluctant for a variety of reasons including the fact that he was actually unpopular among the clergy, mistrusted by Emperor Ferdinand of Austria and there was already a Capuchin cardinal who didn't want a rival as powerful as Fr Joseph appointed. When finally the Pope relented and agreed, the honour would come too late because Fr Joseph died leaving a sick Richelieu without his support to linger on for four more years.

What had these two men achieved in pursuit of Richelieu's ambition to weaken Spain and Austria, destroy Germany and impose Bourbon rule over the Hapsburgs? As Aldous Huxley puts it: "That policy was successful – so successful, indeed, that when Lous XIV carried it to its insanely logical conclusion, perpetual aggressive warfare against everybody, all Europe united against the Bourbons." He went further and stated that the cardinal's actions created "...the social and economic and political conditions which led to the downfall of that dynasty, the rise of Prussia and the catastrophes of the nineteenth and twentieth centuries."[40]

As for Fr Joseph, he was a man both feared and admired. In the event the friar's twin ambitions failed with the rise of Protestantism in Europe and the dominance of the Ottoman Empire. Even when he suffered a stroke he tried to the last to fulfil his duty as spiritual director to his nuns by preaching for hours. Finally he died on 18th December 1638 and was buried in the Capuchin church near the grave of Ange de Joyeuse who had first received him into the order. However, such was the hatred that he had engendered among the people that someone scrawled on his gravestone in French:

Passer-by, is it not a strange thing that a demon should be next to an angel?

8

JEANNE-ANTOINETTE POISSON (1721–1764)

B eauty rather than intellect was Jeanne-Antoinette Poisson's secret weapon and she deployed it with skill and consummate style to allow her star to shine brightly albeit briefly to illuminate 18th century French court life after the death of the Sun King Louis XIV; a remarkable achievement in itself for an illegitimate commoner.

Jeanne-Antoinette was quite literally preened and packaged, prepared and polished for the role Madame le Bon, a fortune teller, is said to have foreseen. One day, her mother was assured, her daughter would capture the heart of a king.[41] She took the prediction seriously, nicknamed her daughter, Reinette (little queen), and began educating her from the age of nine for the royal life ahead and for what was to become her own unique place in history.

Jeanne-Antoinette was born in Paris on 29 December 1721 and was baptised the next day in the church of Saint-Eustache. Her mother was Madeleine de La Motte and her father was said to be François Poisson, a financier who was accused of fraud and was forced to flee the country when Jeanne-Antoinette was only four; conviction for unpaid debts in those days carried the death penalty in France. He was cleared of all the charges eight years later but in the meantime Jeanne-Antoinette and her mother were taken under the protective wing of Charles François Paul Le Normant de Tournehem, a wealthy tax collector. He paid for Jeanne-Antoinette's education, and is generally thought to be her biological father although another financier, Pâris de Montmartel, is sometimes mentioned.

Jeanne-Antoinette attended an Ursuline[42] convent in Poissy and received private tuition with a succession of tutors from the world of Parisian opera and theatre who focused on her elocution. This theatrical training during which Jeanne-Antoinette memorised entire plays would stand her in good stead for the real life role she was to assume. More usual for a young lady with aspirations to join high society as a courtesan, she learned to paint, dance and play the clavichord. Somewhat surprisingly though she also attended the Club de l'Entresol, which today would be described as a 'think tank' for political and economic discussion. It was founded by Pierre-Joseph Alary and Charles-Irénée Castel de Saint-Pierre and was an all male club which met once a week in Paris and was frequented by the likes of Baron de Montesquieu, Horace Walpole and Viscount Bolinbroke. Jeanne-Antoinette became an unofficial guest and quite what these men of letters and political thinkers made of her presence is not recorded but when the time came Jeanne-Antoinette would not be able to resist trying her hand at politics.

Presumably not laying too much store by the musings of a fortune teller, Charles Le Normant de Tournehem arranged for Jeanne-Antoinette to marry his nephew, Charles-Guillaume Le Normant d'Etiolles, at the age of 19. He set them up on a beautiful estate at Etiolles, south of Paris which he gave them as a wedding present. They had two children – a son who died when he was just one year old and a daughter, Alexandrine-Jeanne, whom they called Fanfan. Sadly she also died at the age of nine.

Jeanne-Antoinette's mother must have begun wondering about the prophecies of her fortune teller. Although her daughter had married well she was not moving in royal circles and all that grooming was in danger of going to waste. Jeanne-Antoinette herself clearly decided that she was destined for something more important than married life on the distant outskirts of Paris.

She was regarded as a woman of great beauty and wit and before long she had established her own *salon* at Etiolles which began attracting members of the fashionable Parisian world of painters and sculptors as well as writers including François-Marie Arouet, better known by his pen name, Voltaire.

The Etiolles estate was situated on the edge of the royal hunting ground of the Forest of Sénart which may have proved fortuitous. According to at least one account King Louis XV noticed her deftly driving her phaeton through the woods during a hunt. She must have cut quite a figure and it seems instantly brightened up the life of an increasingly gloomy Louis.

His devoted and pious wife, a Polish princess called Marie Leszczyńska, had borne him 10 children by the time he was just 27 and presumably out of exhaustion if nothing else had lost interest in the king's relentless sexual demands. Louis had turned his attentions to other high born ladies in the court but his third official mistress, the Duchesse de Châteauroux, had just died when his eyes alighted on Jeanne-Antoinette racing through the woods.

She made a more demure entrance to court when she was invited to a masked ball at the Palace of Versailles on 25 February 1745. It was to celebrate the marriage of the king's son 15 year old Louis, Dauphin of France, to the 19 year old, Infanta Maria Teresa of Spain. Jeanne-Antoinette came dressed as a shepherdess and with one aim in mind: to secure the love of the king, who strangely had come as a tree. Evidently she had an instant effect as it is said that her carriage was seen waiting outside the royal apartments the next morning. Whether that is the case or not Jeanne-Antoinette defied the courtiers' assumptions that she would not last long in the king's capricious affections and within weeks she had moved into her own apartment at Versailles directly below the king's. Louis may have been impressed by his new conquest's confidence: she is said to have insisted on succumbing to his charms only on the condition that he made her his official mistress. On 7 May Jeanne-Antoinette officially separated from her husband.

Although well regarded in society, Jeanne-Antoinette was a commoner and urgently needed a title if she was to be presented in court. Louis simply solved the problem by making her the Marquise of Pompadour with her own coat of arms and, on the 14 September that same year, the king's cousin, the Princess de Conti, formally presented her in court. Jeanne-Antoinette's mother must have been thrilled that her work was done but it was short-lived as she died on Christmas Day. It was also time for Madame de Pompadour, as she is better known, to begin to make her own mark on history.

One might divide her role into three areas of influence: the royal bedchamber, the arts and politics. She had competition in the affections for the king but not in Louis's eyes. He adored Madame de Pompadour and became stepfather to her daughter, Fanfan. When the child fell ill he summoned the finest physicians to her side and was heartbroken when she died.

Inevitably there was much jealousy in the corridors of the palace that a mere commoner had managed to steal the heart of the king. She hated the slurs and insults which circulated and the puns on her name known as *poissonades*. At least one lady tried to usurp her as the king's chief mistress.

Marie-Louise O'Murphy de Boisfaily, nicknamed 'la belle Morphyse', tried and failed. She was the daughter of an Irish officer and already one of the king's junior mistresses having being introduced to him by way of a nude portrait commissioned by none other than Giacomo Casanova. Having served as Louis's mistress for two years she thought her moment had come to oust Madame de Pompadour. It was a mistake. A marriage was hastily arranged between her and a provincial nobleman from the Auvergne, Jacques Pelet de Beaufranchet, and she was ousted from court life.

One can only imagine the rows with the king behind closed doors as Madame de Pompadour complained about all the back biting and insults she felt she was having to endure. She probably demanded that Louis did something about it which occasionally he reluctantly did. He even fell out with his best friend the Duke of Richelieu, Louis Francois Armand de Vignerot du Plessis, a soldier and diplomat, who opposed the status and growing influence the king's *maîtresse-en-titre* had acquired, although they were reconciled after her death.

However despite the comments and the salacious cartoons which appeared depicting Madame de Pompadour in vulgar poses, her place in the king's heart and therefore court was entirely secure, not only secure but the great and the good of society and the arts fluttered around her bright flame.

Madame de Pompadour employed all the skills she had learned at the hands of her tutors and staged plays often casting herself in the lead role as a nymph or shepherdess infatuated by the gods.[43] She arranged operas and ballets all to entertain the king and most importantly to ensure that she remained the focus of his affections.

She astutely made sure she maintained an amicable relationship with the Queen who had to tolerate her husband's insatiable appetite for women. Madame de Pompadour showed her all the respect due to a Queen and never tried to usurp her position. Marie Leszczyńska is quoted as saying, "If there must be a mistress, better her than any other." No doubt Louis liked them both all the more for such understanding.

In order to prevent Louis being distracted from other young things at the Palace, Madame de Pompadour acquired lodges and chateaux where she and the king could enjoy their own company perhaps even pretending to be an ordinary couple albeit in luxurious surroundings.

The chateaux were all sumptuously decorated with portraits of her in beguiling and voluptuous poses by artists she patronised like François Boucher, a painter in the Rococo style and François-Hubert Drouais. She may have been maligned by the likes of Thomas Carlyle[44] who called her a "high-rouged unfortunate female of whom it is not proper to speak without necessity" but thanks to her training she became a highly cultured individual whose influence extended beyond commissioning flattering portraits of herself.

Her pursuit of all things beautiful was in large part responsible for a succession of great works of art. Boucher's designs inspired much of the creative genius at the Sèvres porcelain factory – the classic Sèvres pink is called *rose de Pompadour* – and were used in Gobelins tapestries; furniture manufacturers were asked to create pieces for her chateaux. The journalist, Francis Hodgson sums up her contribution: "In literature, sculpture, architecture, the theatre, she knew everyone and cultivated the best. She received Mozart at home a few weeks before she died in 1764. If she had done nothing else she would be prodigious in art history for her role as a patron."[45]

Madame de Pompadour remained the king's mistress for five years. But after suffering two miscarriages in 1746 and 1749, and no matter how much "vanilla, truffles and celery" she reportedly ate to arouse the king's passion, her own sexual desires began to fade and they ceased to be lovers by 1750 – she was still only 29. However she was determined to retain her position of authority when it came to the royal boudoir as well as the affairs of state. She personally selected the more junior mistresses to satisfy Louis while she moved into grander quarters in the palace and turned her attention and influence to other matters. Art, in particular architecture, and more disastrously politics were to distract her.

In architecture her keen eye and artistic judgement didn't fail her, and her brother, Abel, was there to help; when she first became Louis' mistress she had arranged for Abel to follow her to court. On the retirement of Philibert Orry as Director General of the King's Buildings, Abel was given the job of running the operation aged just 18 and ennobled with the title of Marquis de Marigny. Madame de Pompadour's biological father, Charles François Paul Le Normant de Tournehem, was named Orry's official successor.

Together they planned the Place de la Concorde (then called Place de Louis XV) in Paris and the Petit Trianon at Versailles. Beauty to some however is extravagance to others and Madame de Pompadour never held back on any expense – to the point where the people began to notice. During the French Revolution the Place de la Concorde was where they placed the guillotine, which despatched 1,300 souls including Madame du Barry, Louis' chief mistress and Louis XVI, his grandson. The Petit Trianon was only completed after Madame de Pompadour's death and became Madame du Barry's residence.

While no-one doubts Madame de Pompadour's artistic if lavish tastes her political skills were less promising. Whatever she learned at the Club d'Entresol she had either forgotten or misunderstood – a little knowledge was indeed to prove a dangerous thing. But Louis it seems was happy for his mistress to dabble in foreign affairs while pleasures of the flesh distracted him.

Such was her status in court that in 1755 a prominent Austrian diplomat, Wenzel Anton Graf Kaunitz who was ambassador at the Court of Versailles asked for her help in the negotiations which led to the Treaty of Versailles signed in 1756. Austria at the time felt aggrieved at the loss of territory to Prussia. The Treaty was an agreement between France and Austria which said if either was attacked by a third party, assumed to mean Prussia or Britain, the other would come to the defence of its ally. No sooner had the agreement been signed than France and Austria found themselves at war with both Britain and Prussia. It was the start of the Seven Years War which before long involved all the major powers fighting in theatres across the globe: there was the French and Indian War, the Pomeranian War between Sweden and Prussia, the Third Carnatic War on the Indian sub-continent and the Third Silesian War between Prussian and Austria. Essentially though it was a fight between France, Austria and Russia on the one hand against Britain and Prussia on the other. Madame de Pompadour had a lot to answer for.

She can't be held entirely to blame but it was her influence on Louis which helped pull France into the war. In 1757 Frederick the Great of Prussia and his forces inflicted a heavy defeat on the allied armies of the French and Holy Roman Empire at the Battle of Rossbach. The Prussians lost some 550 men, their enemy suffered 10,000 casualties and prisoners. When news of the defeat reached Versailles Madame de Pompadour is said to have uttered the immortal words in comfort to Louis: *Au reste, après nous, le Déluge* (Besides, after us, the Deluge.) By the time the war was over France had lost its North American territories and was virtually bankrupt.

Her meddling in diplomatic affairs was not only damaging to her country but ruthless in her treatment of people who one moment thought they had her support and the next were out of favour. One such victim was Cardinal de Bernis.

Although of noble birth, François-Joachim de Pierre de Bernis, as he then was, came from an impoverished family. But his intelligence and poetry had attracted Madame de Pompadour's attention and she established him in an apartment in the Tuileries Palace in Paris along with a handsome pension. He was appointed French Ambassador to Venice and it was in this role that he had handled the initial negotiations between France and Austria which preceded the Seven Years War. While in Venice he became a sub-deacon and in 1755 he was made a papal councillor of state on his return to France.

But Bernis didn't know which side his bread was buttered. No sooner had he been appointed Secretary for Foreign Affairs than he started trying to rein in some of the excesses of his erstwhile supporter Madame de Pompadour who continued to 'advise' on overseas adventures. He should have known better. There was no doubt a word in Louis' ear casting doubt on the Foreign Secretary's ability and in December 1757 Bernis was banished to Soissons, 100 kilometres from Paris. Only a month earlier he had been elevated by the Pope to Cardinal which was supposed to have given him special authority in the Royal Council.

In time Madame de Pompadour's health began to fail. As well as the effects of two miscarriages she now developed tuberculosis and died on Easter Day, 15 April 1764, at Versailles. She was 42.

She was buried two days later beside her daughter precisely in accordance to the terms of her will: "I wish my body to be carried to the Capuchin Friars in Place *Vendôme* in Paris, without ceremonies in order to be buried in the crypt of the chapel that has been given to me in this church."[46]

Although roundly blamed for much of France's economic woes at the time and the loss of lands it once held, in death Madame de Pompadour was admired for the way she endured the suffering in her final days and will always be remembered for her contribution to artistic excellence. Voltaire wrote: "I am very sad at the death of Madame de Pompadour. I was indebted to her and I mourn her out of gratitude. It seems absurd that while an ancient pen-pusher, hardly able to walk, should still be alive, a beautiful woman, in the midst of a splendid career, should die at the age of forty two."

She had also come upon the scene when life in the court needed brightening as Louis mourned the loss of his mistress. Madame de Pompadour introduced laughter and gaiety; there was music and dancing, plays and opera to distract him. No doubt he should have spent more time on the affairs of state but he was devoted to his Marquise and was sad at her passing. As Louis stood in the rain watching her coffin being carried away from Versailles he said: *La marquise n'aura pas de beau temps pour son voyage.* (The marquise won't have good weather for her journey.)

There was a sense of fun about her which did much to restore her image. A British regiment, the 56th (West Essex) Regiment of Foot became known as "The Pompadours" for its use of her favourite colour purple on the regiment's uniform. The regiment's successor, the Essex, retained both the name and colour. The Pompadour hairstyle is also named after her.

So where does she sit in the gallery of those who have found themselves in the shadow of power? There is no doubt she held King Louis's undivided attention at least for five years and thereafter his devoted friendship. She interfered disastrously in the affairs of state which cost her country dear but she probably contributed more than anyone else to the promotion of artistic endeavour at the time, commissioning works of art, supporting writers and science such as defending the publication of the *Encylopédie* edited by Denis Diderot and Jean le Rond d'Alember. Her influence on some of the great architectural sites in and around Paris and the building of chateaux all to be exquisitely furnished cannot be underestimated.

Her renown if not always her judgement cast a brighter light than others around her. People will always remember the name Pompadour probably more readily than King Louis XV in whose shadow she stood.

9

Charles Maurice de Talleyrand-Périgord (1754–1838)

To serve one master well and faithfully is a worthy achievement, to serve six with widely differing agendas is remarkable and probably unique. Charles Maurice de Talleyrand-Périgord, or Talleyrand as he is universally known, is a prime candidate for our collection. He managed this feat with aplomb and in so doing rightly earned himself the titles of the 'father of diplomacy' and 'prince of diplomats'. Some say he was a traitor to each of his masters as he switched allegiances without apparent qualm to enrich himself. Others argue that he merely served only one as he manoeuvred his way effortlessly through the minefield of politics that was France.[47]

Born on 2 February 1754 in Paris, Talleyrand might have hoped for a military career but he had a club foot as a result of a congenital disorder, Marfan's Syndrome. Unlike his father, Count Daniel de Talleyrand-Périgord, who rose to the rank of Lieutenant-General in the army, the family decided that the young Talleyrand should enter the church, much against his own wishes.

Happily his uncle, Alexandre Angélique de Talleyrand-Périgord, was Archbishop of Reims, and Talleyrand's progress from ordination in 1779 aged 25 to the post of Agent-General of the Clergy, representing the Catholic Church to the French Crown the following year appeared to be effortless. As Agent-General he would come to draft an inventory of the properties of the church proclaiming the "inalienable rights of the church" a position he would deny later in life as matters suited a different master. By 1789 Talleyrand was consecrated Bishop of Autun just as the French Revolution was getting underway. But it was already apparent that the clerical life was not sufficiently interesting and he spent barely three weeks attending to the faithful of his bishopric before being appointed deputy of the National Assembly.

His personal life was also becoming complicated as he enjoyed the new freedoms and liberties which were already being felt in Paris. If you had talent, charm and a quick wit it no longer mattered that you were not of the highest birth, in fact it probably helped. Between 1783 and 1792 he conducted an affair with the Countess Adelaïde de Flahaut and they had a child Charles de Flahaut, in 1785 probably the only child among several reliably attributed to Talleyrand's philandering over the years.

At this time Louis XVI was on the throne in France but after a brief bout of popularity following his accession it was not long before the mood swung against him. At first it was merely high society which found him to be dull-witted but increasingly the nobility opposed his reforms including an increased tolerance towards non-Catholics. Gradually the general population began to have enough of aristocratic rule as well.

Meanwhile Talleyrand, dubbed the Abbé de Perigord, was already eyeing up the potential of a political future and took advantage of the fact that he established a close friendship with Charles-Alexandre, Vicomte de Colonne, who had been appointed Controller-General of Finances. At the time France was virtually bankrupt and Talleyrand supported Colonne's agreement with England abolishing tariffs between the two countries in an effort to increase trade.

In May 1789 Louis accepted that in the face of bankruptcy France had to do something and called a rare meeting of the States-General – a gathering of the Three Orders: the clergy, the nobility and the Third Estate (the common people of France) at Versailles. From the start the key issue was one of procedure: how should they vote – together or as three separate bodies. The king tried to throw his weight about insisting that there should be separate votes and even locked everyone out of the regular meeting place when it looked as though the Third Estate would win the vote. The Third Estate retired to a nearby tennis court and refused to move until they had their way which amounted to the establishment of one Assembly where they would easily out vote the rest. Talleyrand, although not directly involved urged that the king should immediately dissolve the States-General and use force if necessary – he would later remind the Crown of his support. The king rejected this advice. The Revolution was underway.

With unrest in France growing against the monarchy Talleyrand could see the way the politics were moving. He saw no reason why he shouldn't support the effective nationalisation of church properties through a new law called the Civil Constitution of the Clergy even though it was diametrically opposed to the 'inalienable rights' of the church he had proclaimed as Agent-General just a few years earlier. In October 1789 he arranged for all church properties to be handed over to the state in exchange for salaries to be paid by the state and he went so far as to consecrate new bishops to replace the ones who had refused to swear an oath of allegiance according to the new laws. For these actions and possibly with regard to his disinterested attitude towards his flock in Autun and his profligate and licentious private life, Pope Pius VI excommunicated him from the Catholic Church in 1791. Talleyrand was probably indifferent as he had other plans for his future career and he had already been elected President of the Assembly where his 'nationalisation' of the church proved popular.

In 1792 Talleyrand was given his first unofficial diplomatic mission – a visit to England with the aim of keeping England neutral in the impending war with Austria and Prussia. But Talleyrand's mission, actually headed by the Duke de Biron, was always doomed to failure. The revolution in France was not popular among the other crowned heads of Europe; King George III held Talleyrand in contempt, the Prime Minister William Pitt always intended to keep England neutral but had no intention of agreeing to anything the French legation had to offer and the rest of noble society avoided any contact with the pair who represented everything they despised – a lack of loyalty to the crown and their own nobility. Furthermore Talleyrand was not properly accredited. He left empty handed and returned again in April as part of a formal mission headed by Marquis de Chauvelin. In the meantime France had declared war on Austria and unrest against the monarchy was growing in Paris. Pitt did not want to become embroiled in France's problems and reasserted England's neutrality which had nothing to do with anything Talleyrand had to offer on his nation's behalf.

In the late summer of 1792 the so called September Massacres began with mobs running riot through Paris. The monarchy was about to be suspended and the king arrested, found guilty of high treason and executed by guillotine on 21 January 1793. This outrage combined with France's invasion of Austrian Netherlands, present day Belgium, would soon bring England into the war.

It looked as though Talleyrand's diplomatic career was at an end before it had begun. He sought consolation in Surrey among the other exiled nobility dubbed the Liberals who, while hardly welcoming the Revolution, had for a time tried to make the best of it. The impact on the dull lives of the English middle classes was immediate as Duff Cooper quotes in his biography of Talleyrand: "There can be nothing imagined more charming, more fascinating than this colony"; "a society of incontestable superiority"[48] people said at the time.

Finally in 1794 he was expelled from England under the terms of the newly passed Aliens' Act and faced an arrest warrant issued by the National Convention in France as a result of incriminating papers that had been found two years earlier. In fact from his own letters to George-Jacques Danton, a leading figure in the early days of the Revolution who later was himself to die by the guillotine, it is clear that Talleyrand always urged the new order to be faithful to France's Constitution and not seek to expand its territories through armed conflict. Nevertheless at the time Talleyrand, unwelcome at home and in England, sought refuge in America taking up work as a commodities broker and property speculator in Massachusetts.

As a result of excesses even by the appalling standards of the Reign of Terror a new mood took hold in France which opened the way for friends of Talleyrand, notably Anne Louise Germaine de Staël-Holstein, a French writer, to speak in his defence leading to his return. France at this time (November 1795–November 1799) was ruled by the singularly incompetent Directory whose job it was to appoint Ministers. However as anyone with talent had either fled the Terror or was precluded from taking office as a result of terms of the Constitution it was hard to find suitable candidates. By chance Paul Barras, one of the few able leaders of the Directory, happened to be in charge when Talleyrand landed in Hamburg and it was not long before he was allowed safe passage back to Paris and was appointed Foreign Affairs Minister in 1797.

It must have been difficult even for as astute an operator as Talleyrand to judge how the politics in France at the time would unfold. He continued to show his loyalty to the Republican cause, while taking handsome bribes along the way from those who needed his support. While this was regarded as common practice among statesmen in France at the time, Talleyrand expected rewards on a grander scale. When the American President John

Adams sent envoys to France to negotiate an agreement protecting US ships from French privateers it was suggested that a bribe of $250,000 to Talleyrand plus a loan to France of $10 million would smooth the talks. It was rejected out of hand and the mission failed. The matter was made public and there were calls for war with France.

His private life continued to scandalise and impress in equal measure and he attracted the beauties of the day. It was widely assumed that having succeeded Charles Delacroix as Minister of Foreign Affairs, he proceeded to have an affair with Madame Delacroix who bore a child, the future renowned Romantic painter, Eugène Delacroix. Everyone knew that Charles Delacroix was impotent although he underwent a risky operation which was well publicised and apparently miraculously successful. The child's true parentage was never proved one way or the other.

Talleyrand now knew that the government he served was unlikely to last and it was not long before he began flattering by correspondence the successes of the youthful General Napoleon Bonaparte campaigning in Italy. The exiled Royalists for their part thought the tide was turning once more in their favour but they were wrong. Pierre Augerau, a plain speaking soldier, became the new head of the Directory which declared that votes giving greater control to Royalist sympathisers should be declared null and void.

Neither Napoleon nor Talleyrand cared much for the Government they served but both were prepared to bide their time. Napoleon had a supporter in court and Talleyrand recognised the potential power of his general whom he was careful to introduce when he came to Paris as Citizen Bonaparte. Meanwhile in Paris the Jacobins who had taken control of the Assembly had begun attacking the members of the Directory. Talleyrand was a particular object of distaste and, discretion being the better part of valour, he resigned his post in July 1799 leaving an ally, Abbé Emmanuel Sieyès, to take up his position as a Director with the clear intention of organising a coup d'état.

Talleyrand was not idle in his enforced leisure time and increased his long-distance correspondence with Napoleon backing his new campaign in Egypt. It was a shrewd alliance because either Napoleon would triumph and return the conquering hero fit to take power in France or he would be killed and Talleyrand would be able to find others to complete the task he was evidently plotting. As it turned out of course Napoleon's fleet was destroyed by Admiral Nelson in the battle of Aboukir Bay but he escaped and slowly made his way back to France.

Charles Maurice de Talleyrand-Périgord (1754–1838)

While Sieyès was completely confident in his own ability he recognised that he needed a soldier able to carry out the coup. After much searching the problem was solved when Napoleon landed at Fréjus and headed straight to Paris.

Following much plotting and behind the scenes string pulling orchestrated by Talleyrand who was always careful to remain in the background, Napoleon made his move on 9 November 1799 overthrowing the Assembly who were meeting in Saint Cloud and replacing it with the French Consulate. Once again Talleyrand returned to his role in the Foreign Ministry.

In this period Napoleon, the self-appointed First Consul of France, was primarily concerned by two matters: the Royalists and their attachment to the Bourbon princes, and the Jacobins who represented the old revolutionaries. It so happened that his two most influential ministers Talleyrand and Jospeh Fouché, the ruthless Minister of Police, also fell broadly into these camps. Talleyrand with his aristocratic background was once again opening private discussions with the Royalists as he already assumed that Napoleon's rule would not be a long one, and Fouché was firmly on the side of the Jacobins, although he was happy to round up and execute anyone if it suited his purpose. The First Consul erroneously thought he had more to fear from the latter.

Napoleon also wanted one other matter settled – a rapprochement between France and the Vatican. However it didn't help that his Foreign Minister was an excommunicated former bishop living openly in sin with yet another mistress, Catherine Grand. Talleyrand refused Napoleon's suggestion that he take up Holy Orders again so he succumbed to Napoleon's pressure to do the honourable thing and marry Catherine which he did in 1802. But it developed into a loveless marriage and Catherine eventually travelled to England where she lived in luxury provided for her by Talleyrand.

In his pursuit of peace Talleyrand ensured, despite Napoleon's continued interference, that a treaty between France and the United Kingdom was duly signed at Amiens in 1802. It would last only a year but it meant that the UK recognised the French Republic and marked the end of the Second Coalition, an alliance of European monarchs led by Austria and the Russian Empire to defeat Revolutionary France.

However Napoleon, still officially only First Consul, was becoming increasingly autocratic in his behaviour and, with the return of many nobles who were happy to be associated with him, his office was taking on the appearance of a royal court. Despite their apparent loyalty it soon became clear as more and more conspiracies emerged that Napoleon's greatest threat lay precisely with the aristocrats and Royalists gathering around him. Fearing another plot Napoleon, possibly at Talleyrand's prompting, arranged for the arrest and immediate execution of the Duke of Enghien on 21 March 1804. It seems however that the duke was entirely innocent and there is evidence which points to Talleyrand's real guilt in orchestrating the affair despite several denials. Nevertheless for a time at least Napoleon was unassailable and in May that year he declared himself Emperor of the French Republic and made his loyal Foreign Minister Grand Chamberlain of the Imperial Court.

The problem for Talleyrand was that his Emperor was a man of overreaching ambition and despite everything his Grand Chamberlain tried to do Napoleon insisted on expansion and crowned himself King of Italy in the Cathedral of Milan. European heads of state were not going to sit idly by as Napoleon now led his forces into Austria but success followed success and France seemed unbeatable. Talleyrand warned against humiliating a foe who might later prove to be a useful ally but events moved too fast. Urged on by his soldiers and riding on a wave of adulation from home he pressed on. Ulm fell followed by Austerlitz and Talleyrand was ordered by his Emperor to draw up punitive terms for peace which resulted in Austria losing much of its territory and income.

Talleyrand's service to Napoleon was rewarded with the title Prince de Bénévent but while his service may not have been doubted, his loyalty was clearly to France which Talleyrand judged was becoming exhausted by long European wars; Napoleon's separate ultimatums to Prussia, Russia and England did nothing to smooth the path of diplomacy. So Talleyrand began discrete negotiations to engineer a peace between Russia and England and tried to persuade Czar Alexander I to reject Napoleon's demands which he estimated would only lead to more fighting.

Napoleon pressed on with his campaign crushing and humiliating Prussia, declaring a blockade of the British Isles and revealing to Talleyrand that he had every intention of destroying the Bourbons in Spain. Talleyrand considered that his Emperor was out of control and for once thought he should do the wise thing and resign his post as Foreign Minister.

Whether Napoleon suspected his minister of duplicity, was jealous of his influence throughout Europe or just felt emboldened while at the height of his power he relieved Talleyrand of his ministerial duties in 1809 appointing him instead Vice-Grand Elector, a vague sounding position where presumably it was felt he could do no harm. Talleyrand was happy enough because his salary went up and he had less work to do but he knew that it was time to find a new ally and he immediately began correspondence with Louis XVIII, the nation's king in exile since 1793.

Napoleon meanwhile had embarked on his campaign against Spain and in May 1808 following the defeat of Spanish forces at Bayonne, Charles IV of Spain renounced his throne to Napoleon followed on the same day by his son and heir, Ferdinand VII. The Spanish members of the House of Bourbon, along with the Infante Antonio Pascual, were all held in comfortable imprisonment at Talleyrand's recently purchased estate at the Château de Valençay, the implication being that Talleyrand had supported the Spanish adventure which in reality he had tried to resist but failed. As far as Talleyrand was concerned Napoeon had gone too far this time and he said as much to his Emperor: "If a gentleman commits follies, if he keeps mistresses, if he treats his wife badly, even if he is guilty of serious injustices towards his friends, he will be blamed, no doubt, but if he is rich, powerful and intelligent, society will still treat him with indulgence. But if that man cheats at cards he will be immediately banished from decent society and never forgiven."[49]

By 1808 Napoleon finally realised he had overstretched himself. He needed to be sure that while he was fighting in the Peninsular War against Spain and Portugal Russia would come to his aid if Austria decided to win back some of its territories. He therefore sat down at the Congress of Erfurt with Czar Alexander to work out a treaty. Despite dismissing Talleyrand from his Foreign Ministry, Napoleon judged it wise to bring him along to help with the delicate diplomacy. The meeting was of course a failure because Talleyrand spent much of his time secretly advising the Czar how he should negotiate with Napoleon – a courageous and highly risky form of diplomacy but now the rest of Europe realised that Talleyrand was actually on their side.

During the course of the negotiations Napoleon revealed privately to Talleyrand that there was another matter troubling him – he wanted an heir and his wife, Josephine de Beauharnais, was incapable of bearing him children. It fell to Talleyrand to act as suitor and he took the opportunity to introduce him to the daughter of the Emperor of Austria, Maria Louisa. A new bond had been forged not so much for the Emperor as for his former Grand Chamberlain.

In the months after Erfurt Napoleon set off again to Spain but before leaving encouraged Talleyrand to host parties in order that he might be kept informed of the prevailing opinions. Talleyrand duly obliged and on one occasion surprised all his guests by inviting his fiercest enemy, the singularly uncouth Fouché. On his arrival Talleyrand proceeded to engage him in open and apparently friendly conversation. It was of course deliberate because Talleyrand knew that word of this potential dangerous alliance between two such avowed foes would make its way back to Napoleon who immediately fearing that a plot was being hatched against him returned to Paris. He called a meeting of his Privy Council and after some opening remarks launched into a foul-mouthed tirade against Talleyrand. His Vice-Grand Elector listened to it all without batting an eyelid and merely remarked on his way out how unfortunate it was that the Emperor was so ill-bred. In the event Talleyrand returned to court and continued as though nothing had happened remaining in his post. He was biding his time while Napoleon set off again to do battle with Austria. But after the inconclusive Battle of Aspern in May 1809, for the first time it was being suggested that the Emperor was no longer invincible. Then in 1812 Napoleon was again humiliated in his failed invasion of Russia made famous in the painting, 'Retreat from Moscow' by Adolph Norten. The Russian forces refused to fight retreating deeper and deeper into the countryside burning everything behind them. When Napoleon's huge and starving army entered Moscow they found the city deserted and they were forced by hunger and the freezing winter to return home a spent force.

Matters then moved quickly. On 1 April 1814 the French senate established a provisional government appointing Talleyrand as President. The next day Napoleon was officially deposed under the terms of the Acte de déchéance de l'Empereur followed swiftly by the Treaty of Fontainbleau which restored the Bourbons as kings of France. Napoleon was sent into exile on the island of Elba and Louis XVIII returned as a constitutional monarch of France, his powers now greatly reduced.

He assumed the throne at a difficult moment when the borders of Europe were effectively being redrawn by the allies at the Congress of Vienna. France was still technically an enemy state, nevertheless she was represented by Talleyrand who skilfully manoeuvred the major players such that France was protected. He proposed that Europe be restored to its pre-Napoleon boundaries and each guaranteed that they would fight to protect whichever of them might be threatened. Talleyrand wrote to the king: "France is no longer isolated...Your Majesty possesses a federal system which fifty years of negotiation might not have constructed." He went on to list all the steps he had taken to achieve this outcome.

Of course Napoleon wasn't done yet and having escaped from Elba once again, for 100 days, he tried to reclaim his position as emperor. The King and his court were forced to seek sanctuary in Ghent only returning to France after the Duke of Wellington, leading a combined Anglo-Allied force together with a Prussian army under Gebhard von Blücher, defeated Napoleon at the Battle of Waterloo on 18 June 1815.

As for Talleyrand he resigned from the Government and watched and bickered from the side lines for the next 15 years while enjoying his elevation to Grand Chamberlain and with it a big increase in his salary. In the meantime King Louis died in 1824. Talleyrand as Grand Chamberlain was at his tomb to place the flag over his coffin. He was also in the Cathedral of Rheims to witness the succession by Charles X, on 16 September.

Charles proved to be an unpopular king and was forced to abdicate in the July Revolution of 1830 and then leave the country. He was succeeded by King Louis-Philippe I which switched authority from the House of Bourbon to the House of Orleans. On his accession King Louis-Philippe asked a now weary Talleyrand, aged 76, to take up one more post for his country – ambassador at the Court of St James in London – a post he held for four years before retiring to his estate at Valençay. He died on 17 May 1838. It was the end of a remarkable career. He was the ultimate operator and undoubtedly one of the most skilful diplomats in European history and a man who mastered the art of survival as few others.

10

EMPRESS DOWAGER Cixi (1835–1908)

"**P**ower tends to corrupt, and absolute power corrupts absolutely." Lord Acton's words of warning about powerful men may equally have been written about the Empress Dowager Cixi who came to govern China with an unbending ruthlessness for nearly half a century without ever actually being its formal ruler. Dubbed the Dragon Empress in some books her rise to power albeit technically from "behind the curtains", is a story which, as so often, had more modest beginnings.

She was born on 28 November 1835 and given the name Yehonala.[50] She was the eldest daughter of a Manchu official but from an early age she seemed to have had a chip on her shoulder. She felt neglected by her parents and developed a hard streak which probably marked her character for life. She said: 'Ever since I was a young girl, I had a very hard life. I was not happy with my parents, as I was not a favourite. My sisters had everything they wanted, while I was, to a great extent, ignored altogether.'

In the finest traditions of Chinese history there is a mystery about the precise facts of her story. Certainly articles and books written at the time subsequently proved to be little more than malicious fiction. But the reality of her rise to power and the way in which she clung to it to the very end makes clear that she was at the least strong-willed, clever and with a keen eye on where power lay.

At the age of 16 Yehonala was chosen to become a concubine to Emperor Xianfeng, the ninth emperor of the Qing Dynasty, and was taken to the royal harem in the Forbidden City; she was well connected as a cousin of the Emperor's primary wife, Ci An. This wasn't the ordeal it may sound to modern ears as it was a chance to escape what she would have regarded as the childhood neglect she experienced at home. Two years later after the elaborate preparatory rituals she became a royal concubine. But as there may have been many thousands of other concubines vying for the Emperor's attention "promotion" within the ranks of the harem would have required considerable guile and determination – Yehonala had forged both during her unhappy childhood years.

The concubines' role was of course to indulge the Emperor's desires but just as important was to improve his chances of having a male heir. Sons of concubines were regarded as legally entitled to inherit the throne if the emperor's wife had not produced one herself.

Yehonala caught the emperor's attention with her beauty and her singing and it was not long before she became a favourite.[51] Eventually she produced a son called Tongzhi and was elevated to the rank of Second Consort and given the title Tzu Hsi, which means "Empress of the western palace", now written as Cixi. Not only was she one of his preferred concubines but reports suggest that the Emperor even began consulting her on matters of state. She was probably unique among other women in the harem in that she could read and write and would come to help the ailing emperor with his paperwork while at the same time forging her skills in state craft.

When the Emperor died in 1861, critically while staying at the summer residence in Manchuria, he left behind a daughter but no male heir by his wife. This meant Tongzhi was next in line but he was only five. As a result, state business was handled by a regency council of eight officials appointed by Emperor Xianfeng before his death. With so many hands on the levers of power there was inevitably much in-fighting.

Cixi seems to have persuaded the amenable Ci An that they should become co- Empress Dowagers although Cixi had no such position and as a concubine was of a lowlier status than Ci An. Eventually a petition reached Cixi asking her if she would "listen to politics behind the curtains" – in effect become the de facto ruler. Together with Prince Gong, half brother of the late emperor, Cixi and Ci An launched the Xinyou Coup and seized power. As the regents were accompanying Xianfeng's body on the long journey back to the Forbidden City they were stopped and arrested. Two were forced to commit suicide, one was executed and the five others stripped of their authority. Cixi and Ci An became co-regents and Prince Gong took control of the Grand Council in charge of policy making. An Imperial Edict was issued declaring the two Empress Dowagers to be the sole decision makers "without interference" although it wasn't long before Ci An had less and less to do with running state affairs leaving Cixi in charge.

During this time a degree of calm was restored in China; the Taiping Rebellion[52] which had begun in 1850 and Nian Rebellion[53], which started the following year, were crushed and there were even attempts to root out government corruption. The old Manchu elite lost their influence as Cixi gradually replaced them with Han Chinese officials. She was also concerned about the power of Prince Gong who had the support of large swathes of the military. She moved swiftly to clip his wings. Acting on trumped up charges including "improper court conduct", Prince Gong was dismissed from all his positions although he was allowed to keep his title. Her actions may have gone too far as there were petitions for his return. In the end he was allowed back to court although he was restricted to being head of the foreign ministry.

In fact under Prince Gong's guidance and with Cixi's approval foreign relations between the Qing dynasty and Western powers were opened up and attempts were made to modernise China; Gong founded the Tongwen Guan government school where Chinese students could learn foreign languages and study technology. Cixi it seems was prepared to "learn from the foreigners" but she would only go so far. For instance, she agreed to bolster China's navy by buying seven British warships. When they arrived they were of course full of British sailors who assumed no doubt that they would be sailing them. Angered by the "international joke" the Chinese sent the ships back to Britain.

Cixi had tasted power and she was not going to give it up even when Tongzhi reached maturity at 17 and the regency was formally terminated. She was particularly concerned that Tongzhi's new wife, Empress Jiashun, the daughter of a Manchu nobleman, would draw him away from her influence. There was no love lost between the new Empress and Cixi as Jiashun's grandfather had been one of the regents forced to commit suicide during the Xinyou coup. Jianshun tried to pull rank at first and refused to be intimidated by her mother-in-law: "I am a principal consort, having been carried through the front gate with pomp and circumstance, as mandated by our ancestors. Empress Dowager Cixi was a concubine, and entered our household through a side gate."

However Tongzhi was not a strong man. By 15 he had already become something of an alcoholic and was enjoying the company of prostitutes. Perhaps fearing that she would lose all control over her son Cixi ordered the couple to separate. In his loneliness Tongzhi apparently would dress as a commoner and escape the confines of the Qianqing Palace in search of comfort in the brothels of Peking. He eventually contracted smallpox and died on 13 January 1875 – although some rumours suggested he might have had syphilis or venereal disease. He hadn't reached his 18th birthday.

This is where the conspiracy theories emerge because although Tongzhi had no direct heir when he died, his Empress was pregnant and there was some debate as to whether her unborn child should succeed assuming it was a boy. The issue was resolved however when Jiashun and her unborn child died the following March while the discussions were still underway. Her death was put down to suicide from swallowing opium although *The New York Times* said at the time that the death "aroused general suspicion." Had she been driven to it or worse by an overbearing mother-in-law?

Whatever the exact circumstances another vacuum had been created from which Cixi could benefit and she chose her own three year old nephew, Zaitian, to succeed even though he was not directly in line to the throne nor did it follow the rules of succession which stated that the successor should be from the next generation after the late emperor. Cixi got round this by adopting Zaitian on the death of his mother and declaring that Zaitian was actually succeeding Xianfeng; she was effectively airbrushing her own son's short rule out of the history books. The death of Zaitian's mother also left Cixi and Ci An, the two Empress Dowagers, to act as regents. Zaitian was given the formal regnal name, Guangxu, meaning Glorious Succession.

Ci An herself suddenly died on 11 April 1881. She was ill in the morning and dead by the evening sparking instant but unproven speculation that she also might have been poisoned. Whatever the cause the path was now clear for Cixi and in 1884 she took her chance, dismissing Gong as Prince-Regent accusing him of taking bribes and of incompetence in running the military. She now had control.

Guangxu was a sickly child and apparently terrified of the Empress Dowager. He even had to address her as Qin Baba, literally meaning 'Biological Father' which only served to drive home the point that she was the real power in the Imperial household. Having been snatched from his home at the age of four, taken to the Forbidden City and cut off from the rest of his family it seems that the only person he cared for and trusted was his tutor Weng Tonghe.

He must have been relieved upon reaching 17 in 1889 when officially Cixi retired to the new Summer Palace specially built for her six miles from the Forbidden City leaving him, he supposed, to run the country. In reality Cixi was still pulling the strings having 'reluctantly' accepted the advice of court officials to guide and 'aid' the young Emperor to the extent that he visited Cixi every week in the Summer Palace where they took the important political decisions. In personal matters, Cixi's word also held sway forcing Guangxu to select her niece, Jingfen, to become his Empress.

However guided by his tutor, Guangxu could not have failed to have noticed China's steady decline. Britain and France were active in Burma and Indochina and Japan was striding ahead with its modernisation while China seemed stuck in the past. Guangxu decided to act.

He began boldly enough and, unlike Cixi, seemed genuinely determined to pursue policies to westernise China. In June 1898 he announced his 'Hundred Days of Reform' (11 June–21 September) overhauling everything from the military to the railroads and the legal system. There were sweeping changes affecting political, social and economic matters and a new university was to be opened. China was to be modern with a constitutional assembly while retaining its cultural heritage with the Emperor reserving the ultimate authority. Needless to say there were hundreds of officials who opposed everything he was trying to do and they were summarily dismissed. Soon they came running to Cixi asking her to intervene.

Cixi decided to allow Guangxu enough rope to hang himself – rumours were spread fanned by Cixi and her spies about the competence of the young Emperor. The Manchu elite who saw their powerbase slipping away were soon bitter enemies of the Emperor. There could only be one solution and a plot was conceived to overthrow the Emperor, ironically using the support of a military force stationed in Peking and armed with western rifles and artillery – the very tools of modernisation Cixi so opposed.

Inevitably the Emperor got wind of the plot and tried to organise a counter strike. But according to one version of events, one of Cixi's cousins, Jung Lu, who was also said to have been her lover before she became a concubine, had a friend, General Yuan Shihkai, who commanded Guangxu's forces and he warned of the Emperor's intention to strip Cixi of all her remaining powers. General Shihkai at the last moment switched allegiance and ordered his men to fight for Cixi who then boldly returned to the

Forbidden City. The mere sight of her was enough to terrify the Emperor who threw himself to the floor begging for her forgiveness: "I am unworthy to rule. Punish me, as I deserve" which she duly did.

The hapless Emperor was effectively imprisoned in Ying Tai – Ocean Terrace – a palace in the middle of an artificial lake in the Forbidden City with access via a single causeway. He was cut off from the outside world with only the company of his wife, who some say spied for Cixi anyway. Court eunuchs selected by Cixi kept watch along with his guards and an edict was issued declaring Guangxu unfit to be emperor although he remained as titular head and was allowed out for ceremonial occasions.

As for Jung Lu, his loyalty was rewarded when Cixi allowed his daughter, Youlan, to marry into the imperial clan. As a result of her marriage to Zaifeng Prince Chun, Jung Lu became the maternal grandfather of Puyi, called the Xuantong Emperor and the last Emperor of China.

Cixi now had complete control of China and declared war on the European powers which she saw as threatening the empire. The west it was argued was responsible for the opium flooding into China, foreigners had benefitted from inequitable treaties opening the way for foreign companies to establish themselves with special privileges and immunities under Chinese law and last but not least Christianity was on the increase with missionaries spreading out across the country. In short it was perceived as being one-way traffic all in favour of the 'barbarians'. It would end badly but in the meantime Cixi made the most of the absolute power she enjoyed squandering money on jewels, elaborate banquets of 150 different courses not to mention using funds which had been earmarked for rebuilding the navy on her new Summer Palace.

All the while pressure from the much misunderstood western world was building around her. China refused to believe that the 'barbarians' had anything to teach them and Cixi, while tolerating their initiative, seems to have discounted the so-called 'Self Strengthening Movement' whose members were encouraged to travel abroad to bring back anything which might help the country prosper.

Meanwhile a pro-nationalist group once opposed to the Qing Dynasty had re-emerged and had turned its sights on what it saw as the greater evil of western imperialism. It was called The Society of Righteous and Harmonious Fists, dubbed The Boxers by westerners. It consisted of people who had lost out in the wake of what was seen as foreign influence and were made up of well-trained martial artists who came to believe they had special invincible powers. The Boxer Rebellion was born.

In 1897 following the killing of a group of German missionaries, the German navy attacked and occupied Jiao Zhou Bay and from a base in Shandong rapidly expanded mining, factory and railroad building into the interior taking land from local farmers through enforced sales. The killing continued on both sides into 1900. Then in June the Boxers entered Peking and the 55 day siege of the foreign legations began. It was to prove an unequal struggle with the Boxers' swords and spears against the might of an expeditionary force sent by Britain, France, Germany, Japan, United States, Austria, Russia and Italy.

Cixi, belatedly reacting to the growing resentment of the population towards the western powers and particularly the Christian community, knew which way she should turn. At a mass meeting that same month she decided – or at least persuaded the Emperor to decide – that they should back the Boxers even though they were warned that the Boxers may not be an effective military force. She said:

"Perhaps their magic is not to be relied upon; but can we not rely on the hearts and minds of the people? Today China is extremely weak. We have only the people's hearts and minds to depend upon. If we cast them aside and lose the people's hearts, what can we use to sustain the country?" Both sides of the debate at court realized that popular support for the Boxers in the countryside was almost universal and that suppression would be both difficult and unpopular.[54]

It was too little too late. Despite having lost some 1,500 men, the western force eventually marched into the Imperial Palace. The Emperor and Empress Dowager Cixi fled in disguise to Xian in the north west Shaanxi province hidden in the mountains and in September 1901 the Boxer Protocol was signed.

While it is regarded as one of the most unequal treaties the Protocol was not necessarily regarded as a defeat for the Qing dynasty. Before the terms, which included the payment of the equivalent of $6.6 billion dollars to the western countries involved in the struggle and agreement to allow foreign troops to be based in Peking, were agreed a message was sent to Cixi asking if she would accept them. Her advisers urged her to fight on as it would be impossible for the West to conquer the Chinese interior but Cixi being more pragmatic argued it was better to bring an end to war and of course it would allow her to return to Peking and continue with her rule. One of the terms of the Protocol was that Cixi should be regarded as a war criminal and arrested but that clause was dropped.

The Emperor and Cixi eventually returned to the Imperial Palace in January 1902 whereupon Cixi seems to have undergone an immediate change of heart encouraging contacts with Europe and reforms more radical than the ones she had so forcefully opposed. She even had her portrait taken with the new fangled photographic camera to show herself in a new light.

To the very end of her life Cixi managed to control events. Fearing perhaps that the Emperor would try to continue with his more radical reforms after her death, it is now generally agreed that she contrived to have the Emperor poisoned. He died on 14 November 1908 and Cixi died the very next day.

Modern day tests have revealed that Emperor Guangxu's body contained high levels of arsenic. "We took a hair measuring 10 inches, and after analysis, we found its arsenic content was 2,400 times higher than normal," said Zhu Chenru, deputy director of the National Committee for the Compilation of Qing history.

Clearly Cixi herself was too ill to administer the poison so suspicion falls on her favourite eunuch, Li Lianying, but all agreed that only the Empress Dowager herself would have been able to give the order. Even on her deathbed her word was enough to inspire unswerving loyalty. She would certainly have decided that Guangxu should be succeeded by Puyi, the last of the Qing dynasty.

She also had tried to make plans for what should happen after her death always looking for her idea of perfection. She ordered that her tomb, resting among the Eastern Qing tombs near Peking, should be destroyed and rebuilt to a higher standard, covered with gold leaf, ornaments and precious jewels. It was pillaged in 1928, Cixi's coffin was opened and her body thrown on the floor. A pearl which had been placed in her mouth was said to have ended up on the dress shoes of the wife of Chiang Kai-Shek, the political and military leader but no-one really knows. In 1949 the Empress Dowager Cixi's tomb was restored by the People's Republic of China.

As for her legacy, she left behind an enfeebled nation. Her methods were ruthless, even murderous albeit probably in keeping with the tactics of others at the time. Her motives are unclear beyond retaining power for herself; she may have just been ignorant of what the west had to offer and she may have wanted to strengthen China against what she regarded as dangerous outside influences. One thing is clear, for someone without official power she was in command until her dying day.

11

Gerald Fitzmaurice (1865–1939)

As we move into the twentieth century the style of Western diplomacy and behind the scenes fixing becomes more subtle. In this next study, there is less bloodletting, more state craft, and more reliance on word of mouth and the ability to manoeuvre, sometimes in hostile situations, without resorting to force of arms, poison or murder. Diplomacy is no less cunning and the ends continue to justify the means – monetary inducements play their part. Diplomats are still honest men sent abroad to do whatever it takes to preserve the interests of their country – even lie.

Gerald Fitzmaurice was the archetypal English diplomatist skilfully navigating the fiendishly complex Turkish political world. In a review of David Barchard's book, *Out of the Shadows*, a critic wrote: Gerald Fitzmaurice, senior dragoman, or Turkish-speaking consular officer at the British Embassy from 1907 to 1914, is unique in Anglo-Turkish diplomatic history. Though well down the embassy pecking order, his reputation, both in his own lifetime and subsequently, cast a much longer shadow than those of the ambassadors he served. Gertrude Bell, visiting Turkey in 1907, found him 'the most interesting man' in Istanbul. His one-time embassy colleague, Aubrey Herbert, the writer and politician, thought he was cunning as a weasel and as savage. The historian Harold Temperley called him an unrivalled authority.

As we shall see he was one of the second level of British diplomats who, as one commentator put it, took the risks while the ambassadors slept. Despite his relative lowliness which clearly rankled as his promotions were slow in coming, his influence is never doubted.

So who was this obscure man and what made his reputation? He was born in the fishing village of Howth, near Dublin and attended what is now called Blackrock College. The school was new having been founded in 1860 by Père Jules Leman of the French Catholic Order, the Congregation of the Holy Ghost and of the Immaculate Conception, specifically with the aim of training young men for missionary work in the Third World. Indeed it was assumed that the young Fitzmaurice himself would enter the priesthood although interestingly as the school's own website puts it: "In response to changing circumstances, a highly successful civil service training department and university college were established." This was the path of public service that Fitzmaurice was eventually to follow and it was not long before he was distinguishing himself as a gifted linguist.

Discretion being his watchword throughout life he never wrote his memoirs so we have to rely on others' observations, private letters and biographies to fill in the gaps. We do at least know something of his striking appearance: ginger hair, piercing eyes and in later life a full handlebar moustache.

Having received his B.A. from the Royal University of Ireland in 1887, the following year he passed an entrance examination and became Student Interpreter in the Levant Consular Service in Constantinople, where his fluency in Turkish, Arabic and Persian singled him out as a leading 'dragoman'. This was the title given to interpreters in the region but the best of them were more than mere translators; they were also trusted interpreters of nuance and behaviour in the Ottoman Empire where Muslim leaders either refused to learn or claimed not to understand any language other than their own. Their influence therefore could be considerable and the opportunity for conspiracies was abundant. The first Ottoman Grand Dragoman was a Greek called Panavotis Nicosias and Napoleon's own 'favourite Orientalist' was Amédée Jaubert.

The city of Constantinople, which would not formally change its name to Istanbul until the establishment of the Turkish Republic in 1923, was still a major European and Asian crossroads straddling the Bosphorus, the Sea of Marmara and the Black Sea with rail networks into the Middle East and European capitals. At the time Fitzmaurice found himself in post its strategic position was unquestioned and had been recognised as such for centuries with Britain appointing her first ambassador as far back as 1583 when Elizabeth I was queen.

Fitzmaurice's first provincial postings took him to Asiatic Turkey and in time he was appointed political consul then vice consul before returning to the embassy. During this time he witnessed with alarm increasing pressure on the Armenian Christians. As a Roman Catholic Fitzmaurice may not have been entirely impartial.

By late 1895 the massacres of Armenians had increased; many were being forced to convert to Islam and churches were being turned into mosques. The sultan, Abdul Hamid II, was not impervious to criticism from Europe and invited the British embassy to assist in a palace commission of inquiry into the attacks. Fitzmaurice was given the task and, despite fears that his role was doomed to failure and might result in his death, he survived and penned his report which stated bluntly that the conversions had been forced and that the palace itself was behind the massacre of the Armenian Christians. A new commission was ordered and, even though Fitzmaurice's report had been published for all to see in a Blue Book laid before Parliament shortly before his departure, he was assigned to the new inquiry. Despite the obvious dangers, his behind the scenes negotiations led to the reconversion of many of the Armenians and the mosques being re-consecrated as churches.

Fitzmaurice's efforts and skill in difficult if not dangerous negotiations was recognised and he was made CMG – Commander of the Order of St Michael and St George – in June 1887 but he was still officially third dragoman in the Embassy which must have annoyed him as he stood in line behind Adam Block, second dragoman and an infinitely inferior operator. Apart from anything else the work was tedious and Fitzmaurice continually pressed for more challenging assignments.

After a number of short term provincial postings his request was granted by the ambassador, Sir Nicholas O'Conor, but perhaps not as he would have wished.

In 1902 he was sent to apply his knowledge of Turkish politics to assist the floundering negotiations of the Aden Boundary Commission[55] which had been set up by the British and Turkish governments to agree the border between the Turkish province of Yemen and the British Protectorate of Aden. In short the negotiators needed more intellectual muscle and above all wanted to avoid being tricked by mistranslations as had happened before.[56] The task was simple as far as O'Conor was concerned: resolve the situation as quickly as possible but preserve the British position on the border between the Ottoman *vilayets,* or provinces, of Yemen and the Aden protectorate which was part of British India. It is apparent that Fitzmaurice did sterling work but it was a long haul before he was eventually allowed to leave in 1905 with his health suffering having spent so long under canvas. He was given a CB – Companion of the Order of the Bath – by the Foreign Office although he had hoped for more, even a knighthood. But the whole affair had taken much longer to resolve than was hoped and, as Professor Geoffrey Berridge recounts in his biography, Fitzmaurice's own promotion had apparently stalled when he had been passed over for the Chief Dragoman slot on Block's departure.

Finally in 1905 he was made a Junior Consul and effectively second dragoman in Constantinople, a post he took up after a year in England. But Fitzmaurice was not a happy man regarding his appointment to return to the "Byzantine dung heap" and hoped for a more challenging role than the dragomanate had to offer interpreting and guiding for others in the embassy. Even when he became Chief Dragoman in October 1907 he was still dissatisfied, nevertheless, an unmarried man without other distractions, he stuck to the task like the workaholic he was becoming and was made First Secretary the following year.

This marked the breakthrough of Fitzmaurice's real influence in local affairs because in March 1908, O'Conor died and was replaced by Sir Gerard Lowther. This was soon after the so called Young Turks, a secularist nationalist reform party, led a rebellion in July that year against Abdul Hamid II, the last effective ruler of the Ottoman Empire, forcing him to restore the Constitution which he did on 24 July. Abdul Hamid was succeeded in 1909 by Mehmed V who was largely a figurehead.

At first everyone was glad to see the back of Abdul Hamid who was regarded as being too close to Germany but it was not long before "the children", as Fitzmaurice disparagingly referred to the Young Turks in their newly formed Committee of Union and Progress (CUP) in some of his private letters, started making trouble. Above all Fitzmaurice feared they were controlled by Jews, dÖmnes – or crypto-Jews[57] – and Freemasons.

If there is criticism of Fitzmaurice's diplomacy some say it was clouded by this antipathy towards the Jewish people in particular. Writing to B.H. Liddell Hart, the military historian, T.E. Lawrence said: "The Ambassadors were Lowther (an utter dud) and Louis Mallet who was pretty good and gave fair warning of the trend of feeling. I blame much of our ineffectiveness upon Fitzmaurice, the Dragoman, an eagle-mind and a personality of iron vigour. Fitzmaurice had lived half a lifetime and was the Embassy's official go-between and native authority. He knew everything and was feared from end to end of Turkey. Unfortunately, he was a rabid R.C. and hated Freemasons and Jews with a religious hatred. The Young Turk movement was fifty per cent crypto-Jew and ninety-five per cent Freemason. So he regarded it as the devil and threw the whole influence of England over to the unfashionable Sultan and his effete palace clique. Fitzmaurice was really rabid and his prejudices completely blinded his judgment. His prestige, however, was enormous and our Ambassadors and the F.O. staff went down before him like nine-pins. Thanks to him, we rebuffed every friendly advance the Young Turks made."

Whether or not this was true, the CUP became convinced that Fitzmaurice, backed by his ambassador, was against them and this sense of grievance was exacerbated when the British embassy appeared to support a counter revolution which failed. Whatever the real nature of Fitzmaurice's position, it was decided that he could best serve his country elsewhere.

In December 1911 he was sent to the Ottoman province of Tripoli as acting consul general to solve a new crisis following the invasion by Italian forces. The task was made more difficult by the fact that his immediate boss, Justin Alvarez, was vehemently anti-Italian. Nevertheless Fitzmaurice succeeded in smoothing things over with the Italians before returning once again to Constantinople where another challenge awaited him – the outbreak of the First Balkan War in October 1912.

The Balkans had been in a state of crisis since the early part of the century and it was not until the establishment of the Balkan League, an alliance between Bulgaria, Greece, Montenegro and Serbia at the prompting of Russia and directed against the Ottoman Empire, that they were able to win back almost all of the European Ottoman territories. However old differences re-emerged and by June 1913 Bulgaria began attacking her former allies marking the start of the Second Balkan War.

Fitzmaurice's negotiating skills were required in the negotiations between Turkey and the Balkan League in the early part of 1913 but Berridge writes that the CUP began "a discreet campaign for his recall" to London which happened in February 1914. In London he continued his work opposing the policies of the Young Turks and tried in vain to talk up the stock of the Ottoman court and which opponents regarded as merely an attempt "to sustain its cruel, corrupt and capricious ruler."[58]

Meanwhile the outbreak of World War I was looming. The Allies comprised initially the United Kingdom, France and Russia, and the Central Powers, made up of Germany and Austria-Hungary. Ultimately these alliances expanded when Italy, Japan and the United States joined the Allies, and the Ottoman Empire and Bulgaria sided with the Central Powers.

In 1915 Fitzmaurice joined Hugh O'Bierne, a senior British diplomat, in a mission to try and bribe Bulgaria into siding with the Allies. The mission failed because Britain could not offer what Bulgaria demanded, namely the return of Macedonia which had been seized by Serbia during the Second Balkan War. This deal on the other hand was something Germany persuaded them they could supply as Serbia was its enemy. With their agreement secured Bulgaria immediately declared war on Britain forcing O'Bierne and Fitzmaurice to depart empty-handed.

Fitzmaurice was now seconded to the Intelligence Division of the Admiralty Office in London where his and other minds became increasingly exercised by the importance of world Jewry in securing peace. To that end Fitzmaurice we are told advised that Palestine should be offered to the Jews of Constantinople in return for withdrawing their support from the Ottoman rulers.[59] Memoranda at the time suggest this would also have gone down well with the Jewish community in America. Fitzmaurice's knowledge was now highly regarded once again. Lord Fisher, the First Sea Lord, said he was "the most important person in the Eastern Theatre of the War." [60]

But it seems that Fitzmaurice's style, his guile or maybe just his perceived biases brought an early end to his career. Prof Berridge describes this period in these words: "For various reasons, however, he became a nearly man: nearly the negotiator in Switzerland of the formal abdication of the Egyptian khedive (1916); nearly a further recruit to the Arab Bureau in Cairo (later in 1916); nearly consul-general in Moscow following the Bolshevik revolution (1918); and nearly political adviser to General Bridges in Bulgaria (later in 1918). What he did do—prompted not just by the realpolitik of the time but by a long-held attachment to secular Zionism—was to help his old friend Sir Mark Sykes prepare the ground for the Balfour declaration of November 1917, and then to scupper the idea of a separate peace between Britain and Turkey."

It was acknowledged even then that the demands of Arab and Jew over Palestine was a difficult problem which would require the most delicate handling. O'Bierne wrote: "It is evident that the Jewish colonization of Palestine must conflict to some extent with Arab interests. All we can do, if and when the time comes to discuss details, is to try to devise a settlement which will involve as little hardship as possible to the Arab population. We shall then, of course, have to consult experts...I would suggest that we might consult Mr Fitzmaurice."[61]

His idea was never pursued because on 5 June 1916 O'Bierne and all his advisers died when the boat they were sailing on to Russia, HMS *Hampshire*, hit a German mine and sank.

With the end of the war and an armistice between Turkey and Britain Fitzmaurice, 'the Wizard of Stanbul', was nearing the end of his time in public office. He returned to the Foreign Office from the Admiralty in 1919. No longer wanted particularly by the Turks in Constantinople, he served out his remaining time in the news and political intelligence department which was itself closed down. At the age of just 55 he retired to live out the last years of his life in discreet obscurity. He died from a cerebral thrombosis at his home on 23 March 1939.

Fitzmaurice was without doubt an intriguer and a plotter but always with the best interests of Great Britain at heart. He was hard working sometimes to the point of exhaustion, a manipulator and without question a master of his brief when it came to Anglo-Turkish affairs. He undoubtedly earned the 'title' of Fitzmaurice of Constantinople. Was he blinded by prejudice? There are conflicting points of view but all agree that Fitzmaurice was an expert without equal on the complexities of Turkey. Writing his obituary in *The Times*, [62] Professor Harold Temperley said: "The late Mr G. H. Fitzmaurice was a man of the most penetrating insight into the affairs of Near and Middle East and of most remarkable influence. His power of inspiring awe was most remarkable."

Historians and scholars will be able to pore over his many letters to Lloyd George and others but without a definitive personal account one can only speculate about the innermost thoughts of this highly intelligent and dedicated public servant. He undoubtedly operated in the shadows and was prepared to do whatever it took to achieve his masters' ends but never for personal enrichment, although he surely would have liked to receive greater honours. He worked tirelessly in a theatre which today is proving as complex as he feared. He foresaw potential conflict between Jew and Arab and he struggled in vain to seek peaceful settlement throughout Europe; whether his approach would have helped or hindered had he been permitted or been well enough to pursue it is impossible to tell. They still remain the greatest diplomatic issues facing the world today.

12

SERGEI KIROV (1886–1934)

It was in his death rather than in life that Sergei Kirov had the greatest and bloodiest impact on Soviet politics. It might be said that none of our characters enjoyed such brutal loyalty from their master even if the master may have had a hand in that death. It just so happened that he was to become probably the closest friend to the one of the most ruthless leaders the world has known.

Life in the Kremlin at the time was both a relaxed and dangerous experience. In his biography of Joseph Stalin, Simon Sebag Montefiore describes an almost collegiate atmosphere with Stalin and his closest associates dropping in on one another much as one drops in on a neighbour to ask for a cup of sugar. They seemed to live in one another's pockets, their children played together and they dined together enjoying the best that the Soviet Union could offer while the peasants in the countryside starved.

Stalin had succeeded Lenin as de facto leader of the country in 1924 and had introduced a centralised command economy aimed at turning Russia from an agrarian society into a powerful industrial nation. Under his Five Year Plans it was the state which would decide what should be produced and where it should be produced. Of course it created tremendous upheaval as peasants found themselves operating unfamiliar machinery which constantly broke down and then lay idle as spare parts were in short supply. The countryside was devastated, crops failed and famine followed. Failure to reach production targets was a deemed to indicate a lack of loyalty and severely.

Within the walls of the Kremlin loyalty and friendships were also fragile. Everyone wanted to be in Stalin's good books but he was a difficult man and difficult father to all his children with the exception of his daughter, Svetlana. All that really mattered to him was Bolshevism. When one of his sons, Yakov, apparently tried to shoot himself but only succeeded in grazing his chest, Stalin reportedly said, "Couldn't even shoot straight."[63]

The children would also have received little sympathy or warmth from Stalin's second wife, Nadya Alliluyeva, who suffered from mental illness, possibly manic depression, bipolar disorder or a form of schizophrenia. She loved Stalin but also seemed to nag him constantly possibly trying to vie for his attentions with all the other young women who caught his eye or wrote adoring fan letters to him enclosing their photographs. In his own way Stalin did love her but he was ill equipped to cope with her mood swings and nothing was to be allowed to get in the way of his political ambitions.

In the end Nadya's demons drove her to take her own life with a Mauser pistol given to her as a gift by her brother, Pavel. There were also suggestions that the gun was found lying next to the hand she didn't use and that Stalin himself may have been responsible. Her face was bruised suggesting she had sustained blows and the official cause of death for many years was recorded as appendicitis adding to suspicions of a cover-up.

Whatever the truth about Nadya's death, Stalin expressed his grief openly and an elaborate funeral was arranged with horse drawn carriage, honour guard and military bands. It was into this void that the charismatic Sergei Mironich Kirov, the First Secretary of Leningrad (modern day St Petersburg) and a Politburo member stepped. Maria Svanidze[64] wrote: "Kirov was the closest person who managed to approach Joseph intimately and simply, to give him that missing warmth and cosiness."

Kirov was full of joy, constantly singing arias from the operas he loved and at ease with everyone, men and women alike. He too was keen on the ladies particularly ballerinas from the Mariinsky Ballet, which was later renamed the Kirov Ballet in his honour following his death.

Born in 1886, Sergei Mironovich Kostrikov was orphaned as a child. He was brought up by his grandmother before being sent to an orphanage at the age of seven and then to the Kazan Industrial School. But instead of going to university, come the 1905 Revolution, he joined the Social Democratic Party. He was arrested and jailed several times, charged with printing illegal literature. After another year in jail he moved to the North Caucasus, changed his name to Kirov because it was easier to remember and remained there until the abdication of Tsar Nicholas II. He rapidly climbed the Party ladder readily ordering the deaths of thousands of *bourgeois* who failed to follow the Party line in some way. By 1921 he had seized control of Georgia and become manager of the Azerbaijan Party. His loyalty to Stalin would be rewarded in 1926 with the position of head of the Leningrad Party.

Kirov was an outdoor fanatic, accomplished mountaineer and swimmer, curiously in marked contrast to Stalin himself who was generally a sickly person. He suffered from psoriasis and as a result of an accident with a horse-drawn carriage had a slightly shorter left arm which he covered up by constantly puffing on his pipe as he sat and watched his close friend at play. It was an attraction of opposites one might say.

By now Kirov, 'my Kirich', was firmly established as part of Stalin's intimate circle holidaying with him and his family, enjoying health-giving baths at Sochi. How relaxing these occasions were for anyone other than Stalin it is difficult to gauge as no-one dared let their guard down being unsure how Stalin would treat them. He was well aware that many were merely sycophants and he was not averse to using the columns of *Pravda* to criticise even his dear friend. However Stalin's affection for Kirov cannot be doubted; when he visited Moscow Stalin insisted that he should stay in his apartment with his family. The children certainly loved him and put on little doll shows to entertain him.

However, constant plotting, real or perceived, seemed to bubble beneath the surface. On one occasion when Stalin and his entourage were sailing in the Black Sea on a motor yacht, the *Red Star*, shots were fired at the boat from the shore; it might have been an assassination attempt or just a ploy organised by Lavrentiy Beria, Stalin's head of secret police, to undermine Nestor Lakoba who was in charge of security in the region. Nothing was ever what it seemed. Beria launched an investigation and it appeared that the guards opened fire apparently thinking it was an enemy boat. What is clear however is that Stalin also knew that there were always others plotting against him and he would even suspect those very friends standing at his side.

There was no doubt that some did not like the way Stalin was leading the country. A group of regional leaders complaining for example about the famine in the Ukraine or merely that they had not been recognised and promoted in the Party as they felt they deserved gathered to consider who might succeed Stalin. One name emerged: Sergei Kirov.

In what seems like an extraordinarily foolish move Grigory Ordzhonikidze, known as Sergo, invited Kirov to his apartment in the heart of the Kremlin and asked him if he agreed to the plan. Kirov faced an impossible choice: the potential of becoming leader of the country or staying loyal to his friend and mentor, Stalin. He opted for the latter and immediately relayed the information to Stalin himself probably thinking he had made the wiser choice.

The problem for Kirov however was that Stalin, quite apart from feeling betrayed by his old Bolshevik comrades living just yards from him, was now concerned that they thought his dear brother Kirov was his potential successor. Stalin thanked him for his loyalty but at the same time must have considered how he could best avert this latest threat to his authority.

At the time, January 1934, nearly 2,000 delegates were gathering for the Seventeenth Congress which ostensibly elected the Central Committee to run the country for the next four years. Kirov gave a speech praising Stalin as "the great strategist of liberation of the working people" and received his standing ovation. One can only surmise what was going through Stalin's mind as he watched what he may have suspected to be plotters heaping praise on him. Stalin regarded himself as standing alone fighting the cause. No-one could be trusted apart from himself. Even when his own son, Vasily, sought to benefit from the family name, his father shouted: "You're not Stalin and I'm not Stalin. Stalin is Soviet Power."[65] He regarded himself as being somehow separate from the force he had created; he had even changed his name from Iosif Vissarionovich Dzhugashvili to Stalin, meaning Man of Steel, as he thought it made him appear more imposing.

Although Kirov was as nervous as everyone else who came into Stalin's orbit he presumably thought he was safe. He had exposed the plotters and declared his loyalty to his master but that was to misjudge Stalin. No-one and nothing was more important than the cause he was pursuing; he was prepared to sacrifice millions of starving peasants in his fight to deliver a strong, industrialised Soviet Union and it obviously became clear to him that he had to sacrifice the only true friend he thought he had left.

In a carefully choreographed plan he first ordered Kirov to return from his powerbase in Leningrad to be close to him in the Kremlin promoting him to one of the four Secretaries. At first Kirov resisted but he couldn't protest too much because that would also suggest disloyalty putting personal preference ahead of his duty to the Party. Stalin also insisted that Kirov should join him for a summer holiday at his dacha in Sochi. Kirov had no wish to attend but needless to say he could not refuse. It was as though Stalin desperately wanted to keep close to his friend while at the same time not knowing if he could be trusted; nevertheless he was given tasks such as sending him to Kazakhstan to report on the harvest. One minute Kirov was in favour the next he was being publicly bawled out by Stalin.

On 28 November, ominously perhaps, Stalin personally escorted Kirov to the Red Army train taking him back to Leningrad and embraced him warmly on the platform – a Judas kiss as it was to turn out. Three days later Kirov walked into the Smolny Institute accompanied by his personal bodyguard, Borisov, who strangely dropped further behind as they made their way to his third floor office. Was Borisov just getting old and tired or was he deliberately delayed by the guards. Either way Kirov was alone as he passed Leonid Nikolaev who then pulled out his revolver and shot Kirov in the back of the head. Before Nikolaev was able to turn the gun on himself he was knocked to the ground.

At first Stalin is reported to have been shocked by the news – the man reacting normally at the loss of a friend – but then Stalin the leader took control. He insisted on starting the investigation into the murder himself setting up his headquarters in Kirov's office even though he must have known all the facts not least why so many of the guards at the Institute had been stood down and why Kirov, a senior member of the Politburo was protected by only one aging bodyguard.

Nikolaev was dragged before Stalin when he promptly accused Vani Zaporozhets, the deputy NKVD boss in Leningrad and Stalin's man in the city, to his face of ordering him to carry out the assassination. Nikolaev, a former junior functionary who had been expelled from the Party, was unemployed and reportedly bore a grudge against the Party leadership expressing a desire to kill those responsible for his plight. He was the patsy in the crime and paid with his life.

Nikolaev's widow, Milda Draul, claimed her husband must have lost his mind when he discovered she was having an affair with Kirov – an unlikely story as she was plain and Kirov was more attracted to the beauties of the ballet. She was executed three months later while Nikolaev's mother, brother, sisters, cousin and others close to him were arrested and either killed or sent to labour camps. His infant son, Marx, was put in an orphanage and was officially rehabilitated in 2005.

It was also odd that Nikolaev had twice been stopped by guards loitering around the Institute in the previous weeks in what was possibly an earlier attempt on Kirov's life and had been released without charge even though he was found to be carrying a revolver. Lastly Kirov's bodyguard was driven to the Institute by Stalin's NKVD guards to give his explanation as to why he was not with Kirov at the time of the shooting – was he just unfit or was it all part of a plot? By coincidence, Borisov, died on the way in a mysterious crash falling from the truck before he could given his evidence. His widow was committed to an insane asylum.

With undue haste it was announced that Kirov's assassin had been supported by Grigory Zinoviev, the former leader of Leningrad. A law was passed that night ordering the arrest, trial and execution without appeal of all those implicated in the plot against the Party.

The conclusion of Stalin's personal investigation was formally announced at a meeting of the Moscow District of the Communist Party: "Comrade Stalin personally directed the investigation of Kirov's assassination. He questioned Nikolayev at length. The leaders of the Opposition placed the gun in Nikolaev's hand!"[66] Thus started the slaughter or deportation of three million people.

The truth of what happened will never be known although Nikita Khrushchev, who was to succeed Stalin, claimed years later that his predecessor admitted to being responsible. In 1955 he stated: "It must be asserted that to this day the circumstances surrounding Kirov's murder hide many things which are inexplicable and mysterious and demand a most careful examination. There are reasons for the suspicion that the killer of Kirov, Nikolaev, was assisted by someone from among the people whose duty it was to protect the person of Kirov." [67]

It seems clear enough that Stalin loved Kirov declaring that he had been left an orphan by his death, but he was almost certainly also jealous of his popularity, of what he might become and above all the possibility that he might oust him. Nicolai Bukharin's [68]widow is quoted as saying that Stalin could love and hate the same person "...because love and hate born of envy... fought with each other in the same breast."[69]

Kirov's body, minus his brain which was preserved for scientific research, was taken to Moscow for another highly elaborate funeral just as had been staged for Stalin's wife. As the lid of the coffin was being lowered, Stalin stepped forward kissed Kirov's brow saying: "Goodbye dear friend we will avenge you." After the cremation, the following day Stalin placed the urn of ashes in the Kremlin Wall to the sound of trumpet blasts.

As Stalin allowed his avenging net to spread ever wider no-one could escape; everyone with the remotest connection to Nikolaev was implicated. Elizabeth Lemolo, once a great beauty in pre-Revolutionary days, but at the time a penniless widow taking what amounted to handouts from Nikolaev's aunt, was arrested, tortured and executed.

Looking back at the Seventeenth Congress where Kirov and others had heaped praise on the achievements of Stalin, within three years 56% of the 1,996 delegates would be executed or detained. Stalin remembered that when it had come to the vote 300 anonymous ballot papers had shown votes against him and only three against Kirov.

If the consequences of Kirov's friendship had not been so terrifying it might have been possible to find some good in his brief moment in the spotlight. While being responsible himself for the misery and death of thousands, Kirov had belatedly tried in Congress to temper some of the excesses of the Stalinist authority, mistakenly thinking either that his own star was now in the ascendant or that his close relationship with Stalin himself somehow protected him and possibly even carried some weight. He was wrong on all counts. The Marxist scholar Boris Nikolaevsky summed all the plotting and manoeuvring up in this phrase, "One thing is certain: the only man who profited by the Kirov assassination was Stalin."

13

MARTIN BORMANN (1900–1945)

In a snake pit such as the upper echelons of the Third Reich it was important to have the ear of the Führer and even more important to keep all other influences at bay if one wanted to survive. This was Martin Bormann's strategy throughout his brutal career while always being sure to keep in the background, strenuously avoiding the limelight but always having the final word ahead of others in the hierarchy when Adolf Hitler was about to take a decision. He cared not a jot what others thought and would readily cut down anyone who stood in his path, a path which would make him the most powerful figure in Germany during World War II second only to Adolf Hitler himself. And yet he was invisible to most of his countrymen, he was 'the Brown Eminence' who conducted his murderous business quietly and out of sight, with terrible consequences.

There was nothing in Bormann's background or education which suggested that one day he would possess the skills to operate 'behind the scenes' and reach right to the top of the political tree in Germany. There was nothing which obviously singled him out for this delicate path of brutal diplomacy as he was growing up, it was just raw survival instinct.

Like so many in this book, Bormann came from a modest background and perhaps it was that which inspired him to fight his corner so successfully. He was born near Halberstadt, an unremarkable town in the state of Saxony-Anhalt. If anything Halberstadt was noted with terrible irony during the 17th century for having one the largest Jewish communities in Europe.

Bormann was the son Theodor Bormann, a former Prussian sergeant-major who later became a post office employee, and his second wife, Antonie Mennong. He was one of three brothers, but only he and Albert survived to adulthood. Martin Bormann did not excel at school dropping out early to work as a farm labourer on an estate in Mecklenburg. During World War I he served in a field artillery regiment but did not see any action; however it was while he was in Mecklenburg that his politics began to be formed.

He joined a right wing group called Rossbach Freikorps. The first Freikorps was a group of volunteer hussars recruited by Frederick II of Prussia in the 18th century but by the end of World War I the meaning of the word meant paramilitary groups whose membership consisted largely of disaffected soldiers looking for some meaning to their lives and reason for their defeat in the war. The initial target for their venom was Communism and strong anti-Slavic racisim although anti-Semitism had not yet stirred. Above all their purpose was to defend the German military against any perceived betrayal; it seems likely that Bormann would have at least supported if not actually been involved in the so-called Feme Murders[70], politically motivated killings of left wing opponents during the Weimar period which were unofficially supported by the government and which went largely unpunished. Those who were convicted were given lenient sentences and later acquitted. Bormann himself was sentenced to just one year's imprisonment in March 1924 for his involvement in the murder of Walter Kadow, a communist who was killed by Rudolf Höss for supposedly betraying the nationalist, Albert Leo Schlageter, to the French occupying forces in the Ruhr. Bormann was already showing signs that nothing, not even past acquaintances, would stand in his way as Kadow had been his former elementary school teacher. As for Höss he would go on to become commandant of the Auschwitz Concentration Camp.

No sooner had he been released then Bormann joined the NSDAP[71], or Nazi Party, and no doubt during his time as regional press officer in Thuringia or as business manager would have met Hitler for the first time. By 1928 he was climbing the ranks and joined the Sturmabteilung (SA or Brownshirts) Supreme Command. He now had the storm troopers' uniform which in time would earn him the soubriquet, the Brown Eminence. The SA attracted the very worst in society, criminals and cashiered military personnel. As their power and influence grew they were increasingly hated by the professional military high command many of whom were not Nazi party members. But under the leadership of Ernst Rohm the SA would grow to some two million men, twenty times the size of Germany's regular army. However once Hitler was firmly established in power he would purge the SA and Rohm in the infamous Night of the Long Knives reducing the force to something resembling a modest home guard brigade. In its place Hitler had his SS (Shutzstaffel) and Gestapo secret police to manage affairs as the street thuggery style of the SA was regarded as counter-productive to his aims. Furthermore Hitler was concerned about the growing strength and ambitions of the SA. Hundreds were killed and thousands of potential opponents arrested in the purge which lasted from 30 June to 2 July 1934. By the end Hitler was able to declare to the Reichstag on the 13 July that he was "the supreme judge of the German people."

Throughout this time Bormann must have been plotting, manoeuvring and generally ingratiating himself with the fastest rising star in the party. By 1929 he had become close to Adolf Hitler inviting him to be a witness at his wedding on 2 September to Gerda Buch, whose father Major Walter Buch was chairman of the Nazi Party Court. Frau Gerda eventually gave birth to ten children, an act of devotion to the party for which Hitler decided she had earned a medal; Hitler was asked to be godfather of their eldest child tactfully also named Adolf.

In 1933 Hitler now Chancellor, made Bormann a Reichsleiter, or national leader of the NSDAP, a position second only to the Führer and in November of that year he was appointed as a delegate to the Reichstag. He was also made Chief of Cabinet to Rudolf Hess, the deputy Führer, a crucial appointment where his role as personal secretary and right hand man enabled him to learn all about the strengths and weaknesses of others in the Party. He developed his skills as an administrator and increasingly came to be relied upon in all things by Hitler who entrusted him with all his personal finances while he focussed on fighting the war. It was Bormann who arranged the purchase of Berghof at Berchtesgarden and who managed the property portfolio on the Obersalzberg including commissioning the Kehlsteinhaus, or 'Eagle's Nest' which was formally presented to Hitler on 20 April 1938.

For all his instinctive administrative skills Bormann was coarse and uncultured and loathed by most of the senior members of the Nazi party. The boorishness of this squat ill-educated functionary was fatally underestimated however as he silently and diligently made himself indispensable to Hitler. Bormann was never in the front row at major events during the war, he left the spotlight to others but he was always at the Führer's side. In his biography of Bormann, Jorchen van Lang wrote: "Figures like him are easily overlooked. He was never the hero of dramatic scenes, never stood in the limelight."

However when Hess fled to Scotland in May 1941 in his failed bid to bring about an end to World War II, Bormann stepped effortlessly into his post becoming head of the Parteikanzlei, the Party Chancellery, and was appointed Reichs Minister. He knew Hitler was infuriated by Hess's betrayal and calmed him down by giving him a German shepherd dog called Blondie as a present. Bormann knew how to cope with his master's moods.

After Hitler no-one was now more important in the country than Bormann who immediately began using his authority to rein in others, reducing the power of regional managers and taking personal charge of enacting Hitler's decrees. Bormann established the Adolf Hitler Fund of German Trade and Industry, ostensibly to collect voluntary donations from employers' associations to support the NSDAP. But they soon became forced contributions which eventually raised some 700 million Reichsmarks much of which Bormann either used to bribe senior party figures or, as he later perceived that Germany would lose the war, to be siphoned off to offshore accounts when funds would be needed to preserve the cause and protect those high ranking Nazis who managed to escape.

By 1942 Bormann was private secretary to Hitler and effectively deputy Führer. He managed not only Hitler's private affairs but some would argue also managed his behaviour to suit his own ends ensuring that potential rivals such as Herman Goering, Joseph Goebbels and Heinrich Himmler never had any real influence. Bormann had become the gatekeeper to Hitler's office. No-one was allowed to see him without Bormann's approval. He handled all his paperwork as well as his personal finances and when the Führer was away on holiday Bormann gave the orders. Himmler, who was godfather to one of Bormann's children, particularly came to despise Bormann even though Himmler did him the "honour" of boosting his honorary SS number from 278,367 to 555 to reflect his special status.[72] Albert Speer, Minister of Armaments, in his memoirs published in 1966 after serving the full 20 years of his sentence in Spandau Prison noted the intrigues and manipulation as the various leaders tried to curry favour with Hitler. These were intelligent and equally brutal individuals which says much for Bormann's own manipulative skills in keeping them at bay.

Bormann's authority in delivering his master's orders was without question. It was he who signed the decrees calling for the harshest treatment of prisoners and the persecution of Jews. On 9 October 1942 he signed an order stating that "the permanent elimination of the Jews from the territories of Greater Germany can no longer be carried out by emigration but by the use of ruthless force in the special camps of the East." This was followed by an instruction giving Adolf Eichmann and the Gestapo absolute powers over Jews.

Bormann was equally critical of Christians stating that Nazism was "completely incompatible with Christianity".[73] As Alan Bullock wrote in his book, *Hitler a Study in Tyranny*, "In Hitler's eyes, Christianity was a religion fit only for slaves; he detested its ethics in particular. Its teaching, he declared, was a rebellion against the natural law of selection by struggle and the survival of the fittest."

And yet while Hitler wanted to postpone any attack on the churches Bormann pushed ahead with the Kirchenkampf demanding that the clerical influence should be broken once and for all as it was an obstacle to totalitarian authority. Some suggest that Bormann effectively had sole charge of domestic policy while Hitler concentrated on fighting the war.

But not for one moment did Hitler doubt his right hand man. "To win this war I need Bormann," he is quoted as saying.[74] Even when it was obvious that all was lost it was Bormann who was still at his side in the Bunker.

The myth, half truths and rumours surrounding Bormann's last days are typical of the legends that have built up around his life which he managed right up to the end. Certain elements of the story are undisputed. On 29 April 1945 Bormann along with Goebbels, General Wilhelm Burgdorf and Hans Krebs, Chief of the Army General Staff were all gathered in the Führerbunker as the battle for Berlin raged around them and witnessed the signing of Hitler's last will and testament. The next day Hitler married Eva Braun and they then committed suicide – Braun by taking cyanide and Hitler by shooting himself. After their bodies were burned in accordance with Hitler's instructions Goebbels assumed the titular role as Head of Government and Admiral Karl Dönitz, creator of Germany's U-boat fleet, was radioed to be told that he was now President of Germany. All that remained was for Bormann and the others to escape the bunker. He had served his master to the end and now he had to save his own skin. It is at this point that the rumour and conspiracy theories emerge.

Martin Bormann (1900–1945)

One simple theory is that Bormann was killed by an anti-tank shell as he tried to cross the Russian lines but Bormann's long time chauffeur claimed to have spotted him in Munich some time during May 1945. But with the trail running dry and no bodies found people began to assume he was dead. The International Nuremburg Trials tried Bormann in absentia and sentenced him to death for crimes against humanity. His defence counsel argued that one could not sentence a dead man to death.

Over the years journalists and Nazi hunters have scoured the globe following possible sightings of Bormann: was he living with other Nazis like Adolf Eichmann and Josef Mengele in South America having escaped on one of Dönitz's U-boats – one elderly Guatemalan peasant was even arrested for a time in 1967; had he been spirited out of Germany by British Naval Intelligence, given plastic surgery and been living in southern England having handed over all his secrets? It made terrific material for writers with one publisher reportedly paying £500,000 for the rights to a book suggesting that Winston Churchill arranged for Bormann to be smuggled to England so he would reveal where Nazi gold and other riches were hidden in Swiss bank accounts. Other rumours said he escaped disguised as a catholic priest and had celebrated mass in Brazil or that he lived for years as a reclusive millionaire in Argentina.

The reality may well have been more mundane. The remains of two skeletons were found years later in 1972 during repairs to a railway station near where Bormann and Hitler's doctor, Ludwig Stumfegger, were last seen dodging crossfire outside the bunker on 2 May 1945. The bodies had not been shattered by any explosion but traces of glass, possibly from cyanide pills, were found in their mouths.

There was only one difficulty with this theory and that was the German authorities had dug up the ground where the skeletons were said to have been discovered in 1965 and nothing had been found. The rumour mill fired back into action with suggestions that wherever Bormann had been hiding, when he finally died, his body was carefully and surreptitiously returned to the same location.

The remains were removed by the German Government and locked away in a cupboard at the Frankfurt Public Prosecutor's Office where even family members were prevented from seeing them. He was formally pronounced dead by a West German court as late as April 1973. Later in 1999 DNA tests comparing the bones with samples from his son, Martin Bormann, who had become a priest, seemed conclusively to prove that the body was indeed that of Bormann, the mass murderer, but exactly how the remains came to be there will continue to intrigue those who refuse to be satisfied by simple explanations.

For our story however the facts remain as clear as ever. A farm labourer without formal education succeeded in becoming the most powerful figure in Hitler's Germany completely outsmarting every single other figure in the Nazi hierarchy and playing a fateful role in modern day history. In the typical style of the fixer behind the scenes he allowed others to enjoy temporary moments of glory while he stayed at his desk quietly moving the players like pieces on a chess board; they thought they were in charge of events but in reality they were moving to his unspoken command. However once he had risen to the top, Bormann was able to carry out the terrible orders of his Führer and even exceed them if he felt it would help the Party's ultimate and brutal aims. Despite the intrigue and plotting which was a constant throughout this period he was untouchable in his power and in the backing he had from Hitler.

That backing continued to the very end of the war when Hitler was about to take his own life and even then Hitler urged Bormann not to think of himself but of the Party; he didn't want him to take his own life in the bunker but to escape and use the vast wealth which he himself had arranged to be hidden away precisely for that moment and renew the fight.

As with others in these accounts, none of this is in any way to praise Bormann's dark skills it is merely to draw attention to the powerful forces which are not obvious even to those closely watching events. When leaders of nations or heads of organisations appear to be following a course of action, others close by them may be influencing events to a greater extent than is apparent. Bormann was blindly loyal to Hitler no doubt because they shared the same extreme and racist agenda; Hitler for his part believed in his deputy to the very last moments of his life. He believed that Bormann could carry the torch forward. He didn't promote Bormann to President of Germany or to leader of the Party because somehow he knew that Bormann would exert the same control over events as he had done during the strongest moments in the Third Reich. Bormann's job in short was to continue operating in the shadow of power which Hitler trusted would follow his own death. Bormann knew all the secrets; he knew where the cash was hidden, he knew who could be trusted, all he had to do was escape the Allies and their grip on Berlin. Some will always believe that he did regardless of any evidence brought before them.

14

Ted Sorensen (1928–2010)

It would probably be hard to get closer to the man you serve than to be described as someone's 'intellectual blood bank'. Not just an aide or personal adviser but so in tune with the master's intellect that you are actually capable of mimicking his thinking. This is the stuff of ghost writing but when taken to a level where it is impossible to see the joins, it becomes an art form; and when deployed for the most powerful man in the world and at a time of crisis it becomes an essential weapon, part of the arsenal that has to be ready quite literally to win the day.

Theodore Sorensen – always known as Ted – was John F Kennedy's ghost and his shadow long before he became President of the United States. So close had they become that when Kennedy was assassinated it was as though Sorensen himself had been shot. In his autobiography Sorensen said it was "the most deeply traumatic experience of my life...I had never considered a future without him".[75] Later he would quote an Irish lament asking why Kennedy had died leaving the country as "Sheep without a shepherd, when the snow shuts out the sky."[76]

Sorensen was born on 8 May 1928 in Lincoln, the capital of Nebraska. His father, Christian, was a Danish American and his mother, Annis, was of Russian Jewish descent. His father was the state's attorney general and with that pedigree there was a certain inevitability that Ted himself would attend the University of Nebraska, study law and graduate top of his class. While still at university he made his politics clear, setting up the first branch of the liberal group Americans for Democratic Action.

When he moved to Washington in 1951 he went to work for the National Security Agency and for a time with Senator Paul Douglas of Illinois. It was Douglas who introduced Sorensen to the young senator from Massachusetts in 1953. Kennedy and Sorenson began working closely together, travelling the country, talking about their politics and their dreams. Throughout those early years Sorensen was having an immersion course in what made Kennedy tick, learning the way he talked and the phrases he used. A ghost writer and a speechwriter should be invisible in the works they produce, they might find the exact phrase which uplifts a speech but it must sound convincing, writing words the orator is likely to use. By the time Sorensen became Kennedy's chief speechwriter he would have absorbed much of his psyche and political philosophy – he was thinking as Kennedy himself was thinking.

On the way to the White House Kennedy read Herbert Agar's book, *The Price of Union* which described an act of courage by an earlier Massachusetts senator John Quincy Adams. He showed the book to Sorensen and asked him to find further examples. The result of Sorensen's research led to a book written while Kennedy was recovering from back surgery in 1954/55 called *Profiles of Courage*, a volume of short biographies of eight US senators. It became a best seller and although not originally nominated, it won the Pulitzer Prize for Biography in 1957 thanks, according to some accounts, to a little persuasion from Kennedy's father, Joseph, on one of the board members, Arthur Krock, to encourage others to vote for the book.[77]

It wasn't long before people began questioning who the actual author was and whether Kennedy should have agreed to accept the prize. On 7 December 1957 Drew Pearson, a journalist, went on a live TV show called The Mike Wallace Interview and said: "John F Kennedy is the only man in history that I know who won a Pulitzer Prize for a book that was ghost-written for him." When challenged by the host who asked if he knew that for a fact Pearson said he did and alleged that Sorensen was the true author adding: "You know, there's a little wisecrack around the Senate about Jack ... some of his colleagues say, 'Jack, I wish you had a little less profile and more courage." The Kennedys inevitably sued for $50 million unless the network, ABC, issued an apology and a retraction of the allegation. Pearson and the interviewer, Wallace, insisted the story was true but ABC backed down and apologised.

Ted Sorensen (1928–2010)

Sorensen himself seemed to put the matter to rest in his autobiography, *Counselor*, in 2008 when he wrote: "While in Washington, I received from Florida almost daily instructions and requests by letter and telephone – books to send, memoranda to draft, sources to check, materials to assemble, and Dictaphone drafts or revisions of early chapters" adding that Kennedy "worked particularly hard and long on the first and last chapters, setting the tone and philosophy of the book." He also said that Kennedy paid him a sum of money for his contribution to the book while acknowledging that Kennedy deserved full credit for the authorship.

JFK will always be remembered however for his stirring speeches and soaring rhetoric most notably in his inaugural address as President in 1961. He declared that "the torch has been passed to a new generation of Americans" and he challenged Americans, "Ask not what your country can do for you, ask what you can do for your country. My fellow citizens of the world: ask not what America will do for you, but what together we can do for the freedom of man."

No-one doubts the brilliance of the phrasing, equal to many of the great orators, the only issue was who wrote the words. It was a question Sorensen repeatedly faced and he gave this enigmatic reply: "Having no satisfactory answer, I long ago started answering the oft-repeated question as to its authorship with the smiling retort, 'Ask not.'"

There are two theories. In 2005 Thurston Clarke, the historian, was confident that based on new evidence Kennedy wrote the speech, while the author, Richard Tofel, a *Wall Street Journal* executive, was equally certain that Kennedy wrote no more than 14 of the 51 sentences and that if one man was responsible then "that man must surely be not John Kennedy but Theodore Sorensen".

The origin of the quote may actually date right back to Kennedy's childhood days at Choate School in Wallingford, Connecticut where the headmaster, George St. John, liked to challenge his pupils to ask "not what Choate does for you, but what you can do for Choate." But even then there was a degree of plagiarism as St. John was in all probability simply reusing an excerpt from an essay by Dean LeBaron Briggs of Harvard University, where St. John had studied.

As for Sorensen he states quite clearly that "the speech and its famous turn of phrase that everyone remembers was written by Kennedy himself." Whatever the true source, maybe the phrase had stuck in Kennedy's mind, perhaps he had after all been paying attention during his headmaster's addresses or possibly a keen-eyed researcher delving into JFK's history had seen the quote, it lives on today as one of the most memorable speeches of all time.

Sorensen did more than just write speeches. His official title was special counsel and he was a member of the executive committee – Ex-Comm – that Kennedy set up to advise him during the 1962 Cuban missile crisis. One of his duties was to draft exchanges from the President to the Soviet Premier, Nikita Khrushchev. The crisis, triggered by America's failed attempt to overthrow Fidel Castro's regime in the Bay of Pigs[78] fiasco, was conducted on two levels: public exchanges expressing outrage that the Soviet Union was building missile bases on Cuba and the usual behind the scenes diplomatic exchanges between Kennedy and Khrushchev. One assumes that Sorensen's legal and literal skills would have been used to find the right phrase. The Defense Secretary, Robert McNamara, said Sorensen was one of the "true inner circle" members who advised the president throughout the crisis.

Tension was high with Khrushchev demanding that the United States lift its air and sea blockade of Cuba writing on 24 October 1962 that is amounted to "an act of aggression propelling human kind into the abyss of a world nuclear-missile war."

In the end an agreement was reached on the 28 October when the Soviets agreed to dismantle their rocket sites and America promised not to invade Cuba. There was also a side agreement that US rockets armed with nuclear warheads targeting the Soviet Union and based in Turkey and Italy would also be dismantled. Those fourteen days in October were the closest the world came to nuclear warfare during the Cold War – it was not a time for careless words.

On 22 November 1963 Kennedy was assassinated leaving many including Sorensen devastated. He could not imagine life without his leadership and the next day handed in his letter of resignation to President Lyndon Johnson. It was refused and Johnson persuaded him to stay and help him with his speeches including drafting Johnson's first address to Congress and his 1964 State of the Union. But it was never going to be the same relationship built up over years; his writing could be just as elegant but Johnson was not Kennedy and in February 1964 Sorensen left the White House.

Ever the Kennedy insider, Sorensen advised Senator Robert Kennedy in the 1968 primary campaign against Vice President Hubert Humphrey. But on the night of 4 June Robert Kennedy too was assassinated by the Palestinian, Sirhan Sirhan. The following year Soensen lent his support to

Ted Sorensen (1928–2010)

Senator Edward Kennedy following the Chappaquiddick Island incident advising him on how he should explain away the hours of delay the senator took to report the accident. On 18 July Kennedy's car was driven off the island's Dike Bridge leaving his passenger, Mary Jo Kopechne, trapped inside. Kennedy failed to report the accident to the police until the next day when Miss Kopechne's body was recovered. Kennedy pleaded guilty to "leaving the scene of an accident after causing injury" and was given a two month suspended jail sentence.

The spin Sorensen may have suggested in a vain attempt to make the incident at Chappaquiddick look better probably counted against him when the new President Jimmy Carter put his name forward as director of the Central Intelligence Agency. In addition he declared himself a conscientious objector to his draft board shortly after World War II – a man who was allegedly prepared to gloss over the death of a young woman and yet was not able to fire a weapon in defence of his country was not the person the Senate was looking for to run its spy network. In his autobiography Sorensen also blamed his failure to secure the post on his two failed marriages and because he wrote an affidavit in defence of releasing the Pentagon Papers (see Charles Colson below).

Although he tried to secure the nomination as Democratic candidate for New York Senator he failed and continued to focus on his extensive work as a partner in the law firm Paul, Weiss, Rifkind, Wharton & Garrison. His responsibilities and clients included advising US corporations how to expand their operations overseas and foreign governments among them Central Asian countries, President Anwar Sadat of Egypt and Nelson Mandela.

But Sorensen always kept an attentive ear to the American political scene and when he was nearly 80, despite having suffered a stroke which had left him nearly blind, he thought he had identified a new young Democrat in the JKF mould, Barack Obama. In an interview with the *New York Magazine* in February 2008 he noted: "They said Obama, born black in America, really didn't have a chance to be president, he should run for vice-president, wait a few years. They said Kennedy, baptized a Catholic in America, didn't have any real chance to be president, and he should run for vice-president and wait a few years. They said Obama's too young, a senator in his first term; when Kennedy started out, they said he was too young, a senator in his first term. That got me more interested."[79]

He still had cards to play and felt he could make a difference. He wasn't writing as much but he still had powerful contacts he could call. Sorensen revealed that he had lunch with JFK's daughter, Caroline, and told her that this was her father's man which led to the Kennedy clan giving its blessing to Obama. Sorensen would only say modestly: "I had a small role in that."[80] Some reports say he also had a hand in Obama's powerful inaugural address in 2009 'A New Birth of Freedom' a phrase from the Gettysburg Address with shades of Martin Luther King and echoes of Kennedy stressing the need for shared sacrifice and a new sense of responsibility to answer America's challenges at home and abroad. "Today I say to you that the challenges we face are real. They are serious and they are many. They will not be met easily or in a short span of time. But know this, America – they will be met. On this day, we gather because we have chosen hope over fear, unity of purpose over conflict and discord," he declared.

Regardless of his politics Obama can deliver a speech and Sorensen recognised the skill. He played a significant role in the making of President Kennedy and in his own words had a small part in the making of President Obama.

He suffered a second stroke and died on the 31 October 2010 aged 82. In the true style of the shadow player he remained forever in the background but his contribution was remembered. President Obama said on hearing the news of his death: "I got to know Ted after he endorsed my campaign early on. He was just as I hoped he'd be – just as quick-witted, just as serious of purpose, just as determined to keep America true to our highest ideals."

Sorensen was no idle dilettante with a gift for the written and spoken words he recognised their power and how to use them to the greatest effect. Others can judge whether or not Kennedy and Obama were good presidents but at a time of crisis he was able to provide the phrases which turned America away from nuclear war. Why they found themselves in that predicament is another matter but when Sorensen stepped into the White House offering advice it made a difference. Kennedy was able to draw on his intellectual blood bank, along with the advice of others to be sure, and offer the soothing words which turned the two most powerful nations in the world away from mutually assured destruction. He wasn't a field operator, the Senators didn't want him running the CIA for them and nor did the voters want him representing them in the Senate, but he was on the edge of history for most of his life and it is possible that it was his words, his spin, which ensured that at least one catastrophe was averted.

He never made policy but he could accurately reflect what his masters wanted to say and to the end he found the felicitous phrases when even the masters he so admired sometime fell short. "There were articles and books written that JFK could not realistically deliver all the hopes he raised," he said watching Obama struggle. "But I responded to that by paraphrasing Browning, 'A president's hopes must exceed his reach, or what's the presidency for?'"[81]

15

Robert Maheu (1917–2008)

The golden rule of the fixer is to stay in the shadows delivering the policies of your master. For most of his colourful life Robert Aime Maheu did just that operating around the world with governments and gangsters, tycoons and billionaires but he is best known for a period when he became the front man for a master who retreated into the shadows himself never to reappear.

Maheu was born in Waterville, Maine, on 30 October 1917, graduating from Holy Cross College in 1940 before moving on to Georgetown University in Washington D.C. It was while still at university that his future career path would be decided. His country needed him for the war effort.

He was approached and recruited by the Federal Bureau of Investigation (the Central Intelligence Agency was not founded until 1947) to work as a counter-intelligence officer posing as a Canadian businessman and Nazi sympathiser. His mission, which he readily accepted, was to gather information about German military activity while at the same time feeding false information to two German spies who were said to report directly to Hitler. He evidently performed the task well and the two Germans were later arrested with Maheu's help.

In 1947, now certain about his chosen career and supremely confident in his own abilities, he left the FBI and established his own private investigation business which he preferred to think of as a consultancy which just happened to be staffed by former FBI colleagues. One of his first clients was the newly formed CIA. They needed what was termed 'cut out' operators – people who could undertake clandestine work which was completely deniable if they got caught. In short they needed people to do their dirty work.

Robert Maheu (1917–2008)

One of his first assignments arose was when US President Eisenhower became infuriated by the actions of the new left wing Cuban government of Fidel Castro which had seized US assets in the country and given its allegiance to the Moscow at the height of the Cold War. Castro had to be got rid of, but how? There were two options: military action or assassination. America would try both.

As Maheu put it: "In the winter of 1959–60, however, the CIA still thought it could pull off the invasion (of Cuba). But it thought the odds might be better if the plan went one step further – the murder of Fidel Castro. All the Company needed was someone to do the dirty work for it. Professional killers. A gangland-style hit."

Washington decided to enlist the support of an unlikely ally – the Mafia. They were equally furious with Castro because he had seized their hotels and lucrative casino businesses on the island and they wanted to do something about it. However the US authorities could not be seen to be plotting anything directly with the Mafia, they needed a go-between, a cut out to handle the negotiations.

According to CIA documents now in the public domain Colonel Sheffield Edwards, Director of Security, recruited Maheu in August 1960 to make contact with 'Handsome Johnny' Roselli, the West Coast representative of the Chicago Mob who ran operations in Hollywood and Las Vegas. At a meeting in the Hilton Plaza Hotel in New York City Maheu portrayed himself as a representative of a group of international corporations which were also suffering under Castro's regime rather than the CIA and offered to pay Roselli $150,000 if he had Castro assassinated. Roselli declined but agreed to introduce Maheu to two other mobsters, Sam Giancana, boss of the Chicago Outfit, and Santo Trafficante Jr., the Tampa, Florida boss. Before the revolution in Cuba which brought Castro to power, Trafficante[82] was one of the leading Mafiosi figures and had been expelled as an 'undesirable alien.' The Mafia certainly had the motivation to help the Agency; Giancana reportedly said that the CIA and the Cosa Nostra were "different sides of the same coin."

Maheu set up a meeting on 12 March 1961 between Jim O'Connell, chief of the CIA's operational support division, Roselli, Trafficante and Giancana at the Fontainebleau Hotel, Miami Beach. At this meeting O'Connell handed over poison pills and $10,000 to Roselli to be used against Castro.

Several attempts were made on Castro's life – according to his bodyguard, Fabian Escalante no fewer than 638 over the years – including exploding cigars, poisoned scuba diving suits and straightforward Mafia-style shootings.

When he gave evidence to the Church Committee[83] in 1975 Maheu justified his role in the plot against Castro by saying he thought America "was involved in a just war."

In later life when Maheu came to write his memoirs[84] he gave this explanation of his role: "Though I'm no saint, I am a religious man, and I knew that the CIA was talking about murder. They (CIA bosses) used the analogy of World War II, 'If we had known the exact bunker that Hitler was in during the war, we wouldn't have hesitated to kill the bastard ...' But in my mind, justified or not, I would still have blood on my hands ... If anything went wrong, I was the fall guy, caught between protecting the government and protecting the mob, two armed camps that could crush me like a bug."

Every single attempt on Castro's life failed and the programme was eventually stopped or at least postponed as Washington prepared to launch a military assault by proxy on Cuba.

While still in office President Eisenhower authorised a $13 million fund to the CIA to train a paramilitary group called Brigade 2506 in Mexico to carry out an attack. When President John Kennedy defeated Eisenhower in the 1960 election and heard about the plan he gave it his backing. On 15 April eight B-26 bombers supplied by the CIA attacked Cuban airfields and returned to the United States. The next night the main assault party setting off from Guatemala landed on Playa Girón in the Bay of Pigs. At first they established a bridgehead overwhelming the local defence but by 20 April under the direct leadership of Castro the Cuban army forced the invaders to surrender. They were interrogated in public before being sent back to the States. It was a complete humiliation for the US Government.

Maheu described the CIA as his 'first steady client' paying him $500 a month retainer but his undercover activity had already attracted another powerful and reclusive operator, the industrialist billionaire Howard Hughes who began using his services on a freelance basis around 1955 but the relationship was wholly unique. Maheu never actually met Hughes in all their time working together. All communication was by telephone.

To begin with Hughes used Maheu to keep tabs on his girlfriends and any of his rival suitors. He was a playboy and film-maker discovering a number of stars such as Jane Russell and Jean Harlow and he married the actresses Jean Peters and then Terry Moore. Maheu's job was to keep track of those Hughes loved as well as those by whom he felt threatened.

In 1966 Maheu moved from Los Angeles to Las Vegas and began to work full time for Hughes, effectively running Hughes's hotels and casinos. While his boss remained hidden from public view Maheu, the behind the scenes fixer, stepped into the limelight. It was a complete reversal of the fixer role. He said of Hughes: "He was the King of Vegas and as his surrogate, I wore the crown."

Hughes had ambitious plans for the Strip and it was Maheu's job to deliver. To begin with Hughes had only intended to stay in the Desert Inn for ten days but after three months in the penthouse suite the hotel owners tried to evict him. Hughes's response was to arrange for Maheu to buy the hotel. He had ambitious plans not just for the hotel but the whole of Las Vegas and he had money to spend having sold his stake in Trans World Airlines for $546.5 million. Before long he was the third largest landowner in Vegas having snapped up the Sands, the Castaways, the Frontier, the Silver Slipper and the Landmark along with 25,000 acres of prime real estate worth a total of some $300 million at the time.

Brian Greenspun, president and editor of the *Las Vegas Sun*, said: "When he came here in 1966, Bob spearheaded Howard Hughes' efforts to buy up a number of mobbed-up hotels on the Strip. Only men with Mr. Hughes' money and vision and Bob Maheu's tenacity could have succeeded in ridding Las Vegas of mob influence...Without Bob Maheu, Las Vegas would be a very different and a far less successful place today."

Maheu in classic fixer style became the gatekeeper to Hughes speaking to him and getting his instructions in long phone conversations. Although he was never allowed to meet him, others could not even speak to him.

Having secured his property portfolio in Nevada Hughes had another task for Maheu. At the time Hughes was trying to win federal approval for some new airline acquisitions and he decided that the wheels of government needed oiling, so Maheu was ordered to deliver two bundles of $50,000 each in cash to Charles Rebozo, a close aide of Richard Nixon ostensibly as a contribution to his campaign fund. It was a barely welcome gift as Nixon blamed the revelation that Hughes Corp had loaned his brother, Donald, $205,000 for his election defeat by Kennedy in 1960. Nixon was also so concerned that one of his former employees, the Democratic National Committee Chairman, Larry O'Brien, knew about Hughes's donations that he had O'Brien's Watergate offices broken into but as everyone now knows the burglars were caught in the act.

Hughes also had environmental concerns about the protection of Nevada's water supply and nuclear weapons' testing in the state. On two occasions Maheu travelled to Washington with $1 million in cash to persuade first President Lyndon Johnson then Nixon to call off the testing programme.[85]

By 1970 Maheu had fallen out with Hughes or more likely had fallen out with the group of carers assigned by Hughes Corp executive, Bill Gay, to look after the increasingly ailing and tormented man. The carers were dubbed the 'Mormon Mafia' because most were members of the Church of Jesus Christ of Latter-day Saints. Maheu was fired probably at the instigation of Gay and set up a new company, Robert A. Maheu and Associates.

Two years after he left, Maheu was sued by Hughes who claimed he was "a no-good son of a bitch who robbed me blind". Maheu sued for defamation and Hughes settled out of court. But to the end it is clear that Maheu had a soft spot for Hughes who eventually died at the age of 70 on board his private jet travelling to his home in Houston. Maheu believed he had died from neglect. In 2004 he said: "My heart still bleeds for what happened to Howard Hughes. I often said after I got off the phone with him that I just finished talking to the poorest man in the world. He was so unhappy."

Maheu's client list during his working life was varied if not wholly above board. In the midst of his plotting to kill Castro, he was hired by Giancana to place a wiretap in the home of comedian, Dan Rowan, whom Giancana suspected of having an affair with his girlfriend, Phyllis McGuire, lead singer of the McGuire Sisters. The wiretap technician was caught red handed and immediately pointed the finger at Maheu who in turn arranged for the CIA to get the then Attorney General, Robert Kennedy, to drop the charges.

Later Roselli who had introduced Maheu to the other mobsters felt that he wasn't getting enough help from the Agency to fight deportation and told the *Washington Post* journalist, Jack Anderson, all about the Castro plot before giving evidence to the Church Committee. It was too much of a betrayal for some people and days later Roselli's decomposing body was found in a 55 gallon oil drum floating in Dumfoundling Bay off Miami Beach. He had been shot and his legs sawn off. He had broken the Mafia code of silence, *omertà*.

Maheu had only been in business on his own account for a few weeks when he was offered five thousand dollars by the Greek shipping billionaire, Stavros Niarchos, to use his dark arts to sabotage a deal which would have handed his rival, Aristotle Onassis, a monopoly on shipping Saudi Arabian oil. It was a deal also vehemently opposed by Vice President Nixon for the obvious damage it could do to US interests in the region.

Robert Maheu (1917–2008)

The Jiddah Agreement required Onassis to supply five hundred thousand tons of tanker shipping to create the Saudi Arabian Maritime Company. The company would be free of Saudi taxes get a guaranteed 10 per cent of the country's annual output and at the same time weaken US influence with the Saudis. Onassis later told the writer, Peter Evans: 'I was about to stick my finger into the American pie' – a pie dominated by four major American companies. In his biography on Onassis, *Nemesis*, Peter Evans states that Nixon is alleged to have shaken Maheu's hand saying: "And just remember, if it turns out we have to kill the bastard don't do it on American soil."

Maheu was being given carte blanche to carry out murder on behalf of the US Government – a licence to kill. Maheu's eldest son, Peter, who also became a private investigator, justified the plan in this way: "If you think paying $3 or $4 a gallon for gasoline today is bad, you can imagine what we would be paying if my father did not play a major role in scuttling that deal." His youngest son, Robert, said his father was a man of "strong values and ethics who always acted in a manner he felt was in the best interest of his country." In the end all it took for the deal to be called off was a wiretap of Onassis's phone calls which were released to the Saudis.

Much later Maheu is also said to have devised another anti-Onassis scam arranging for Prince Rainier of Monaco to slash Onassis's 52% stake in a company that owned Monaco to less than a third, although Maheu always coyly and Sphinx-like denied any involvement.

Other alleged activities by Maheu's office included the making of a soft porn film for the CIA using look-alikes of President Sukarno of Indonesia and a Russian woman. Parts were distributed in the country in order to discredit Sukarno. It was a job.

To this day private investigator firms around the world are digging and delving into private, corporate and government affairs. Seldom if ever do these inquiries lead to public exposure or worse still a court case with all the downside of media exposure. The modus operandi as in the case of Onassis and his wiretaps is simply and discretely to make the information available to a third party; the deal then goes away or a belligerent party, perhaps the claimant to a family fortune, backs off. The last thing any investigator or consultancy wants is public exposure. Those who need to know of their existence can easily find out; banks and lawyers use them all the time in the process of due diligence and, on occasion, rules and laws are bent and even broken.

The fact that Robert Maheu broke cover and placed himself at the very forefront of Howard Hughes's empire is wholly unique. The other activity, his involvement in the plot against Castro and his dealings with the Mafia, are unlikely to be repeated in the present day but the 'research work' undoubtedly continues.

Maheu was the archetypal fixer who judging by the accounts of his own family members always had his country's interests at heart – the ends he believed justified the means. He may even have felt he had no choice in the matter once he had been recruited by the FBI at university. The thrill of it all was probably too much to resist and once hooked as a student there was no turning back. He had conspired and lied for the good of his country and that was the path of his life. Whether or not he really had a licence to kill is debateable but his career is said to have inspired the series of action spy movies, Mission Impossible starring Tom Cruise. Maheu didn't have the gadgets that the films make great use of but he most certainly had the connections. He served several US administrations, he knew his way about the criminal underworld and was trusted by them, and he was sufficiently astute to be handed the unofficial role of 'chief operating officer' by one of America's richest and most secretive business tycoons.

Maheu also managed to survive when things went wrong, another attribute of the successful go-between. When Howard Hughes's life became ever more eccentric he was happy to move on, when plots went awry Maheu somehow was never blamed for the failure and above all he managed to serve many different masters on both sides of the law without apparently getting his fingers burned. Consultancies like his still operate on the basis that they will come up with a plan which the client must approve of but the outcome particularly when moving on the edge of the law can never be certain.

Maheu survived to enjoy a comfortable retirement enjoying talking to reporters smiling his enigmatic smile giving nothing away because nothing could be proved.

He died on 4 August 2008 of congestive heart failure at the Desert Springs Hospital in Las Vegas, a city he had helped create, probably taking the best of his secrets to the grave.

16

Malcolm MacDonald (1901–1981)

Malcolm MacDonald was the inspiration for this short book. By the time our two families got to know each other he was serving as High Commissioner in Kenya but he was always described as a 'roving ambassador'. He was Britain's trouble shooter in some of the hottest spots in the world, soothing ruffled feathers, building friendships with his charm and throughout playing down his own importance. "I am merely the runner," he would say of his

role at important conferences. Despite his eminence in the international diplomatic community he was down to earth and, as far as I was concerned as a budding journalist, always had time to give advice and lend a helping hand. He displayed no airs and graces standing on his head if he thought it would entertain the youngsters in his midst and by all accounts displaying the same acrobatic skills, walking on his hands, in front of presidents or prime ministers when he thought it might lighten the mood. It was this easy manner which enabled him to negotiate and cajole as he travelled the globe. Few other people can claim to have been adopted by a tribe of headhunters, rehabilitated an imprisoned terrorist to the point where he became president of his country and all the time never straying from his upbringing or his traditional roots.

In one sense Malcolm MacDonald was destined to move in rarefied circles and one might say started at the top and stayed there. He was born on 17 August 1901 at Lossiemouth in Scotland, the second of three sons among six children of Ramsay MacDonald who was to become Britain's first Socialist prime minister.

The family moved to a flat in London's Lincoln's Inn Fields where the politically active visitors the young Malcolm would have met included Keir Hardie, a fellow Scot who rose from humble beginnings to become the first leader of the Labour Party.

MacDonald was educated at Bedales School in Hampshire between 1912-1920 where he seemed to excel in all things but his academic work. Nevertheless he did win a minor history exhibition to Queen's College, Oxford where he read modern history obtaining a second class degree staying on for one more year to take a post graduate diploma in economics and politics earning a distinction in 1924. During his time at Oxford he got his first taste of political debate joining the Oxford Union. After university he probably developed his obvious love for overseas travel when he was part of a three man Oxford debating team touring in the United States, Canada, Hawaii, Fiji, New Zealand, and Australia.

His first formal experience in politics was as a member of the London County Council between 1927 and 1930 until finally, at his third attempt, he was elected as the Labour member of parliament for the Bassetlaw division of Nottinghamshire. For the next ten years his professional life could hardly be described as behind the scenes but it was during this period that he refined his innate negotiating and diplomatic prowess which his country would call on time and again even though he remained determined in later life to keep a low profile refusing all honours save that of Order of Merit from the Queen.

In 1931 following the formation of the National Government, MacDonald was appointed parliamentary under-secretary in the Dominion Office[86]. Even at that early stage and in a relatively lowly position he was used as a secret negotiator carrying messages from his father, Ramsay, to Mahatma Gandhi during the protracted negotiations leading to India's independence. He made an impression in Whitehall and between 1935–1940 he was cabinet minister as Secretary of State for Dominion Affairs and Secretary of State for the Colonies. His future career in international affairs was already taking shape.

Another idiosyncrasy was also developing – his working style. MacDonald worked long but disjointed hours which would upset his staff who had to keep up. He would start work early, take a nap after lunch, return to work and, at this early stage in his youthful life, would enjoy partying into the small hours with the stars of London's theatreland such as Ivor Novello, Noël Coward and Laurence Olivier. Even in what passed for retirement, he would follow a strict regime of working, resting, long uninterrupted periods of letter writing and of course his favourite high tea in the afternoon with cakes and sandwiches which allowed him to forego heavy evening meals. Even if he had to attend dinner parties which he did at our house in Kenya on occasions, he would discretely gather his cutlery in front of him and eat nothing while entertaining other guests with his conversation. He remained the lad from Lossiemouth where everyone had high tea, never supper.

Another name that would have crossed MacDonald's radar at this time would have been Jomo Kenyatta who had taken to giving speeches in England and writing letters to the newspapers between 1931 and 1948 raising issues about the plight of his countrymen in Kenya particularly regarding what was called 'the destocking of the Kamba Reserve.' The colonial government had decided that there was over-grazing by cattle and that herds of cows – the principal currency of the tribes – should be reduced. One of the colonial officials sent a memo to MacDonald saying: "Mr Kenyatta is becoming increasingly mischievous." They would soon be hearing more from him.

Meanwhile one of MacDonald's first diplomatic duties was to help solve the Anglo-Irish Trade War which had flared up in 1932 following the election of Eammon de Valera and his Fianna Fail Party. De Valera immediately imposed tariffs on goods imported from Britain and abolished 'land annuities' – money that the British government had loaned to Irish farmers and which the farmers had agreed to repay. MacDonald succeeded in finding a settlement to the dispute with de Valera, some say largely thanks to their shared interest in ornithology; typical MacDonald tactics to defuse a situation.

MacDonald lost his seat in the 1935 general election but was back in Parliament when he won the by-election in Ross and Cromarty the following year. He was briefly Health Minister in the Churchill government in 1940 working on food rationing, provision of air raid shelters and the early stages of the National Health Service. But Churchill didn't get along with MacDonald despite flattering appeals and persuaded him to take up a post in Canada as British High Commissioner. He remained there from 1941–1946 becoming close to Mackenzie King, Canada's longest serving prime minister. King was an authoritative but not a charismatic leader and must have admired MacDonald's more relaxed style. While in post he advised

King on numerous issues including the conscription crisis when Canadians were divided over sending troops to fight against Germany in World War II, how he should manage the political situation following the exposure of Igor Gouzenko, a cipher clerk in the Soviet Embassy, who revealed Stalin's efforts to steal nuclear secrets[87], and how to calm concerns about what was dubbed the American Invasion of Canada.

In June 1942 Japanese forces attacked the Aleutian Islands and occupied Adak and Kiska, the first time American territory had been occupied since 1812. Faced with what they perceived to be a real danger of an attack on the American mainland, the construction of a land route to supply bases in Alaska was deemed essential. It was MacDonald who suggested that this could be construed as an 'invasion' of Canadian territory and alerted King to the potential diplomatic issue. King probably had other concerns on his plate but later admitted to MacDonald that the road "was less intended for protection against the Japanese than as one of the fingers of the hand that America is placing more or less over the whole of the Western Hemisphere."[88]

While he was in Canada he met and later married a beautiful war widow called Mrs Audrey Rowley by whom he had a daughter, Fiona. Among the distinguished guests at Christ Church Cathedral in Ottawa to witness the ceremony was the Prime Minister, Mackenzie King. But MacDonald was not the stay at home family man and it was not long before he was on his travels again. When Fiona wrote about her father later in life she said, "I thought of him more as a statesman than a father."

After the war ended MacDonald eagerly seized an opportunity to escape party politics in favour of the world of diplomacy. He was appointed Governor General of Malaya, Singapore and British Borneo in 1946 arriving with great fanfare and a guard of honour at Changi Airport in Singapore to be greeted by Lord Louis Mountbatten, Supreme Allied Commander South East Asia. It was a delicate period. Before MacDonald's arrival the British government had been working on a plan to unite the nine Protected Malay States and the Colony of Straits Settlements (which included Singapore, Malacca and Penang) into one Malayan Union. It was not a popular idea and the sultans and many Malay officials made their point by boycotting MacDonald's swearing-in ceremony on 22 May 1946. He decided that the best way to break the ice was to invite them all to a tea party at his residence in Penang. It worked and it was not long before MacDonald concluded that the Malayan Union idea was a non-starter not least because it would have disempowered local leaders. Difficult negotiations continued including efforts to satisfy the demands of the Chinese and Indian residents who began to feel they were being left out of the discussions. The Colonial Secretary, George Hall, thought it might boost McDonald's standing in the talks giving him added authority if he were given a title. Hall suggested that MacDonald should accept the honour of being made a Knight of the Grand Cross of Michael and St George (KCMG – or Kindly Call Me God as it was affectionately known). MacDonald demurred. He said later, "I was averse to honours, and especially to those which carried titles. They seemed to me to make false distinctions between a few human beings and millions of equally worthy others – to establish something like a caste system in our society."[89]

He emphasised this preference for informality by going to work in open neck short sleeved shirts, refusing to join the whites only Tanglin Club in Singapore preferring the mixed race, Island Club, and letting it be known that he did not want visitors bowing before him even though as Governor General he represented the King. Mountbatten thought this a step too far but MacDonald ignored him.

Finally on 21 January 1948 the Federation of Malaya Agreement was signed at King House by all the Malay rulers and Sir Edward Gent, the first and last governor of the short lived Malayan Union. MacDonald eventually fell out with Gent over his handling of growing unrest and murders in the plantations. Gent eventually declared an emergency believing it would all be over in a matter of weeks – in fact the Malayan Energency would last for twelve years. In the end MacDonald recommended Gent's recall to London which Whitehall accepted. On the flight home Gent's plane collided with another aircraft on its approach to London and he was killed. MacDonald was full of remorse.

It is at this stage that his success as an international fixer really took flight as in time his responsibilities were expanded to take in the whole of South East Asia. His approach to the Dominions and Commonwealth was regarded as different and refreshing. He was quoted by an Australian reporter as saying the strength of the Dominions was "in the sum of the strength of its parts. The stronger, the more self-contained and self-reliant Australia grows, the better for Britain as well as for the Commonwealth." MacDonald's attitude in all his diplomatic postings around the Empire was to empower the local leaders to achieve their independence. When he became governor of Malaya he said in a broadcast, "We are not here to divide and rule. We are here to unite and get out."

The gradual evolution of the Commonwealth began as far back as 1884 when the Prime Minister of the day, Lord Rosebery, described the growing independence of the British colonies as becoming a 'Commonwealth of Nations'. Its first statutory recognition was in the Anglo-Irish Treaty of 1921 where the wording the 'British Commonwealth of Nations' was substituted for 'British Empire'.

In 1948 MacDonald took on a new brief as Commissioner-General for the United Kingdom co-ordinating Britain's relationships in the whole of South East Asia and Africa. During this turbulent time successive governments kept him in post such was their regard for his ability and the relationships he had developed at every level from state leaders to the tribal elders. He was constantly on the move travelling to Vietnam, Colombo, Laos and Siam (Thailand) always seeking to calm troubled situations and all the time loving every minute: "I thus became almost like a bird on permanent migration, alighting for a brief busy while in this or that land, and then taking off again to fly elsewhere."[90]

One of MacDonald's greatest pleasures at this time was escaping from the formalities of life in Singapore into the jungles of Borneo travelling up river and getting to know the tribal people. It was here he met and was befriended by Temonggong Koh, paramount chief of the Iban people, a tribe of headhunters, who adopted him as his "son". On these travels MacDonald would often dress in his MacDonald tartan kilt "to show them that they were not the only wild men in the world."[91]

While in Singapore MacDonald showed how important he regarded youth and the future generations by helping found the University of Malaya and Singapore in 1949. He said later, "Some of the most fascinating and enjoyable work I had to do was concerned with the University and nothing was more important, of course, than trying to help the 'rulers of tomorrow' in Malaysia to become experienced and wise."

By the time MacDonald came to depart for a new posting as High Commissioner for India in 1955 he had succeeded in uniting conflicting forces particularly among the Chinese, all the while resisting the wrath of his masters in London for what they probably regarded as a cavalier style. *The Straits Times* editorial declared: "It is significant that, on a day when Malcolm MacDonald's London critics fired another of their angry salvos at him, some 10,000 people gathered in Singapore to present him with a silver casket and the Freedom of the City. Rare is the ambassador who can, at the end of his sojourn in a country which has become so sensitive about colonialism, accumulate this amount of genuine goodwill for Britain."[92]

The Indian posting came at a difficult point when India was attracting suitors from the Soviet Union as well as China. Britain on the other hand as a colonial power saw its influence declining. It was MacDonald's job to manage and maintain those military and economic ties at which he was largely successful not least because Jawahalal Nehru, the country's first Prime Minister, approved of MacDonald's principled stand against the British attack on the Suez Canal[93]. He had once accepted a dare from Nehru after a dinner to walk on his hands while Nehru himself stood on his head. Somehow in the midst of his work and travels between Britain's extensive offices on the continent, he found time to write a book entitled *Birds in my Indian Garden*, one of half a dozen publications. But India was not a happy posting for MacDonald who found Nehru and other officials set in their ways and unreceptive to his advice.

In 1960 MacDonald tried to retire but the following year he was called upon to be co-chairman and leader of the British delegation at the International Conference on the Settlement of the Laotian Question in Geneva which lasted from 16 May 1961 to 23 July 1962. By the end of their discussions 14 nations pledged to respect the neutrality of Laos. It is clear from government papers now in the public domain that MacDonald established close links with the Chinese authorities and Chou-en-lai, the first Premier of The People's Republic of China, who said MacDonald was "the only capitalist we can trust." He was able to travel extensively throughout the country reporting back to London that he had seen "hundreds of thousands" of Chinese, visited communes, factories and steel mills. He said that the country's leaders had "gone through an 'agonizing reappraisal'; that they have learned their lesson, and that, although they know the country is still vulnerable to nature, they have become more practical, more realistic and more patient."[94]

In 1963 he was persuaded by the Colonial Secretary, Duncan Sandys, to become Britain's last Governor and Commander-in-Chief in Kenya during the delicate period leading up to the country's independence under its first President, Jomo Kenyatta. The issue on his arrival was the choice between a regional style government or a stronger central government. At the time MacDonald thought the regional approach stood more chance of winning the support of minority tribes.

The drive to independence was hurried through in 11 months rather than the anticipated two years and general elections were held at the end of May 1963 with MacDonald demanding total impartiality from his colonial officials. He had heard that London had secretly instructed district commissioners to lend their support to KADU (Kenya Africa Democratic Union) against the rival Kenyatta led KANU (Kenya Africa National Union). Their objection to KANU was a prejudice against Kenyatta who had served seven years in prison for his leadership of the Mau Mau[95] rebellion. Typically MacDonald chose to make up his own mind about the people with whom he was dealing. Whereas Whitehall dismissed Kenyatta as "a pretty big devil, a bad man on the whole" who liked a drink, MacDonald rather liked him and noted at receptions how he only took soft drinks.

KANU won a clear majority in both the House of Representatives and the Senate. Kenyatta was duly elected prime minister and regional assemblies were selected.

It is tribute to MacDonald's diplomat skills and friendship with Kenyatta and other important Kenyan politicians like Tom Mboya that he was welcomed back to the country as High Commissioner. He remained in Kenya until 1965 after which he began his roving ambassador role in earnest for Harold Wilson's Labour Government being posted back to Africa at a time of great upheaval on the continent especially with Nigeria's civil war and coping with the illegal regime of Ian Smith in Rhodesia. With masterly understatement MacDonald wrote to his wife Audrey on 22 August 1967, "It is quite a job trying to cope with the affairs of a dozen different countries in different parts of eventful Africa."[96]

In his renewed retirement MacDonald kept active and retained his great interest in young people becoming Chancellor of the University of Durham, President of the Voluntary Service Overseas as well as accepting the presidency of the Royal Commonwealth Society. Despite having no official title or position there wasn't a world leader or senior diplomat who didn't know his name or would read his hand-written letters with interest and attention. He could open any door in any embassy and was generous enough to use his influence to help those, such as budding journalists like me, who wanted to meet distinguished figures they would otherwise have never got to see.

'Our Man Anywhere' as he was known by some probably achieved more than any other diplomat simply by being true to himself, never pulling rank and always being charming. If it meant doing a few handstands to break the ice then that is what he did. He seemed to be interested in what everyone else had to say and as a result was interested in everything from his love of ornithology to Chinese ceramics, from photography to least the important student with whom he had time to discuss their ambitions and dreams.

He declined repeated offers of a knighthood or peerage. He had become a member of the Privy Council in 1935 and only in deference and duty to the Queen did he accept his Order of Merit in 1969.

He suffered a heart attack and died on 11th January 1981 when he went out into his garden on a cold night to check his plants. He was 79. When I attended his funeral in the little St Peter's Church at nearby Ightham in Kent I remember it as being a sombre gathering with a handful of diplomats among the family and friends in dark mourning clothes. In contrast at the service of thanksgiving for his life at Westminster Abbey on 3rd March 1981 it was a more upbeat mood with favourite hymns and the Queen Mother's piper, David Duncan, playing the lament.

In his commemorative address, Sir Shridath Ramphal, the Common-wealth Secretary-General said he possessed the highest diplomatic qualities; he was "the supreme interlocutor". And he summed up the modesty of his character in these words: "Confident of his own strength, he did not need to prove it; conscious of his country's might, he saw no need to flaunt it. Incapable of superior airs, he was at ease with people the world over and, inevitably, they with him. He wore his patriotism lightly; unswerving, yet never intense, and blended always with a deep awareness of a wider brotherhood."[97]

On his death his "blood brother" one of the headhunters in Borneo asked the family if they would send part of his body to be buried in his adopted land. Fiona recalls: "We said no, but thought that it might be appropriate to send his kilt and we did just that."

Malcolm MacDonald in the kilt, shaking hands with a headhunter.

17

General Hossein Fardoust (1917–1987)

Uniquely in this collection of studies, Hossein Fardoust was identified early in life for the role he was to fulfil. What remains unclear in his story is where did the power lie around the gilded Peacock Throne. Who was really pulling the strings? Conspiracy theories abound to the present day.

When he was still a child Fardoust was selected by unseen hands to be the playmate of the man who would become the Shah of Iran, Mohammad Reza Pahlavi. He was allowed to attend a private school in the grounds of the palace established to instruct sons of the privileged few who were close to the royal family. This was followed by a four year spell in Switzerland accompanying Pahlavi, now 11, to Le Rosey Institute boarding school. It was the first time an heir to the throne had been sent overseas for his education. The decision to send the young crown prince abroad was influenced by his father's close and sophisticated adviser, Abdolhossein Teymourtash, who had himself been educated in Russia, was well read and multi-lingual. The prince's father, Reza Shah, was a strong determined figure who wanted to modernise his country, dealt ruthlessly with his opponents (mostly the Shiite clergy) and probably terrified his sensitive son who would have stood to attention in his father's presence. It is inconceivable that Fardoust would have been chosen without careful vetting. Just to keep an eye on the prince, Fardoust later claimed in a book[98] he wrote about his time in office that a young valet, Ernest Perron, was also sent to Le Rosey to befriend Pahlavi. It obviously worked because on their return to Iran Perron was appointed to the palace. Again precisely to whom Perron was actually reporting remains in doubt although Fardoust clearly suggests that it was to foreign intelligence services, probably Britain's MI6. According to his biographers the prince had a miserable time in Switzerland where he was constantly being watched and never allowed to get into trouble or behave like all the other boys in his class playing in the surrounding countryside or climbing in the mountains.

Fardoust was born in Tehran in 1917, the son of a gendarmerie officer. He attended the military elementary school in 1925 before being 'selected' as Pahlavi's friend and then going to school in Switzerland in 1931. On his return he joined Iran's military college becoming a lecturer.

When World War II broke out Iran found itself in a strategic and some considered vulnerable position. Its oil reserves were seen as vital to the Allies but Reza Shah himself was thought to be siding with the Axis forces even though Iran was officially neutral. To maintain essential supply lines to the Soviet troops fighting on the Eastern Front, British, Soviet and some Commonwealth forces invaded Iran on 25 August 1941 in an assault codenamed, Operation Countenance. Expecting to be dethroned Reza Shah abdicated in favour of his son, Mohammad Reza, and went into exile in South Africa. For a time there appeared to be a vacuum into which political factions, suppressed under Reza Shah and including the clergy, merchants, nationalists and the Communist Tudeh Party, flexed their muscles once again. Not for the last time, the young and inexperienced shah, still only 21 and suddenly dropped into turbulent waters, hesitated. He needed his advisers around him.

Fardoust appears to have been the shah's closest confidant and played a leading role in the events at this time not least those surrounding the fate of Azerbaijan. While the Persian Corridor was being used to support the Soviet Forces it was always understood that Allied forces, which by now included the United States, would withdraw from Iran at the end of the war. However in what became known as the Iran-Azerbaijan Crisis of 1946 Stalin at first refused to give up the Iranian territory his forces now occupied until eventually he succumbed to diplomatic pressure from Washington and accepted a deal struck by Tehran. The Iranian prime minister at the time was Ahmad Qavam who flew to Moscow and negotiated directly with Stalin. The deal which Qavam, nicknamed the old fox, hammered out with the Soviets granted them oil concessions in the north of the country but no sooner had the Russians pulled out, than the agreement was promptly rescinded. While Qavam may have been prime minister it appears that Fardoust was the shah's eyes and ears on these occasions and it was in this role that he became what he himself described as "the second most powerful man" in the regime.

The influence of the west was never in doubt either. Outside forces had brought the shah to the throne and as a constitutional monarch with little experience, he presumably was grateful to his backers. But gradually over time he would cling to the power he could wield as a result of the intelligence gathering he built around him. However what he and his allies thought was a well informed spy network failed to understand the mood of the people. Nevertheless to begin with it was Fardoust's job not only to keep his monarch informed but also to feed information to his Western masters in effect acting as the go-between in the delicate relationship.[99]

Oil was the lifeblood of the country, it was what had brought the shah to power and it produced the riches which would bewitch the west and mesmerise the shah himself. However in March 1951 the Majlis, the Iranian Parliament, passed a bill introduced by the Prime Minister Dr Mohammad Mosaddegh, who had been jailed by the shah's father, nationalising the Anglo-Iranian Oil Company (AIOC) which was widely thought to be benefitting from a one sided concession arrangement. The international reaction to the nationalisation was swift, Iranian oil was boycotted and the vast Abadan oil refinery producing 10% of all oil output was forced to shut down operations.

Fruitless negotiations dragged on. The shah tried to fire Mosaddegh but riots broke out and not for the last time protestors railed against perceived western interference in Iran's domestic affairs. The shah no doubt longing for the power his father once exercised even offered to leave the country – he was dubbed the 'suitcase shah' for always being ready to pack up his bags at the first sign of trouble.

Elections were held and Mosaddegh was returned but as the country's economy, so dependent on oil wealth, was suffering from the boycott the mood on the streets began to change and the shah and his international backers saw an opportunity.

The danger of Iranian oil assets falling into the hands of communist sympathisers and the threat of a domino effect throughout the Middle East was used as the excuse for a coup in 1953 codenamed Operation Ajax, by the CIA, and Operation Boot by Britain's MI6.

Mosaddegh, obviously in favour of the nationalisation of AIOC and therefore against Western interests, was arrested by soldiers and sentenced to death on 21 December 1953, a sentence later commuted to life imprisonment under house arrest. Fazlollah Zahedi was appointed as prime minister but he was just titular head of a military junta. The coup handed the shah unlimited powers backed by his armed forces and supplemented by a new secret intelligence operation, SAVAK, whose officers and agents it is accepted were trained by the CIA, Israel's intelligence network Mossad and MI6 and tasked with suppressing any opposition to the shah. Fardoust was made deputy head of SAVAK but everyone assumed he ran the operation.

For two days it looked as though the coup might fail as the arrest of Mosaddegh faltered. The shah fled the country but a mob, which declassified documents show was funded by the CIA, was bussed into Tehran and backed up by tanks, marched on Mosaddegh's home and seized him. Hundreds were killed in the exchanges and Mosaddegh supporters were rounded up and imprisoned; all orchestrated by SAVAK.

However no single organisation even an intelligence gathering network would be allowed to run without some checks and balances and Fardoust was put in charge of the Special Intelligence Bureau of Iran, described as a SAVAK within a SAVAK, which he ran for 20 years. In this position Fardoust was not only receiving information about opponents to the shah but was also able to watch SAVAK officers themselves. This information would prove useful later when the tide turned suddenly against the shah.

In his own book, Fardoust admits that he made all his notes in pencil which allowed him to change details and thereby keep secret the real information about the shah's growing unpopularity as the regime began to stumble. The unanswered question was did he do this because he could not bring himself to pass on bad news or was it on the instruction of his Western bosses in the CIA and MI6? The motive is unclear as when the revolution swept through Iran everyone, including the international community, seemed to be taken by surprise by its scale and impact.

Fardoust and his officers received extensive training in the dark arts of intelligence gathering, torture and interrogation from Iran's western supporters. The creation of SAVAK itself can be traced back to the arrival in Iran of Brigadier Norman Schwarzkopf Sr., father of General 'Stormin' Norman' Schwarzkopf who would later command the coalition forces in Operation Desert Storm which drove Saddam Hussein's Iraqi troops out of Kuwait. It was a return to familiar territory for Schwarzkopf Sr., because he had been invited by the Iranian parliament in 1942 to help train the local police to suppress Soviet-backed separatists intent on destabilising the political situation in Azerbaijan.

His job in 1953 however, it is claimed, was to galvanise the shah to stage the military coup and to train those loyal to him to rise up against Mosaddegh. It was these supporters who would form the nucleus of the feared SAVAK which had unlimited police powers and crushed all dissent.

According to *Encyclopædia Iranica*: "This organization was the first modern, effective intelligence service to operate in [Iran]...Its main achievement occurred in September 1954, when it discovered and destroyed a large Communist Tudeh Party network that had been established in the [Iranian] armed forces."

The size of SAVAK membership is impossible to gauge but according to documents released after the 1979 Iranian revolution there may have been as many as 15,000 full-time agents plus thousands of informants.

The coup of 1953 engineered by western forces marked an irreversible change for the country. The shah was now the undisputed head of state, an authoritarian monarch backed by a loyal military, an intelligence service of undeniable strength and supported behind the scenes by the combined strength of the CIA, Mossad and MI6. So long as the Soviet-bloc was kept at bay everyone was happy. Everyone that is except the people whom the shah mistakenly became convinced supported him. Those who did speak out were arrested, imprisoned and killed by SAVAK.

The shah's demeanour changed markedly over the years. When he first succeeded his father he would walk into a meeting of his prime minister and other senior advisers – his cabinet – pull up a chair and ask what was on the agenda addressing everyone by name in almost casual conversation. Within 20 years, as one eye witnessed told me, he had changed as he believed his authority was beyond question. His cabinet by then would gather punctually and he would enter the room waiting for the Prime Minister to pull out his chair. With a mere glance he would ask what was on the agenda and in turn he would look imperiously down his nose addressing each cabinet member as "Minister of Finance or Minister of Defence..." depending on the topic, refusing to use their actual name. The minister would answer nervously hoping his reply would find favour. On one occasion the most junior economics adviser in the room dared to correct the shah on the meaning of gross domestic product. The shah exploded throwing down his pen and stormed out of the room. The prime minister rushed after him to apologise for such impertinence and returned later with the surprising news that the adviser had been right to explain the point. In time that same adviser rose to an important rank in the cabinet himself but by then he had learnt a lesson and he became the quietest man in the room, only speaking when he was directly addressed. This he said was out of fear of saying the wrong thing or of falling out of favour such was the atmosphere the SAVAK wanted to maintain. The shah mistook it for respect.

In 1961 the shah, now full of confidence, launched his White Revolution promising land reforms and western style modernisation and some people began to believe in a better life, however what he could not deliver was true democracy. The sharpest criticism came from the clergy and in particular a priest in the holy city of Qom, Ayatollah Ruhollah Khomeini. He argued in his sermons which were taped and distributed in Tehran that the emancipation of women was against Islamic law and that in any case the shah was merely a puppet of Western powers. What the shah believed, or perhaps was led to believe by the sycophants around him, was that all the people loved him. He would say to the end: "I can claim to have the pulse of my people in my hand."

There is no written independent evidence of what Fardoust was saying to the shah at the time but it is known that the military leaders – army, navy and airforce – would line up outside his office to give their reports on a regular basis but no-one wanted to bring him bad news. The blame for any unrest was placed on Khomeini.

In June 1962 the ayatollah was arrested sparking riots which once again the shah seemed incapable or unwilling to put down with force. In the end the prime minister sent in the army and hundreds died and Khomeini was sent into exile in the holy city of Najaf in Iraq. But if they hoped that would keep him quiet they were wrong. His sermons grew in strength and he openly criticised the Americans who had been granted immunity from any prosecution. "These people can commit any crime they want in Iran," he said.

In 1967 the shah at last confident in his own authority crowned himself King of the Kings, Emperor of Iran, and his third wife, Farah Diba, as Shahbanoo or Empress. Rising oil prices were swelling the government coffers enabling him to deliver on many of the promises of his White Revolution adding to the illusion that all was well in the country. Most commentators seem to agree that the shah genuinely wanted to improve the lot of Iranians and the status of Iran in the world. The problem was he wanted Iran to become westernised and his people did not agree.

On 15 October 1971 he hosted a lavish gathering of 50 heads of state to mark the 2,500[th] anniversary of the founding of the Persian monarchy by

Cyrus the Great. The shah was convinced, and no-one disabused him, that he was somehow the latest in a divine line of kings. As the world leaders were carried in a fleet of luxury coaches being fed fine food and drinks along the way to the invitation-only festivities they were unaware that Fardoust's SAVAK had been busy rounding up 'troublemakers' to keep the streets clear. But the opposition ensured the press were on to the story and instead of coverage about the wonders of the Iranian dynasty and its history, the papers were full of reports about people being arrested to silence any opposition. Amnesty International began speaking up against widespread human rights violations, false imprisonment and torture. The celebrations were overshadowed by endless media reports of abuse and the people felt insulted. Not only were they not allowed to take part in the celebrations but increasingly they felt the benefits of the oil boom were not reaching the more deprived rural parts of the country. There was another growing anger: even those who were enjoying some of the oil wealth, the educated and privileged youth in Tehran, were beginning to resent the authoritarian monarchy and yearned for democracy.

The shah seemed blissfully unaware that the tide was turning. He was basking in his new found oil power over his Western masters and as a member of OPEC (Organisation of the Petroleum Exporting Countries) he seemed to take pleasure in announcing yet another price hike. He went on television to lecture the west's 'permissive society' for squandering precious energy. Nevertheless he was regarded as an ally and would have enjoyed being a guest of President Nixon at the White House.

However, all along the lavish living, jet setting and skiing holidays in Switzerland were driving a wedge between himself and the vast majority of his people who were predominantly rural and followed the teachings of the Shia Muslim clerics. When in January 1977 the newly elected US President Jimmy Carter arrived in Tehran he toasted the shah in champagne from crystal glasses saying, "Iran, because of the great leadership of the Shah, is an island of stability in one of the more troubled areas of the world." How that went down in the mosques of Iran can only be guessed.

To add insult to injury shortly afterwards an article, obviously inspired by the shah's advisers, appeared in the papers accusing Khomeini of being a British agent. It was the spark which set off the explosion. Riots broke out first in Qom and spread throughout the country to Tehran. One aide to Khomeini said later that the shah did everything wrong to unite all the disparate factions against him. Despite the broadcast of his sermons, many if not most Iranians had not heard of the obscure cleric, but by singling Khomeini out for criticism he became the figurehead which represented the entire Shia community and the focal point of the revolution.

Martial law was declared but the following day, 8 September 1978, thousands gathered in defiance for a religious demonstration in Tehran's Jaleh Square. Soldiers ordered them to disperse but they refused and shots were fired. The questions remain: who fired first? Was it the troops or, as some claim, were there professional agitators in the crowd firing on the Iranian troops to provoke retaliation? Either way both troops and demonstrators died in the exchanges.

In an attempt to placate the mobs, the shah broadcast a message in November saying, "I have heard your revolutionary message." But a scapegoat was required and he ordered the arrest of a number of ministers and advisers based on a list of some 500 names compiled by SAVAK. Among them was the former prime minister, Amir-Abbas Hoveyda.

It was a futile gesture and, bowing to the inevitable, on 16 January 1979 the shah packed his bags once more and left the country for the last time accompanied by his empress. With the shah now out of the country, Hoveyda's guards abandoned him to the revolutionaries. He was subjected to what amounted to a mock trial before Sadegh Khalkhali, dubbed the 'hanging judge', and was executed.

This was the fate of many who were assumed to be supporters of the old regime, but for Hossein Fardoust there was another outcome. Surprisingly he was one of a few prominent military figures who did not leave the country after the revolution. He of all people in his pivotal role in the establishment and running of the hated SAVAK should surely have been one of the biggest targets and on the first available flight out of the country. However something or someone must have given him confidence to remain and far from running it is believed that he had a direct hand in the creation of SAVAMA, the secret intelligence operation of the new Islamic Republic. It is alleged that he was able to survive and even enhance his position because he was able to hand over a list of former SAVAK officials and intelligence garnered through years of surveillance of both government and opposition figures.

His presence, even leadership of SAVAMA was picked up by the media. *The Washington Post* wrote: "Though it came to power denouncing the shah's dreaded SAVAK secret service, the government of Iran's Ayatollah Ruhollah Khomeini has created a new internal security and intelligence operation, apparently with a similar organizational structure and some of the same faces as its predecessor. The new organization is called SAVAMA. It is run, according to U.S. sources and Iranian exile sources here and in Paris, by Gen. Hossein Fardoust, who was deputy chief of SAVAK under the former shah, Mohammad Reza Pahlavi and a friend from boyhood of the deposed monarch."

The conspiracy theorists shouted that because Khomeini seemed to adopt SAVAK and its operatives he himself must secretly have had Washington's covert support despite all the rhetoric and the storming of the US embassy which followed. Nothing of course will ever be admitted.

Throughout his career Fardoust deliberately kept himself out of the public eye even at formal events. One insider said many claimed to know him, but that was typical Persian bluster and they may only have seen him at a distance. But everyone knew him by reputation and the wisest always tried to avoid him.

Fardoust made his first and last public appearance in April 1987 when he gave an interview on television denouncing the shah and his entourage for corruption. He alleged that he had 10,000 full-time investigators just to keep track of the theft being carried out by the monarch and his courtiers. He even claimed that the marriage of the Shah to Princess Fawzieh of Egypt, his first wife, was entirely contrived by British intelligence presumably as a marriage of convenience. Just three weeks after Fardoust's interview was broadcast the Iranian authorities announced that he had died from "old age and other natural causes."

The shah had ruled his country for nearly 38 years. From the moment he assumed his position until his final departure from the country he had been propped up by outside forces. Internally it had been the work of his own brutal intelligence operation which had kept his enemies in check but it had also left him remote and out of touch. Fardoust, if we believe his own words, was the second most powerful man in the kingdom and was standing just behind the shah's throne throughout his rein. Like many of his predecessors who have worked in the shadows he apparently built his own insurance policy in the form of a dossier probably on friend and foe alike. Armed with so much intelligence he made a smooth transition into the arms of the Iranian revolutionaries but how he really came to meet his end remains a mystery.

The speculation will continue regarding the identity of the real puppet masters throughout the shah's reign and indeed after the 1979 revolution.

General Hossein Fardoust (1917–1987)

The shah's widow defends his corner saying he was a man who had his people at heart which may well have been true but at the same time he was happy to deploy all the levers of power at his disposal to cling to office and the most dangerous lever was operated by his childhood companion, Hossein Fardoust.

18

Ralph David Abernathy (1926–1990)

When Ralph Abernathy was still a boy he
knew that he was going to grow up to be
a preacher. He noticed how the preacher was the
most admired person in the community and it was
an ambition his mother encouraged.

Abernathy was born in Lindon, Alabama on 11
March 1926 one of 12 children. His father, William,
the son of a slave, worked as a sharecropper before
saving enough money to buy a 500-acre farm in
Marengo County later becoming a leading light
among African Americans in his community, the first African American to
vote in Marengo and the first to serve on a grand jury.

After school Ralph Abernathy went to Alabama State College where he
earned a bachelor's degree in mathematics and later in 1951 a master's in
sociology at Atlanta University. Even while still at college Abernathy showed
the first signs of the life that lay ahead when he was elected president of the
student council and led protests demanding better living accommodation
for students and a better cafeteria.

True to his first dreams, while continuing his studies at college he
became a Baptist minister and after graduation served as a minister at the
Eastern Star Baptist Church in Demopolis, Alabama eventually becoming
a full time minister at the First Baptist Church in Montgomery at the age of
26. Three years later a new preacher called Martin Luther King Jr., arrived
at the nearby Dexter Avenue Baptist Church and the two men became firm
friends although their characters were quite different: King was a gifted

preacher with ideas, Abernathy was more practical if old fashioned in his ways but able to turn dreams into reality. Above all the two men agreed that to achieve their goals of equal rights they should adopt a non-violent approach in all their protests.

The catalyst for the work they would do together occurred on 1 December 1955 when Rosa Parks, a black seamstress from Montgomery, tired after a long day at work, refused to give up her seat on a bus to a white passenger when the 'colored' section was full. At the time African-Americans were required by law to give up their seats to white passengers if the bus was full. She was reported by the driver, James Blake, arrested and fined.

This act of defiance had happened before but this arrest marked a key moment in the civil rights movement. Parks was a member of the National Association for the Advancement of Colored People (NAACP) but this time the churches came together to coordinate the protest and formed the Montgomery Improvement Association (MIA). The relatively new preacher Martin Luther King was appointed its president, Abernathy a senior aide and together they planned a boycott of the buses from the basement of King's church, today renamed the Dexter Avenue King Memorial Baptist Church.

For the next 381 days the 17,000 African-Americans of Montgomery boycotted the buses either walking to their jobs or relying on car pools to ferry them to and from work threatening to cripple the bus company whose revenues plummeted. Throughout this time King and Abernathy were in and out of jail for their protests. Abernathy's home and church were fire-bombed even after the US Supreme Court gave blacks and whites equal status on buses and the boycott had ended on 20 December 1956.

The following year Abernathy, King and Bayard Rustin formed the Southern Christian Leadership Conference (SCLC) – King was made president and Abernathy secretary-treasurer. The conference adopted the motto: "Not one hair of one head of one person should be harmed." Despite endless harassment and multiple arrests the partnership between the two men was enduring. In 1961 King persuaded Abernathy to give up his pastor's role and devote all his time to the SCLC. One of their associates in the movement, Hosea Williams, said they made "the greatest team...Martin wouldn't make a decision without him."

The formation of the SCLC was not without its own internal difficulties. On 10th January King invited about 60 black ministers and community leaders to the Ebenezer Church in Atlanta to set up an organisation primarily aimed at bringing about the desegregation of buses in the south. There was a follow up meeting the next month and initially a group was formed calling itself the Negro Leaders Conference on Nonviolent Integration. This name was eventually dropped in favour of the SCLC and the brief was widened from its narrow focus on bus segregation to all forms of segregation. It was a modest enterprise with one small office and a single full time staff member based on Auburn Avenue, Atlanta. [100]

To begin with the organisation did not have the overwhelming support of either black churches or their communities. Faced with violent opposition from the white community including the police and the Ku Klux Clan some churches and their pastors were too frightened to sign up. Many black leaders felt the question of segregation should be challenged in the courts rather than by boycotts which provoked arson and bombings on their properties. There was also the strong belief that it was not the job of the churches to be politically active and certainly not to organise, even lead, marches and demonstrations. On the other hand there were already signs particularly among the younger activists that the protests planned did not go far enough and they advocated occupations and sit-ins.

Despite this opposition the SCLC campaign had developed its own momentum. In December 1961 its supporters joined the Albany Movement in Georgia which was fighting segregation in the state. It was unsuccessful at the time but the protestors were still perfecting their tactics and the demonstrations continued, moving to Birmingham, Alabama where for the first time the protests attracted international media coverage not for the message of protest but for the brutal response from the police.

The Birmingham Campaign began with boycotts but then expanded into sit-ins and marches led by Fred Shuttlesworth, the outspoken pastor of Bethel Baptist Church, aimed at provoking mass arrests and filling up the jails. Shuttlesworth asked King and his colleagues to help them drive home their message of anti-segregation as racially motivated bombings increased. Birmingham was dubbed 'Bombingham'. He told King, "If you come to Birmingham, you will not only gain prestige, but really shake the country. If you win in Birmingham, as Birmingham goes, so goes the nation." To-gether they organised intensified action and launched Project C standing for Confrontation.

Tactics on both sides became extreme: the protestors trained schoolchildren to join the marches and the police used tear gas, fire hoses and dogs against them. As the situation worsened President Kennedy ordered in Federal troops to restore order. By the time calm returned some 3,000 people had been arrested – the majority high school children. King himself was arrested and while locked up he wrote his famous Letter of Bingham Jail in response to a statement by eight white clergymen condemning the tactics of King and the SCLC. He wrote: "Injustice anywhere is a threat to justice everywhere. We are caught in an inescapable network of mutuality, tied in a single garment of destiny. Whatever affects one directly, affects all indirectly... Anyone who lives inside the United States can never be considered an outsider..."

The tactics in Birmingham had also differed radically from Albany which was perceived as a failure for the cause. In Birmingham they focused on the downtown shopping areas and government district calling for fair hiring and desegregation. King said: "The purpose of ... direct action is to create a situation so crisis-packed that it will inevitably open the door to negotiation."[101]

The March on Washington for Jobs and Freedom on 28 August 1963 marked the highlight of King's career with his 'I Have a Dream' speech. In fact the march was organised by a multitude of civil rights groups which included the SCLC; with his administrative skills Abernathy would have been at the forefront as an estimated 2–3,00,000 marchers converged on the city and made their way from the Washington Monument to the Lincoln Memorial. A riot was expected but did not materialise – there were songs by the likes of Joan Baez and Bob Dylan, appearances by celebrities of the day such as Harry Belafonte, Sidney Poitier and Charlton Heston, and a multitude of speakers including King's famous address:

...I have a dream that one day this nation will rise up and live out the true meaning of its creed: We hold these truths to be self-evident: that all men are created equal.
I have a dream that one day on the red hills of Georgia the sons of former slaves and the sons of former slave owners will be able to sit down together at the table of brotherhood.
I have a dream that one day even the state of Mississippi, a state sweltering with the heat of injustice, sweltering with the heat of oppression, will be transformed into an oasis of freedom and justice.
I have a dream that my four little children will one day live in a nation where they will not be judged by the color of their skin but by the content of their character.
I have a dream today...

There was also criticism from unexpected quarters. Malcolm X, the firebrand spokesman for The Nation of Islam, dismissed it as a picnic. This was perhaps an early sign of growing dissent about the direction and forcefulness of the protests including the violence of the Black Panther Movement whose members carried loaded guns.

Throughout this campaigning Abernathy was always at King's side and undoubtedly subject to the same inquiries by the Federal Bureau of Investigation who were looking for everything from links to the Communist Party or personal failings such as extramarital affairs. But King was rapidly moving out of officialdom's normal reach. On 14 October 1964 he received the Nobel Peace Prize for his non-violent campaigning to combat racial inequality and the work he and Abernathy were doing in the SCLC continued without let up.

In 1965 they helped organise the Selma to Montgomery Marches – three separate marches to the Alabama capitol culminating in what became known as Bloody Sunday when the state police clashed with the civil rights demonstrators on 7 March.

As though he was trying to cover as much ground as possible perhaps fearing that his time was short King began to expand his campaigning speaking out against all poverty and on 4 April 1967 turned his wrath against the Vietnam War. Some described it as the most controversial speech of his life and it cost him the support of many of his allies.

Then that fateful day on 4 April 1968 in Memphis dawned.

King and Abernathy and the rest of their entourage had flown to Tennessee to support the striking sanitation workers who had staged a walk-out demanding equal pay and working conditions with white workers. Their flight had been delayed because of a bomb threat – not an unusual occurrence for King who had become philosophical about life. On 3 April he delivered his last address to a comparatively small gathering and referred to those threats:

"And some began to say the threats... or talk about the threats that were out. What would happen to me from some of our sick white brothers? Well, I don't know what will happen now. We've got some difficult days ahead. But it doesn't matter with me now. Because I've been to the mountaintop. And I don't mind. Like anybody, I would like to live a long life. Longevity has its place. But I'm not concerned about that now. I just want to do God's will. And He's allowed me to go up to the mountain. And I've looked over. And I've seen the Promised Land. I may not get there with you. But I want you to know tonight, that we, as a people, will get to the Promised Land! And so I'm happy, tonight. I'm not worried about anything. I'm not fearing any man. Mine eyes have seen the glory of the coming of the Lord!"

As usual King and Abernathy were booked into the same room 306 at the Lorraine Motel in Memphis. In fact they stayed in the same room together so often that is was dubbed the 'King-Abernathy Suite' according to the evidence the motel owner, Walter Bailey, gave to the House Select Committee on Assassinations.

Just after 6pm on 4 April King was standing on the second floor balcony of his room when he was shot by a single bullet. Abernathy was first on the scene and cradled King in his arms. He cried: "Martin, it's alright. Don't worry this is Ralph. This is Ralph."[102] There was still a pulse despite his severe injuries and he was taken to St Joseph's Hospital but never regained consciousness. He was 39 years old.

Witnesses claimed to have seen James Earl Ray, a fugitive, running from a rooming house opposite the hotel. Later a package including a rifle and binoculars with Ray's fingerprints were found. After an international manhunt was launched Ray was arrested at London's Heathrow Airport and extradited back to the United States. At his trial he was convicted and sentenced to 99 years. He died in prison. Conspiracy theories continue to circulate for years. In 1998 the King family brought a civil action for just $100 against Loyd Jowers, a restaurant owner whose erratic testimony claimed the shot had been fired by a Memphis policeman and that the Mafia and other parties, without naming the US government, were involved. By the end of the hearing the jury found that Jowers and other unspecified governmental agencies were all part of a conspiracy to kill King.

The world had lost a powerful and charismatic leader while Abernathy had lost his closest friend. It was a mutual affection. In his last speech King had spoken directly to Abernathy almost as though he knew something was about to happen and needed to acknowledge their close relationship. Turning to him he said: "Ralph Abernathy is the best friend that I have in the world." It was as though he was anointing Abernathy as his chosen successor.

The shooting sparked a wave of riots in Washington D.C., Chicago, Louisville and many other cities. King's family and supporters called for calm and non-violent action but divisions in the movement began to appear. Some more militant factions wanted the protests to be more forceful. This was the moment for Abernathy to step from the shadows. He was appointed as the new leader of the SCLC and he tried to fulfil the plan for a Poor People's Campaign in Washington D.C. Huts were built in the middle of the capital to drive home the point and the plan was to present their grievances to President Lyndon B. Johnson but the protest only succeeded in landing Abernathy back in jail.

Sometimes the shadow cannot hold the seat of power and without King's charisma and influence the SCLC began to disintegrate, debts built up and Abernathy resigned in 1977. It may have been that the mood among African Americans was changing and demanding a more aggressive form of protest than even King himself had always advocated. The movement lacked discipline and violence replaced peaceful protest – Abernathy realised that his time had come and gone. He may also have acknowledged privately to himself that he was no Martin Luther King; an able lieutenant but not the person to stand in front of the crowds and whip them into effective but peaceful action. He was a second in command.

Inevitably arguments developed over the 'heritage' of the King name and the real history of what had been achieved, much as years later the Mandela family in South Africa was reduced to squabbling over Nelson Mandela's name. In 1978 Abernathy objected to a six hour documentary about King's life which he dismissed as "a distortion of history." Later Abernathy published his own autobiography the year before his death entitled, *And The Walls Came Tumbling Down* in which he talked frankly about King as an adulterer. He was immediately accused of betraying the name of Dr Martin Luther King but he defended himself saying he was only writing about what others had covered before in public. He added that while he did not approve of King's behaviour he understood it because they had both been away from home over such long periods campaigning throughout the country.

Abernathy was briefly involved in public controversy in 1980 when he endorsed Ronald Reagan's Presidential campaign which again brought a rebuke from Mrs King who called Reagan a "war hawk."

Abernathy's moment in the spotlight away from King was short lived and he saw out the last of his years as pastor of the West Hunter Street Baptist Church in Atlanta. Despite what might be regarded as a failure to pick up King's baton his contribution to the civil rights campaign was widely acknowledged. Andrew Young, the former Mayor of Atlanta, said on Abernathy's death on 17 April 1990 that he would be remembered as a man who performed "a silent labour that was very much needed," and as a "jovial, profound, loving preacher who gave his life in the service of others."

Ralph David Abernathy (1926–1990)

President Bush said in a statement: "I join with all Americans to mourn the passing of the Rev. Ralph Abernathy, a great leader in the struggle for civil rights for all Americans and a tireless campaigner for justice."

Abernathy never objected to being overshadowed by King, they were a team and they relied on each other; one plodding and methodical, the other capable of great oratory which could move not just a large crowd but a country. Without Abernathy many doubt that King would have been organised enough to have succeeded as he did. His role was always to remain faithfully in the shadows to serve the person who had specifically selected him as his right hand man. Abernathy did not make international headlines, his name is not instantly recognisable and he never gave speeches which today, years later, are remembered and quoted. But he was one of the faithful servants who never sought the limelight and did not seek to enrich himself as a result of his privileged position. He will forever remain in the shadow of his gifted and closest friend.

19

CHARLES COLSON (1931–2012)

There were two Charles Colsons. The first described himself as 'a hatchet man' to a US president, the second was a born-again Christian. While acknowledging his epiphany just as he was about to be jailed although dismissed by some as a smokescreen to win a lenient sentence, we will focus here largely on his first life when  even the most powerful man in the world turned to him for his services.

Colson was born on 16 October 1931. The son of a Boston, Massachusetts lawyer it was assumed that the legal profession was always going to be his chosen career but he also had a strong patriotic streak. While still at school he organised a fund raising campaign during World War II to collect enough money to pay for a new jeep for the army[103]. He was also politically motivated and at 17 he signed up as a volunteer to help Robert Bradford's 1948 re-election campaign as the Republican Governor of Massachusetts. Although Bradford lost, Colson would later claim that he learned 'all the tricks' of running a dirty campaign at that time including planting fake news stories about opponents and using the names of dead people on ballot papers. He was preparing himself unwittingly for the life which was to make him infamous.

After school he earned a BA with honours at Brown University and his Juris Doctor from the George Washington University Law School. But the political bug had bitten and before qualifying as a lawyer he worked for the Assistant Secretary of the Navy (Material) and campaigned for the Republican Leverett Saltonstall in his successful bid for the Senate, subsequently working as his Administrative Assistant until 1961. By this time he had married Nancy Billings who had borne him three children and was already contemplating separation. They would divorce three years later when he married Patricia Ann Hughes.

However the other important introduction Colson made while working on the Saltonstall campaign in 1956 was with Richard Nixon, then the US Vice President to Dwight D. Eisenhower. There was an instant rapport and Colson immediately threw in his lot to help Nixon run for the Presidency in 1960. He was devastated when John F Kennedy got into the White House but his mind must have been made up by then, his future lay in politics not the law.

However he had to bide his time so he established his own practice, Colson & Morin, in 1961 which soon made a name for itself in Boston and Washington D.C. circles and before long was attracting heavy hitters to the payroll; people like Edward Gadsby, the former chairman of the Securities Exchange Commission and Paul Hannah, general counsel of Raytheon, a company specialising in defence and national security. Successful though the practice evidently was Colson had other ambitions and by 1967 he had agreed to remove his own name from the company letterhead which now became Gadsby & Hannah. Within two years Colson quit and joined Richard Nixon in the White House as Special Counsel to the President.

Colson had got what he always wanted, a seat at the top table and, typically of many but not all of our shadow players, he didn't seem to want any more for himself. He was content to serve the President who in turn came to regard him as the son he never had. Colson would later be happy when a comment he himself wrote in an internal memo was leaked to the press saying that he would "walk over his own grandmother" to ensure that Nixon was re-elected. The quote was recycled and embellished but its central message was clear, the patriotic lawyer from Boston Massachusetts would do anything and resort to any trick to protect his master.

Rupert Cornwell, writing in *The Independent*, said, "What is certain is that each played to the other's base instincts – Colson to his boss's vindictiveness and paranoia, the President to his aide's ruthless devotion to the cause."[104]

No sooner has a President been elected than he starts calculating what he can achieve in his first years of office to ensure that he gets re-elected for a second term; the first term is in large part devoted to securing four more years. It was in pursuit of this aim that Colson achieved notoriety and displayed his loyalty to his President becoming what The Washington Post said was "one of the most powerful presidential aides, variously described as a troubleshooter and as a master of dirty tricks."

Like many, Colson was the gatekeeper to Nixon's office. He would arrange private meetings for the myriad of special interest groups who sought some favour – industrialists, lobbyists and veterans' organisations – in fact anyone whose political persuasion aligned with the Republican Party. According to the special files on Colson held in the US National Archives, it was Colson's role to broaden the White House lines of communication and arrange presidential meetings with these groups.

Colson oversaw exactly who was invited to meet the president, reviewed presidential appointments and most importantly drew up a list of those who were not in favour. He famously produced a document which became known as Nixon's Enemies List. John Dean, White House counsel, said in a memo dated 16 August 1971: "This memorandum addresses the matter of how we can maximize the fact of our incumbency in dealing with persons known to be active in their opposition to our administration; stated a bit more bluntly—how we can use the available federal machinery to screw our political enemies."

It seems that Colson would resort to any tactics if he believed it would help Nixon. It was reported that he hired Teamster Union thugs to beat up anti-war protestors and even suggest firebombing the Brookings Institute[105].

Although he basked in the tough guy image of trampling over his grandmother not all leaks were welcome and half way through his time in office Nixon decided something had to be done about the flow of information, real or imagined, out of the Oval Office. With dark humour a covert unit called The Plumbers was established with a budget of $250,000 to start plugging those leaks and Colson recommended E. Howard Hunt, a former CIA officer, to take the lead working alongside Gordon Liddy. Liddy was the youngest Bureau Supervisor in the FBI headquarters in Washington D.C. and described by one supervisor as a wild guy.[106]

Liddy and Hunt's first task was to organise a break-in to the Los Angeles office of Dr Lewis Fielding who was psychiatrist to Daniel Ellsberg, a military analyst working for the Rand Corporation. Ellsberg once a supporter of the Vietnam War had access to secret government papers which revealed that the US government knew from an early stage that America was unlikely ever to win the war and that prolonging it would cost many more lives than was being admitted. When Ellsberg had a change of heart about the war he copied the documents and released them first to Neil Sheehan, a correspondent on the *New York Times* who agreed not to write anything until he was given the go ahead. But Sheehan broke his promise earning himself a scoop based on Ellsberg's information and material from other sources. The *Times* later wrote that the so-called Pentagon Papers "demonstrated, among other things, that the Johnson Administration had systematically lied, not only to the public but also to Congress, about a subject of transcendent national interest and significance."

Nixon had no intention of being ensnared by anything else Ellsberg was about to publish and dispatched his plumbers to find out if there was any psychiatric data which might be used to discredit Ellsberg and the anti-war lobby. But the burglary on 3 September 1971 discovered nothing although Ellsberg later said a file had been left open in the office suggesting its contents had obviously been read.

Colson always denied having authorised the break-in but admitted leaking information from Ellsberg's confidential FBI file to the press. Years later when he came to write about his life in public office, Colson expressed his regret for attempting to cover up the incident.[107]

Nixon's concern was not so much that the story was political dynamite for the Johnson administration, but that it also could cast a light on the low moral standards of others who sat in the White House. H.R. Haldeman, Nixon's Chief of Staff, was heard discussing on the Oval Office Tapes on 14 June 1972 the impact the Pentagon Papers had on all presidents. He quoted Donald Rumsfeld, who was a legal adviser and a member of Nixon's cabinet at the time: "Rumsfeld was making this point this morning... To the ordinary guy, all this is a bunch of gobbledygook. But out of the gobbledygook comes a very clear thing.... It shows that people do things the president wants to do even though it's wrong, and the president can be wrong."

Drawing on the tricks he had learned as a staffer for Saltonstall, Colson then authorised Hunt to start digging for dirt into Senator Edward Kennedy's life. In his own book[108] Hunt wrote that Nixon was particularly interested in exactly what happened on Chappaquiddick Island when Miss Mary Jo Kopechne died in 1969 and about any extramarital affairs.

By 1972 Nixon and Colson were beginning to think hard about the President's second term in office and Liddy was appointed to the Committee to Re-elect the President, known as CREEP, which had the brief of improving and extending the work of the Plumbers. Various wild ideas were mooted to embarrass the Democrats including trying to photograph Democrat campaign officials in compromising positions with prostitutes.

Most were rejected but one was given the go-ahead: a break-in to the Democratic National Committee offices in the Watergate complex.

There were two break-ins which Liddy supervised and it was on the second occasion, 17 June 1972 that the five burglars were caught red-handed. Liddy admitted running the operation from the nearby Watergate Hotel. He was sentenced to twenty years which was later commuted to four and a half years.

Although the storm was breaking around them with fresh revelations, including a slush fund controlled by the Attorney General, John Mitchell, to finance intelligence gathering about the Republicans, Nixon was re-elected for a second term on 7 November 1972 in one of the biggest landslide victories the country has ever seen. However Colson must have seen what lay ahead and on 10 March the following year he resigned from the White House once again returning to law as senior partner of Colson and Shapiro in Washington D.C. although he couldn't entirely break his ties with Nixon and served as his special consultant for a few more months.

Colson himself was never convicted of any wrongdoing over the Watergate scandal. While the president he had served with unswerving loyalty was forced to resign on 9 August 1974 thereby avoiding certain impeachment and being thrown out of office, Colson himself struck a deal with the prosecutors exercised the Fifth Amendment and pleaded guilty to the lesser charge of obstruction of justice over the Ellsberg break-in. He was sentenced to one to three years but only served seven months in a minimum security prison in Alabama and was released in January 1975.

Before his arrest Colson claimed that he was taught the error of his ways when a close friend, Thomas Phillips, chairman of Raytheon Company, gave him a copy of C.S. Lewis's *Mere Christianity*. After reading it Colson says he became an evangelical Christian and joined a prayer group. In his own memoir Colson admits to being torn between a desire to be truthful and a desire to avoid conviction on charges on which he believed he was innocent. Some might say in the end he chose the route of self-preservation. When the story came out that he had repented for his sins and was now a committed Christian the press was merciless in its ridicule claiming it was all a typical Colson contrived scam to win a more lenient sentence. "If Mr Colson can repent of his sins, there just has to be hope for everyone," sneered *The Boston Globe* of its own hometown boy. Ellsberg noted that he never apologised to him for the one crime of which he was convicted.

It is easy to be cynical about Colson's change of direction, his Pauline conversion, but we can take it here at face value. His early life was as the classic fixer, the servant of a powerful man who was prepared to do anything even break the law if he felt it was in the best interests of the presidency. He like others with great intellectual gifts was blinded by what he perceived to be the right course of action – the ends always justifying the means. Nixon was the political leader he had always supported and he was determined to help him get into power and once there remain in office. If that meant trampling over his grandmother, digging any dirt on his master's enemies, even risking jail, so be it.

Colson was in that category of shadow player – a man who clearly enjoyed his power; he did Nixon's bidding but he was also a manipulator playing to his master's vices. If Nixon thought he had opponents, Colson would give him a long list of his enemies. If the president wanted to be surrounded by friends, Colson would organise supporters to troop into the Oval Office. Colson had a clear agenda even if those closest to the President didn't know what his latest plan was; there was no love lost between Haldeman and Colson, the former once complaining that "Colson was always doing things behind my back."[109]

When he had served his curtailed prison sentence Colson devoted his time and his intellect completely to his new found calling. He wrote copiously and he worked tirelessly for prison reform. While he was in prison he was granted a three day release to attend his father's funeral during which time he came across some of his father's papers in which he discovered that they had a shared interest in the plight of prisoners, the way they were treated and their fate after they had served their sentences. This Colson says in his memoir, *Born Again: What Really Happened to the White House Hatchet Man*, helped convince him that he had a calling from God. On his own release he set up the Prison Fellowship in 1976 which grew into a nationwide organisation. This was followed in 1983 by the founding of the Justice Fellowship calling for reforms in the US criminal justice system. He must have enjoyed being invited back to the White House by President George W Bush to present the results of a study he organised – the faith-based initiative, InnerChange.

But it seems he could never quite let Watergate go and he chose to give an interview in 2005 criticising Mark Felt, the FBI man revealed as the mysterious Deep Throat who guided *The Washington Post* reporters, Carl Bernstein and Bob Woodward, in their investigations. Colson with some gall said Felt should have known better than to disclose the results of a government investigation to the press, this from a man who had learned in his earliest days in politics how to plant stories in newspapers to suit his cause. His attack brought a swift response from Ben Bradlee, *The Washington Post* Executive Director and the only other man to know Deep Throat's identity before it became public. He said he was "baffled" that Colson and Liddy were "lecturing the world about public morality". He said, "As far as I'm concerned they have no standing in the morality debate."[110]

Nevertheless Colson eventually found himself rehabilitated. He was given the right to vote once again when Governor Jeb Bush of Florida, the state where he was living, restored his civil rights, he was awarded honorary degrees and with no little irony was presented with the Presidential Citizens Award by President George W. Bush standing together in the Oval Office. He donated the royalties of his book to his prison ministry along with the $1 million Templeton prize awarded to the person who has done most to advance the cause of religion.

Colson was in the White House plotting and conniving ruthlessly as Nixon's fixer in chief for four years (1969–1973) and for 35 years he worked to promote his religious convictions and rehabilitate the prison system. If it was just a ploy or a smokescreen it was sustained with extraordinary dedication.

Michael Cromartie, vice president of the Ethics and Public Policy Center, said on Colson's death in 2012, "He played political hardball for keeps. He was ruthless. He wanted to win at all costs and he had a reputation as a person who wanted to win at all costs ... I think if he's going to be remembered for anything, he's going to be remembered as a person who had a complete turnaround in his life."

The writer, David Plotz, gave this assessment of Colson. He was "Richard Nixon's hard man, the 'evil genius' of an evil administration." While Colson himself admitted that he was "valuable to the President ... because I was willing ... to be ruthless in getting things done."[111]

For all his good work it seems that even he realised he would always be remembered as President Nixon's right hand man prepared to go to any lengths, to break any rules if he thought it would keep his master in power. Some argue that the two men were made for each other. *Time Magazine* wrote: "...Haldeman contends, the crafty Colson became a Nixon intimate by deliberately appealing to Nixon's vindictive instincts. And that volatile combination of the unchecked worst in both Nixon and Colson, Haldeman suggests, was the cause of Watergate."[112] Perhaps he did recognise in the end that he had been wrong but there will always be those who cannot quite bring themselves to believe that he was not just another 'evil genius.'

20

TARIQ AZIZ (b. 1936)

Tariq Aziz is perhaps the most unusual member of our cast of shadow players in that political circumstances in Iraq rather than personal idiosyncrasies forced him to become the public face of Saddam  Hussein's dictatorship, his master's voice. With his fluent English, heavy glasses and bushy moustache he cut a benign almost professorial figure. He was the most recognisable face of the regime, constantly travelling the globe trying to win friends, carrying messages from his leader in the style of fixers and go-betweens down the centuries to give to anyone who would listen. Today he languishes as a frail, old man in prison always protesting that he was just a politician and quietly questioning whether the fate of Iraqis is now any better than it was under Saddam's rule.

Our family arrived in Baghdad some years after Brigadier General Abd al-Karim Qasim had seized power overthrowing the Hashemite monarchy in 1958. Even then Iraq suffered from constant revolution and regime change. It was perfectly normal to fly into the country and find a different group in charge, stopping cars from the airport pointing their machine guns in the window just to check who we were. Britons at that stage were not the enemy however – Iraqis were too busy vying for power among themselves.

In 1963 Colonel Abdul Salam Arif, the leader of the Iraqi Revolutionary Command Council who had played a major role in overthrowing the monarchy, staged his own coup ousting Qasim. But Arif himself was never secure. In the autumn of 1964 a plot among supporters of the Ba'athist Party[113] was discovered and its leaders were arrested – among them one

Saddam Hussein. However on 13 April 1966 in what was widely suspected as being an act of sabotage, Arif was killed when his Royal Iraqi Air Force de Havilland Dove crashed. He was succeeded as President by his brother, Abdul Rahman Arif. But Abdul Rahman was weak and on 17 July 1968 he was woken in his bed to be told he too had been overthrown in a bloodless coup but at least he was allowed to seek exile in Turkey. Ahmed Al Bakr became President and Saddam, then deputy leader of the Ba'ath Party, was appointed Deputy Chairman of the Revolutionary Command Council and Vice President responsible for the security services. It was from this security base that Saddam was able to increase his standing in the party until finally Bakr stood down in 1979 for 'health reasons' in favour of Saddam. Bakr eventually died in 1982.

Although today Iraq is torn apart by inter tribal and religious rivalry it was once regarded as the cradle of civilisation, home of the Sumerian people and where the first form of writing was born in the 4th century BC. Baghdad city was built in the 8th century and became a centre of learning in the Middle Ages. By the twentieth century the country was a mandate under British control and in 1932 independence was granted to the Kingdom of Iraq installing the Hashemite monarchy. The tragedy for the country today is that there is no talk of civilisation and even the brutal regime of Saddam Hussein is missed by many for its order if not its methods.

Tariq Aziz is from an Assyrian family, the son of a waiter, and uniquely among Saddam's secular government a Christian member of the Chaldean Catholic church. He was originally called Michael Yuhanna but with eye to a future in politics changed his name to Tariq Aziz to make it more acceptable to the Muslim majority in power.

After studying English at Baghdad University he joined the Ba'ath Party in 1957 and within four years had become both editor of the newspaper, *Al-Jamaheer* and the party's own paper, *Al Thawra*. As a prominent party activist Aziz would have been close to Saddam and soon after the revolution in 1968 he began rising through the party ranks becoming minister of information, a member of the Regional Command and then in 1977 he was appointed to Saddam's Revolutionary Command Council, the ultimate decision making body in the country. Two years later Aziz was made deputy prime minister and his life began as a globetrotting diplomat explaining Saddam's policies to the world combining the role for much of that time with foreign minister.

Iraq is important not just because of its oil wealth but also because of its geographical location with Syria and Turkey to its north, Jordan to the west, Saudi Arabia and Kuwait to the south and Iran to the East. According to Aziz, Iraq's new government was focusing on development at the time. He denied any particularly close links with the Soviet Union, which is something the West feared, but reminded interviewers that it did not regard the United States as an ally either. Indeed it had broken off diplomatic relations for a time with Washington following the Arab/Israeli War in 1967, and was more interested in establishing links with France and other European nations.

However as they were travelling back from a meeting of the non-aligned states[114] in Havana in 1979 Aziz said he was instructed by Saddam to start improving relations with the US: "He told me, Tariq, we are going to be the leaders of the non-aligned, and it doesn't look well if we don't have diplomatic relations with the other superpowers. We have very good relations with the Soviet Union. We have to look pure non-aligned. We have our differences with the United States concerning the Arab-Israeli conflict. So, I would like you to start preparing carefully, without any hurry, the resumption of the relationship between us and the United States."[115] Although Aziz was not yet the foreign minister (he was appointed in 1983) he was already beginning to take the lead role in international diplomacy for his country.

But Iran with its newly proclaimed Islamic Republic demanded Aziz's immediate attention and it was getting personal. In April 1980 members of the Iranian backed Islamic Dawa Party threw a hand grenade at him in the middle of Baghdad killing a number of bystanders. The attack was to become the prelude to the prolonged Iraq-Iran War which broke out in September that year when the Iraqi army and air force invaded Iran. Saddam was worried that the Islamic revolution which had toppled the Shah would spread into Iraq sparking a popular uprising by the Shia majority which had been suppressed and side-lined in Iraq. Far from being unprepared for the attack, Iranian forces quickly stopped the Iraqis in their tracks and by 1982 had pushed them back. The war itself would continue for another six years despite repeated calls by the United Nations Security Council for a ceasefire. It was a primitive campaign fought out in trenches lined with barbed wire and indiscriminate and extensive use by Iraq of chemical weapons including mustard gas.

Washington, which had been stunned by the Khomeini revolution, made no secret of its support for Saddam, openly discussing its agenda in Congress. As full details later emerged the extent of that support became apparent. ABC's Nightline reported: "It is becoming increasingly clear that

George Bush, operating largely behind the scenes throughout the 1980s, initiated and supported much of the financing, intelligence, and military help that built Saddam's Iraq into the power it became", adding "Reagan/ Bush administrations permitted – and frequently encouraged – the flow of money, agricultural credits, dual-use technology, chemicals, and weapons to Iraq."[116]

Throughout the negotiations to broker a ceasefire including meetings in New York and standing at Saddam's side when he met the former US Defence Secretary, Donald Rumsfeld, in Baghdad in 1983, was Aziz. At the same time he also flew regularly to Russia which was officially neutral in the conflict but still maintained a steady supply of armaments to Iraq.

Eventually a ceasefire was agreed and both sides withdrew their forces but while the fighting with Iran was over, Saddam was turning his wrath on the Kurdish population. Thousands of troops, fighter bombers and helicopter gunships were unleashed on the Kurds in the north wiping out entire villages using poison gas in his genocidal al-Anfal[117] campaign. It was reported that 100,000 Kurdish civilians lost their lives[118]. The Kurds who had been backed by Iran had long resisted the Iraqi regime and yearned for an independent homeland. The chemical assault on the village of Halabja which had been taken over by the Kurdish peshmerga fighters was the single worst attack where 5,000 died.

Saddam's campaign to rid himself of the Kurdish resistance continued into 1989 when he was satisfied that the problem had been eradicated; 90% of Kurdish villages had been razed to the ground, thousands had been killed and possibly millions interned and disappeared in camps or had fled the country.

But politics continues and behind the scenes diplomacy never sleeps. The US had lost its main ally in the region, the Shah of Iran, upsetting the balance of power. Discreet and not so discreet talks between Washington and Baghdad had been continuing since 1979 when Saddam allowed the CIA to open an office in the country. As the guard changed rapidly at the White House the mood music became even warmer. Zbigniew Brzezinski, National Security Adviser to President Jimmy Carter had even appeared on national television to say that he saw no fundamental incompatibility of interests between the United States and Iraq.

So when Aziz flew into Washington in 1984 he was sure of a good welcome. He met the new President Ronald Reagan and Vice President George Bush and once again formal diplomatic relations were restored between the two countries – it suited everyone. Aziz said in an interview later, "It's not in our philosophy to sever diplomatic relations with countries with whom you have some differences, or even some enemies, because after all, you need to talk, even to your enemies, if you have enemies. So we did it, and it worked. It worked for a while." [119]

But the financial cost of the war against Iran had been high. It had borrowed some $80 billion mostly from Saudi Arabia and Kuwait and was struggling to repay the money due to the falling price of oil. Saddam asked his fellow Arab nations to help support the price by cutting down on production but his appeal fell on deaf ears with the United Arab Emirates and Kuwait even exceeding the quotas agreed by OPEC. Furthermore Saudi Arabia and Kuwait were not inclined to write off the debt Iraq owed and there was a complete silence from Washington.

Saddam then started claiming that Kuwait had been stealing Iraq's oil by slant drilling across the border into its Rumaila oil field but he may just have been angered by what he saw as Kuwait's overproduction of oil which was helping keep the price of a barrel of oil low and costing Iraq $/ billion annually in lost revenue. While still in office Aziz said there had been no long term plans to invade Kuwait but later he would suggest that Saddam was mentally unstable when he gave the order to attack. Whatever Saddam's real motive, on 2 August 1990 Iraqi troops invaded and within 48 hours the Kuwaiti forces, which had actually been stood down the previous month, were defeated; those who were not killed or captured fled into Saudi Arabia or Bahrain. The Emir of Kuwait and the rest of the royal family had escaped into Saudi Arabia. Saddam proudly proclaimed on 8 August that Kuwait was now the 19th province of Iraq and named his cousin Ali Hassan Al-Majid, as the new military governor.

But the consequences of his action so soon after the economically debilitating war with Iran were punishing. International reaction was instant and tough economic sanctions were immediately imposed on Iraq. The US urged other nations to join a coalition against Iraq. Aziz claimed later that he had tried to dissuade his leader, "I asked Saddam Hussein not to invade Kuwait," he said, "But I had to support the decision of the majority. When the decision was taken, I said to him this is going to lead to war with the US, and it is not in our interests to wage war against the US." [120]

Intensive diplomatic negotiations followed with America insisting that there could be no preconditions to Iraq's immediate withdrawal. Aziz flew to Geneva for some last minute bargaining with US Secretary of State, James

Baker, early in January 1991 but he had nothing to offer except a warning. He was asked by a reporter, "Mr. Foreign Minister, if war starts...will you attack?" His response was, "Yes, absolutely, yes."

On 17 January coalition forces drawn from 34 countries launched their first aerial bombardment and the very next day Iraq responded by firing the first Scud missile towards Israel. It was hoping to provoke a response and draw them into the war which in turn might lead to Arab nations withdrawing their support for the coalition. President Bush was able to convince the Israeli Prime Minister Yitzhak Rabin not to retaliate by promising to deploy Patriot missiles to defend Israel.

The aerial attacks were followed by a ground assault on 24 February. The coalition forces drove deep into Iraqi territory before a ceasefire was called 100 hours after the ground attack had begun. As the Iraqi troops pulled back they torched more than 600 oil wells causing huge environmental as well as economic damage. The last fire was put out ten months after it had been set alight.

After the war Iraq was left with few friends and tied down by United Nations' economic sanctions imposed by the Security Council on 6 August 1990. They amounted to a total financial and trade embargo and their original purpose was to compel Iraq to withdraw from Kuwait, pay reparations for the damage it had inflicted and eliminate its weapons of mass destruction. Everything but medicines and essential food imports was banned but in time it was assumed that there was an unspoken additional purpose to the sanctions and that was the removal of Saddam Hussein. This became official US policy in 1998 with the passing of the Iraq Liberation Act in October 1998.

The sanctions hit home and soon the UN was itself concerned about their impact. An inter-agency report stated that "Iraqi people may soon face a further imminent catastrophe, which could include epidemic and famine, if massive life-supporting needs are not rapidly met." Restrictions were then eased to allow an Oil for Food programme to alleviate the humanitarian crisis.

Over the next decade Aziz could be found travelling the globe trying to make deals where he could. On 26 July 2000 he was back in Moscow to meet President Vladimir Putin at the Kremlin as part of a three day visit to the country. Russia repeatedly called for an easing of the sanctions which were affecting civilians as well as Saddam's regime. Britain opened a secret channel of communication between a junior minister for foreign affairs, Peter Hain, and Aziz in a bid to avoid any further conflict.

The war rhetoric was stepped up with the 9/11 attack on New York. Some in the George W. Bush administration saw it as an excuse to remove Saddam even though there was no link between Iraq and the attack. Bush announced his 'War on Terror' ramping up the temperature. The prime objective was to remove Saddam Hussein – many regarded it as unfinished business from his father's defeat of Iraqi forces in the first Gulf War.

Aziz kept pushing hard in his diplomatic mission to avoid war even taking time to visit Nelson Mandela in January 2003 and winning his support for a peaceful outcome. Mandela asked, "Why does the United States have to behave so arrogantly?" adding, "Their friend Israel has got weapons of mass destruction but because it's their ally they won't ask the United Nations to get rid of them."

Just nine days after Colin Powell, the US Secretary of State, was making his presentation to the UN Security Council on 5 February 2003 using computer generated images of a 'mobile biological weapons laboratory' in Iraq which was later proved to be based on false information, Aziz, the Chaldean Catholic, was at the Vatican for an audience with Pope John Paul II. He wanted to assure him about "the wish of the Iraqi government to co-operate with the international community, notably on disarmament".[121] The Pope also took the opportunity to make it clear to the world that he was against any war against Iraq. His wish was rejected and of course just over a month later on 18 March the shock and awe bombing of Baghdad began. On 24 April Aziz surrendered to US forces.

Soon after the invasion Bush stated that Aziz was one of those responsible for hiding the weapons of mass destruction. *USA Today* reported: "President Bush expressed unshakable confidence about finding banned weapons in Iraq and complained that Tariq Aziz, one of Saddam Hussein's closest deputies, is not cooperating with U.S. forces who have him in custody. Bush said the deputy prime minister, the most visible face of the former Iraqi government other than Hussein, 'still doesn't know how to tell the truth.'"[122] Aziz put it differently when he was interviewed later about Iraq deliberately trying to conceal weapons of mass destruction: "I was in charge of supervising the work of UNSCOM. I attended hundreds of meetings with them at hundreds of sites, but they were committed to proving the untrue. Bush was going to war regardless."[123]

In April 2008 Aziz was found guilty for his role in the deaths of 42 merchants executed for sanctions profiteering and sentenced to 15 years, and another seven years for the deportation of Kurds from northern Iraq.

Then in 2010 he was sentenced to death for crimes against humanity by the Iraqi Supreme Court but at the time of writing, nearly three years later, the execution order has not been signed. It says something about Aziz's reputation that his sentence provoked almost universal outrage led by the Vatican. A spokesman, Federico Lombardi, said the Church opposed the death penalty and that leniency towards Aziz would "foster reconciliation and the reconstruction of peace and justice in Iraq after great suffering".

The Pope's appeal was echoed by the UN Secretary General, Ban Ki-Moon, who said the death sentence should be cancelled; by the European Union foreign policy chief Catherine Ashton who said that his execution would be "unacceptable"; by Amnesty International who condemned the use of the death penalty; by the Greek President Karlos Papoulias and the Russian Foreign Ministry who called for clemency.

It seems that Aziz simply had seen and learned too much from his privileged position. Not only does he know what happened under Saddam, but embarrassingly perhaps he knows about life in Iraq under the economic sanctions, perhaps he knows about the bribery that went on over oil for food deals and other commercial contracts. Commentators questioned the impartiality of the courts.

But Aziz is not a well man, reportedly suffering from depression, diabetes, heart disease and ulcers. He has had a stroke and through his lawyer, Badie Aref, has said, "I would prefer to be executed rather than stay in this condition."

In all probability he will see out his final days in his Iraqi prison away from the spotlight which followed his every move. A very public figure who nevertheless was overshadowed by his tyrannical master.

21

Jósef Hieronim Retinger (1888–1960)

Depending on one's point of view few people in recent modern history have had as great an impact on the world today as Jósef Retinger. Obscure, retiring possibly secretive and forgotten in death, his creation today directly affects the lives of hundreds of millions. In his own life he knew every world leader and businessman of importance and founded an organisation which some claim amounts to the shadow government of the world or at the very least an important branch of it. On the other hand he may just have been a man who worried about the planet and advocated a united approach to the problems of the environment, population growth and economic thinking. Conspiracy theories abound and no answers ever emerge but there are some facts upon which a story can be based before we reach a crossroads which takes us down a path of evil control or simply enlightened questioning. Was Retinger the shadowy figure behind wars, tectonic economic shifts and the rise and fall of governments or did he simply create what amounts to an important think tank not to mention the European Union itself?

Retinger was born in Krakow in 1888 when Poland was still part of the Austro-Hungarian Empire. His father was a lawyer working for Count Wladyslaw Zamoyski, a well connected, rich and highly educated nobleman who became guide and mentor to the young Retinger when his father died; it was as though his life at the top table of Europe was pre-ordained giving him access to the most important players and ultimately decision makers.

Retinger was a brilliant student and was awarded his PhD in literature from the Sorbonne in Paris at the age of 20 – the youngest ever recipient at the university. Early plans to join the priesthood – he entered the Jesuit seminary in Rome – were quickly set aside at the prospect of having to remain celibate as he embraced the bohemian world of Paris. Thanks to introductions from the Count he was soon mixing with artists like Pierre Bonnard, writers such as André Gide and the composer Maurice Ravel. However, evidently restless in his search for new experiences, countries and knowledge Retinger went to Germany and enrolled at the University of Munich to read comparative psychology. He also became fluent in several languages over the years.

A group of friends from various political groups urged Retinger to go to England in 1911 and start promoting Polish interests even though Poland still did not exist as an independent state. He took his new wife, Tola, with him and quickly made many new friends, among them Joseph Conrad the Polish author who had adopted British citizenship and his wife, Jessie; they were all on holiday together in Poland when World War I broke out and there was a scramble to get the Conrads out of the country to Vienna by train.

Retinger seemed to know everyone that mattered even at that early stage in his life and he tried to use his contacts to persuade Austria to break off its alliance with Germany. He organised meetings with Herbert Asquith, the British Prime Minister, George Clemenceau, Prime Minister of France, Viscount Northcliffe, the British publishing magnate, and the French General Henri Berthelot all to no avail. Indeed his interference in matters of state only succeeded in getting him declared *persona non grata* in Austria and the Germans putting a price on his head.[124]

With his marriage failing and now unwelcome in Britain, Retinger found sanctuary in Mexico during the 1920s and was soon advising both the union leader, Luis Morones and the future President Plutarco Calles.

He fell in love again and in 1926 married Stella Morel, daughter of the British labour pacifist and politician Edmund Morel. They had two children but Stella died in 1933 and Retinger's effortless rise to the top stalled; he struggled to survive as a writer but kept in touch with his contacts who included General Wladislaw Sikorski, the Prime Minister of the Polish Government in exile.

When World War II broke out Retinger parachuted into occupied Poland to support the underground movement at the age of 56 giving him the record as the oldest man to make a combat parachute jump. His motives even then were challenged by senior figures in the Home Army (the *Armia Krajowa*) and suspicious members of the resistance made an attempt on his life by poisoning him.[125] He survived and made it back to London where he convalesced in the comfort of the Dorchester Hotel.

Having witnessed so much destruction in Poland and throughout Europe those who knew him said he made it his "personal mission in life to bring about a united, peaceful Europe."[126] It is however at this point that we reach the crossroads in our story. Was the man who had been awarded a Medal for Courage in the Cause of Freedom by King George V in 1948 (he never attended the ceremony) a genuine peace loving patriot who wanted nothing more than a harmonious Europe? Alternatively, was he about to embark on the most devious plan for what some argue was nothing short of eugenics on a global scale, control of the world's population, eradication of the weakest links and all controlled by a handful of people answering to no-one but their own private and highly secretive clique?

Some facts are agreed. Along with Paul van Zeeland, the former Prime Minister of Belgium, he co-founded the European League for Economic Cooperation (ELEC) in 1946 whose aim as its title suggests was to reach a consensus and unity particularly in monetary aspects in Europe. Members of the Kronberg Conference, named after the hotel where the group first met, gathers every year to agree policy to promote greater integration, cooperation and understanding among nations. The ELEC led directly to the founding of the European Economic Community which became the European Union we all know today.

Retinger went one step further when he called together a small group of the most influential businessmen and politicians initially from Europe and America to a private meeting in a room at the Hotel de Bilderberg in Oosterbeek in the Netherlands from 29 to 31 May 1954. He had the backing of Prince Berhard of the Netherlands and Paul van Zeeland. The purpose was for all the invitees to be able to discuss any topic they wanted and to express their most private opinions freely and off the record; in particular it was to cement relations between Europe and America. The intention was for its wise counsel to filter back to the respective countries – a sort of consensus on the best way forward might emerge.

Retinger wrote later about his reasons for calling the first meeting: "A few years ago a large number of people began to feel anxious about a growing distrust of America which was making itself manifest in Western

Europe and which was paralleled by a similar distrust of Western Europe in America. This feeling caused considerable apprehension on both sides of the Atlantic and in 1952 I felt that it was of the first importance to try to remove this suspicion, distrust, and lack of confidence which threatened to jeopardize the post-war work of the Western Allies."

Such was the success of the first meeting, attended by 50 representatives from 11 countries in Western Europe and 11 Americans, that it was agreed to make it an annual event meeting in different locations. Retinger was the appointed the permanent Secretary of the Conference which became known as the Bilderberg Group. It continues to meet every summer and attendance is by invitation only. Security is extremely tight and until recently the list of 'guests' was always kept secret. In 2013 for the first time a list was released showing that among the guests were the British Prime Minister, David Cameron, Henry Kissinger, the former US Secretary of State and the head of the IMF, Christine Lagarde.

It is this very secrecy which fuels the concern about the real or imagined purpose of the gathering. In 2001 Lord Healey, one of the founders of the Group and former British Chancellor of the Exchequer, dismissed any notion of world domination, "To say we were striving for a one-world government is exaggerated, but not wholly unfair. Those of us in Bilderberg felt we couldn't go on forever fighting one another for nothing and killing people and rendering millions homeless. So we felt that a single community throughout the world would be a good thing."[127]

Four years later, Viscount Davignon, the former European Commissioner for Industrial Affairs and Energy, told the BBC, "There will always be people who believe in conspiracies but things happen in a much more incoherent fashion... When people say this is a secret government of the world I say that if we were a secret government of the world we should be bloody ashamed of ourselves."

What is clear is that it has become a club of the most influential world figures with an uncanny knack of inviting politicians shortly before they come to make their mark in their own countries. Bill Clinton was just the governor of Arkansas when he went to the conference in Germany in 1991 – a year later he was President of the United States. Margaret Thatcher was still three years off becoming Prime Minister of the United Kingdom when she was invited to attend and it is said was somewhat overwhelmed at her first meeting. Tony Blair was a backbencher in the House of Commons not even leader of the Labour Party when got his call in 1993 and Herman van Rompuy, hardly a dominant figure in Europe, was unanimously elected President of the European Council seven days after addressing the Bilderbergers in 2009.

The problem say the conspiracy theorists is that the 'unity' of nations with such different backgrounds under umbrella organisations like the EU smacks too much of the hidden agenda to create a One World Order. It is even suggested that they want to remove the weakest in society – there will be the rulers and there will be the slaves. This is said to be the shadowy agenda of the modern Illuminati, a secret society established in 1776 in Bavaria to combat superstition and religious interference and influence in public life. Today it is accused of masterminding a secret plan for world domination by infiltrating its supporters into all walks of life. The conspiracy view takes it further and accuses various think tanks including the Club of Rome and the Committee of 300 of orchestrating everything from wars and economic decline to famines and disease in order to achieve their alleged ends: one world government, one currency, one authority to bring order to the chaos; by introducing policies such as NAFTA – the North America Free Trade Agreement – it is claimed that hundreds of thousands of Americans were deliberately being put out of work as a result of cheap imports. Does it make sense, they ask, to have one European Union with no borders allowing free migration which imposes burdens on countries' infrastructure, benefits programmes, schooling and housing?

The Committee of 300 is said to sit at the top of the tree among all the secret societies. Founded in 1727 by a group of British aristocrats, the Committee it is claimed showed their hand in an article in *Neue Freie Presse* in 1909 which contained a statement by Walter Rathenau, former Foreign Minister of Germany and an industrialist, who said, "Three hundred men, each one of whom knows each other, lead the economic fortune of this continent and choose their successors from among themselves." Leading this organisation it is alleged are the Rothschild family, other financiers and members of various European royal families.

The Club of Rome is another think tank founded in 1968 which describes itself as "a group of world citizens, sharing a common concern for the future of humanity." In 1972 it published a report entitled *Limits to Growth* which warned that economic prosperity could not grow indefinitely because of limited natural resources. Was this just the first important warning for the good of mankind or a more sinister suggestion that there were too many people and some were surplus to requirements? The allegation by the conspiracy theorists is that the Club of Rome is merely the foreign relations arm of the Committee of 300 from whom it takes its orders.

It all sounds fanciful and beyond reasonable belief when the whole plot is said to encompass the Vatican, the Knights of Malta, various intelligence agencies, Freemasons and others, yet when the world's leading bankers and financiers, the most powerful political leaders and diplomats gather secretly at different locations around the world to talk off-the-record without any apparent decisions being reached it raises questions. The most pertinent recent question brought up in the British Parliament in 2013 when the Bilderberg Conference was being held in the UK was why did none of these brains spot the approaching banking collapse in 2008? It is easy to see the conspiracy answer – the collapse was orchestrated.

Those who knew Retinger don't recognise this as a secret plan that he wanted to fulfil: "Retinger was motivated by lofty ideals, not wicked schemes, when he first called the Conference together at the Bilderberg Hotel in Holland."[128]

Retinger himself realised from the outset that his motives and those of his colleagues would be misinterpreted. He wrote in 1956: "In order not to be accused of starting an unofficial political 'mafia', we decided from the outset not to consider ourselves a policy-making body but to have as our principal aim the smoothing over of difficulties and tendencies among countries and the finding of a common approach in the various fields – political, cultural, economic, and social. Moreover, we do not contemplate taking any direct action. We draw the attention of existing organizations to the points in question; what those organizations do remains their own responsibility. For this side of our work, however, we have always had the tacit approval of the Governments of the countries to which the participants belong."

At the very least it is reasonable to feel uneasy when such highly connected men and women travel from around the globe for unscripted, unrecorded exchanges which purport to reach no conclusions, advocate no plan of action and benignly hope that the invitees will take home with them the thoughts and concerns expressed at their meetings. In June 2013 Michael Meacher, MP, said in the House of Commons, "130 of the world's biggest decision-makers don't travel thousands of miles simply for a cosy chat." In reply Kenneth Clarke, a government minister, laughed off the conspiracy theories saying, "We go there for the chance of having an off-the-record, informal discussion with the range of people you described, who are indeed distinguished but who are not remotely interested in getting together to decide anything."[129]

The world is full of unexplained events which simply add fuel to the conspiratorial fire. When the Balfour Declaration was revealed in 1917 promising a homeland to the Jewish people in Palestine, the British government was still secretly contemplating allowing a Turkish presence which would have been anathema to the Jews. But at a celebration welcoming the declaration on 2nd December hosted by Lord Rothschild, leader of the Jewish community and attended by Robert Cecil, assistant foreign secretary, and Sir Mark Sykes, assistant secretary to the war cabinet, some at that celebration knew secret negotiations were going on but said nothing.[130] Who decided that the Shah of Iran was surplus to Western requirements? Having installed the Hashemite King Faisal in Iraq, who determined that it was time for regime change, gave their backing ultimately to Sadam Hussein and then later approved his downfall? He was the West's ally in the region, we armed him and courted him and yet a swift military action of 'shock and awe' was unleashed against him led by the United States backed by Britain. Why was the Vietnam War allowed to continue even when Washington realised that victory was impossible? Who was to gain by the deaths of more American soldiers? More recently what sense can be made of the Arab Spring where in Egypt President Hosni Mubarak, again the West's friend, was toppled followed by free and fair elections which were then overturned barely a year later with the help of the military and the quiet acquiescence of the West; it wasn't really a military coup people argued. What is to be made of Syria where President Bashar al-Assad is known to have chemical weapons and used them just like Iraq, but on this occasion the West decides it is not appropriate to intervene to save ordinary citizens? What is the West's agenda for the Middle East the most volatile region of the world? By July 2013 America seemed reluctant to be the world's policeman and it was left to Saudi Arabia to make itself ready for any potential threat; satellite images showed Saudi missiles being pointed not only at Iran but also Israel, another staunch friend of America.

The man in the street almost never knows why such things are allowed to happen when they do and only at a much later date discovers that events did not unfold quite as they were portrayed at the time. It is for this reason that secret societies, even ones apparently born out of good intentions, cause suspicion.

When the chain smoking Retinger died from lung cancer in London on 12 June 1960 having not enriched himself one iota and having rejected all honours save that of the Medal for Courage which seems to have been forced upon him by King George V, he may well have died a contented man. He had set in motion an organisation which would blossom or explode depending on one's point of view into the European Union and he had created a forum for private debate where he hoped important and difficult issues could be discussed freely. Or perhaps he was worried that the Bilderberg Group was getting out of control with ambitions far greater and more sinister than is admitted.

From a very young age Retinger was immensely well connected. At his funeral in London, attended by five British cabinet ministers but not many others, Sir Edward Bedington-Behrens, a distinguished soldier and advocate of European cooperation, said: "I remember Retinger in the United States picking up the telephone and immediately making an appointment with the President, and in Europe he had complete entrée in every political circle as a kind of right acquired through trust, devotion and loyalty he inspired."

Retinger used those connections to great effect, expanding his network of friends around the world; whether he was using them for good or ill is so far unknown. What is clear is that two of the enterprises he established survive today, one the ever-enlarging European Union whose laws certainly transcend boundaries and his Bilderberg Group whose invitations are still considered to be desirable even irresistible by political leaders, financiers and industrialists the world over. If the Bilderberg Group is not a shadow government it chooses to remain in the shadows, happily laughing off dismissively any suggestion that there is any agenda other than peace and prosperity to all men.

As for Josef Retinger who left this world discretely and without fanfare, he was undoubtedly a man with a contacts book that was without equal. A number of our list of shadow players had similar access to the most powerful players, the question will remain – did Retinger use his access to give orders or merely to offer advice?

22

GEORGE MITCHELL (b.1933)

It is never too late to take up the burden of being a go-between as the Democrat George Mitchell proved when he retired from the US Senate. What he then embarked upon was a determined effort on behalf of two presidents to resolve two of modern history's more intractable problems far away from American shores but inextricably bound to them. For one he was hailed as a hero and at the same time condemned as the architect of an abject surrender to terrorism, for the other he ultimately had to admit that he had failed as the competing sides were never going to agree – at least not in his lifetime.

Mitchell's style in his political life and his later role as a fixer and peacemaker can best be described as low key. If anyone wanted to avoid the limelight it was Mitchell quietly going about his business while others gathered in the media spotlight all too ready to give their well-rounded sound bite. He was described as America's 'gray man' and regularly as an éminence grise moving constantly and patiently between the opposing sides of an argument until agreement or at least consensus could be reached. He once said, "Conflicts are created, conducted and sustained by human beings; they can be ended by human beings."

Mitchell was born in Waterville, Maine on 20 August 1933 into a family which might have suggested the role which he would one day lead. His father, George, a school janitor, was of Irish descent but had been orphaned and adopted by a Lebanese family while his mother, Mary (née Saad) had emigrated to the United States from the Lebanon when she was just 18. His early life was hard. He was one of five children and worked shifts also as a janitor as he made his way through school intending to become a teacher with a modest ambition to become mayor of his local town.

However in 1954 he joined the US army rising to First Lieutenant and served as a counter-intelligence office in Berlin. By then he had changed his mind and wanted to become a lawyer. In 1961 having completed his studies through a part-time programme at night he received his law degree from Georgetown University. He served as a trial attorney for the Antitrust Division of the Justice Department but in 1962 he got his first taste of political life when he spent three years as one of Senator Edmund Muskie's assistants. Although he lost a campaign to become Governor of Maine, he had been spotted and was appointed US Attorney for Maine by President Jimmy Carter and in 1979 he was made a federal judge. The following year he succeeded Muskie when he resigned from the Senate to become US Secretary of State. He served out the remainder of Muskie's term then was re-elected in his own right in 1982 with 61% of the vote. Mitchell's style and manner earned him praise from both sides of the Senate and for six consecutive years he was voted 'the most respected member' of the chamber serving as Senate Majority Leader from 1989 until he left in 1995 having turned down an offer from President Bill Clinton to become a Supreme Court Judge. However his toughest challenges still lay ahead.

In 1992 Northern and Southern Ireland were trying once again to reach out to each other when Mary Robinson became the first President of Ireland to visit Belfast. But the fighting in the north continued when loyalist gunmen killed five Catholics in a bookshop in Belfast and later in the year the IRA blew up a forensics laboratory in the city. Across the Atlantic Bill Clinton was on the presidential campaign trail when he suggested that he would like to appoint a Special Envoy to Northern Ireland in a bid to end the troubles by sending an independent go-between. The announcement, aimed squarely at the Irish-American vote infuriated London as US Presidents had traditionally steered well clear of the debate even though it was common knowledge that sympathetic groups in America supported the IRA throughout the seventies.

The idea languished in the long grass until the following year when Clinton met the Irish Taoiseach, Albert Reynolds, on St Patrick's Day in Washington. They sang 'When Irish Eyes Are Smiling' together but Reynolds made it clear that there were major obstacles before peace talks of any kind could be resumed. In his address Reynolds said: "We live in a time when ambitions for peace are tempered by the realization that old animosities and deep distrust often live long in the human heart. They can give rise to terrible and prolonged violence... Twenty-five years of conflict, the loss of over 3,000 lives, and an immeasurable quota of human suffering have not and cannot advance the search for a lasting and equitable settlement." In reply Clinton pledged America's support for what he called "your courageous peace initiative."

Washington appeared to be taking sides in 1994 when the Sinn Fein leader, Gerry Adams, was given a visa to visit the United States and met Clinton. Once again London was furious as many regarded Adams to be a senior member of the Provisional IRA and as such directly implicated in the bloodshed, something Adams always strenuously denied. The Americans argued that by agreeing to meet Adams they were increasing their influence over the republicans and their chances of bringing them to the negotiating table.

In 1994 having gained concessions from the British government including the release of IRA prisoners and a reduction in military patrols a ceasefire was declared and Adams urged Washington to play a 'nudging role'[131] in searching for peace. The following year Mitchell was appointed Special Envoy and the British Prime Minister, John Major and John Bruton, who had succeeded Reynolds, agreed that Mitchell should chair an international commission on the disarmament of the paramilitaries. It was still not a breakthrough in the peace talks which had been stalled for 15 months but as John Major said it "concentrated the mind." It had been a long time coming. Talks had been going on in one form or another since the eighties and in November 1994 the British Government revealed that they had been having secret discussions with the Provisional IRA despite previous denials.

In his own account of the start of the negotiations Mitchell, the practised listener, allowed the parties to rant on. Recalling his first meeting with the Rev. Ian Paisley, the unionist minister apparently could find nothing to like about the envoy with an Irish background. Paisley answered every approach by Mitchell with "No. No. No. No." Mitchell said, "I was accustomed to rough-and-tumble political debate but I'd never experienced anything like this."

A trained negotiator, much like a hostage negotiator, has to listen and keep on listening and that was always Mitchell's tactic acutely aware of the history and every stumbling block along the way that would lead to peace. Later Mitchell would describe the standoff and ultimate agreement in this way: "... long-time enemies came together to form a power-sharing government, to bring to an end the ancient conflict known as the 'Troubles'. This was almost 800 years after Britain began its domination of Ireland, 86 years after the partition of Ireland, 38 years after the British army formally began its most recent mission in Ireland, 11 years after the peace talks began, and nine years after a peace agreement was signed. In the negotiations which led to that agreement, we had 700 days of failure and one day of success. For most of the time, progress was nonexistent or very slow..."

Having succeeded in agreeing to the principle of disarmament, the first step in the Northern Ireland Peace Process, Mitchell spent the next four years negotiating between all parties involved. His meetings were conducted in private, even secretly; publicity wasn't Mitchell's style and a wrong word may have been easily misinterpreted.

The suspicion was always that the ceasefire would not hold and that the real aims of the protagonists had not changed. On 13 August 1995 when Adams was addressing a crowd in Belfast City Hall someone called out "Bring back the IRA" to which Adams replied: "They haven't gone away, you know." And therein lies the doubt even today.

The lengthy and carefully chosen words of the Good Friday Agreement were released on 10 April 1998 at 5.36pm more than 17 hours after the official deadline had passed and after a number of calls to both sides from Clinton urging them to stick to the task. Mitchell said, "I am pleased to announce that the two governments and the political parties in Northern Ireland have reached agreement."

When he was asked in 2009 what had been the key factor in reaching an agreement Mitchell said "The two messages [political leaders] were getting, and really they're still getting from their constituents, are 'Look, we want this settled. We don't want this conflict to continue.'"[132]

The Agreement included provisions for a devolved, inclusive government, troop reductions, prisoner release and polls on the unification of Ireland among others but it was a fragile deal. On Saturday 15 August a group now calling itself the Real IRA carried out a bombing in Omagh killing 29 people and injuring hundreds of other – it was the single worst attack of the Troubles.

Who had really won? For the people of Northern Ireland clashes between Protestants and Catholics continue. The Republicans from the south are unlikely to achieve their dream of a united Ireland as that would require a majority vote by the largely Protestant north which wants to remain part of the United Kingdom. Tensions between the two religious groups remain high but the real loser according to some is that we have given in to terrorist threats. The opponents of the Agreement say terrorists have been released from prison, gunmen have been allowed to become politicians and there was outrage in the media when the Queen shook hands with Martin McGuinness, the former IRA commander and Northern Ireland's Deputy First Minister in June 2012. An IRA bomb, we were reminded, murdered the Queen's cousin Lord Louis Mountbatten.

Fragile deal or not Mitchell was seen as being the honest broker seeking to bridge the difficult sectarian divide. He was nominated for the Nobel Peace Prize, was awarded an honorary knighthood from the Queen and the Presidential Medal of Freedom, America's highest civilian honour for his work in Northern Ireland.

Back in Washington, Mitchell returned to his legal practice occasionally being criticised for his work on behalf of the tobacco lobby but in 2009 President Barak Obama had another Gordian Knot for him to cut through – the Israeli-Palestinian crisis. His success in Northern Ireland had enhanced his reputation as a political fixer but now as Special Envoy to the Middle East he had an even older war to end. Accepting the challenge he recognised the difficulties ahead, "The situation in the Middle East is volatile, complex, and dangerous." And he was in no doubt what would be required: "This effort must be determined, persevering, and patient. It must be backed up by political capital, economic resources, and focused attention at the highest levels of our government. And it must be firmly rooted in a shared vision of a peaceful future by the people who live in the region." [133]

He would have had a good idea of the trouble he was walking into as in 2001 he had chaired a presidential committee into the Israeli-Palestinian crisis and produced a report warning Israel against expanding its settlements and urging the Palestinian authority bring a halt to militant activity in its territory. Both forlorn hopes and now things were getting worse.

2008 had closed with Hamas[134] ending its six month truce with Israel and launching rocket attacks into the country. The Israelis immediately responded with a 24 day bombardment which left some 1,500 Palestinians dead. Israel declared its intention to wipe out Hamas which was considered to be a terrorist organisation by the United States and Britain as well as Israel. Human rights watchers regarded Israel's punitive strikes as a war crime. It was not an auspicious time to begin searching for peace in the Middle East.

Mitchell's appointment was interpreted by most as positive move. David Aaron, a US diplomat with long Middle East experience said: "It reflects a serious commitment by the new administration to addressing the Arab-Israeli crisis. He has real negotiating experience in Northern Ireland and the Middle East and he understands the requirements of both sides." While Abraham Foxman, national director of the Anti-Defamation League, told *The Jewish Week* that "Senator Mitchell is fair. He's been meticulously even-handed."

The question was what could he do to make a difference? It looked as though Obama was determined to show willing but the obstacles were considerable. As usual Mitchell's tactics were to listen to what the opposing sides had to say. Within a week of being given the task he was travelling throughout the Middle East beginning in Cairo and making visits to Jordan and the West Bank, Turkey and Saudi Arabia. He met the future Israeli Prime Minister, Benjamin Netanyahu in 2009 and continued his patient excursions through the region seeking common ground.

The gulf between the parties always seemed too wide. Mitchell was keen to press for Palestinian statehood which was out of the question as far as Netanyahu was concerned. Any suggestion that the Israeli West Bank settlements should be halted was another non-starter, if anything Netanyahu wanted them to be expanded.

While Mitchell was anxious to help rebuild the stricken Hamas-controlled Gaza Strip with a promised injection of $900 million, Israel continued to bomb what they said were illegal tunnels used for smuggling in weapons. The Palestinians said they were being used to bring in much needed medical supplies.

Reflecting on what he had achieved in Northern Ireland and hoping for a similar compromise in the Middle East he said: "It was a political agreement which represented the best that could be achieved at that time. When you make a political compromise you accomplish as much as can be accomplished under the circumstances which exist at the time. So the result is that you get an agreement that viewed years later with the benefit of hindsight will necessarily be imperfect and not have accomplished what you want. But this was about what could be done at that time."[135]

He seemed to be saying that no-one has all the answers and no-one is always right. He declared as much to Colonel Oliver North during the Iran-Contra affair[136] in 1987 when he asked him to "remember that it is possible for an American to disagree with you on aid to the Contras and still love God, and still love this country, just as much as you do".

George Mitchell (b.1933)

The highlight of his shuttle diplomacy was direct talks between Netanyahu and the Palestinian President Mahmoud Abbas in September 2010 hosted by Obama in New York. From the outset neither side sounded optimistic, Netanyahu warned: "This will not be easy. True peace, a lasting peace, will be achieved only with mutual and painful concessions from both sides." Abbas was calling for an end to Jewish settlements on the West Bank. When the talking started Netanyahu refused to stop the construction of the settlements and negotiations soon faltered. There was nothing even Mitchell could do or say to bring the two men back to the table and finally in May 2011 he resigned.

Acknowledging that he had taken on 'the toughest job imaginable' Obama said, "His deep commitment to resolving conflict and advancing democracy has contributed immeasurably to the goal of two states living side by side in peace and security."

The US Secretary of State Hillary Clinton added her own tribute: "As well as anyone in his generation, George understands the slow, hard work of diplomacy, the art of compromise and the indispensable role of American leadership in the world."

Mitchell may not have pulled off the impossible but he remained true to himself throughout his career in public life. He was both the peacemaker and a man who treated all men fairly but without favour. When the shareholders of Walt Disney had a very public falling out with their chairman, Michael Eisner, in 2004 it was Mitchell they turned to in a bid to calm the troubled waters. And when he was asked to conduct an investigation into the use of steroids in the Holy Grail of national baseball he pulled no punches. His report revealed widespread use of performance enhancing drugs and Mitchell wasn't afraid to name names singling out some of the game's top stars.

Above all Mitchell seems to have faith in human nature even when the going gets tough. When the Northern Ireland peace talks looked like floundering yet again, he had soothing words: "Maybe I'm a hopeless optimist and maybe I'm blinded by my affection for the people of Northern Ireland, but I do believe they are going to somehow work their way through it without a complete collapse of the process."

He was right on that occasion and one suspects that if there is another conflict in another part of the world, Mitchell would say there is always hope. He is the go-between par excellence who was able to interpret and polish sometimes harsh opinions and carry them to the other side so that they sounded more amenable. When Dr Paisley barked "No. No. No. No" at him he may have flinched inwardly at the inflexible rhetoric but he would probably have simply adjusted his glasses and thought: "Maybe, there's another way."

23

Peter Mandelson (b.1953)

Peter Mandelson was not the first spin doctor the world has seen but he was probably the finest practitioner of the 'dark art' in modern day politics. He also demonstrated the shadow player's greatest gift is the ability to survive not one but two setbacks in his career and to go on to serve more than one master. Having shown everyone else how to play the game using all the techniques that today's technologically savvy world has to offer there have been many who followed in his path, but no equals.

Mandelson was always going to find a home in politics. He was born on 21 October 1953 in Hampstead, North London which was something of a Labour Party stronghold. He was the son of Mary and 'Tony' George Mandelson and the grandson of Herbert Morrison, the former Labour Deputy Prime Minister. Harold Wilson, the Prime Minister, had a house just up the road and the young Mandelson was invited to visit on occasion. Before going up to Oxford University to read philosophy, politics and economics where he joined the university's Labour Club he flirted briefly with the communism – "more for social than political reasons" he later claimed. In September 1979 he was elected to Lambeth Borough Council but 'retired' in 1982 apparently disillusioned by the parlous state of Labour politics.[137] The Party needed to modernise. It was beset on the one hand by the Militant wing and on the other it seemed stuck in the past. In 1983 Michael Foot led a disastrous election campaign against Margaret Thatcher who was enjoying huge popularity following the victory in the Falkland Islands. Foot had decided that the party manifesto, *A New Hope for Britain*, should include all the resolutions passed at the party conference including unilateral nuclear disarmament, withdrawal from the European Economic Community, abolishment of the House of Lords and the renationalisation of British Telecom, British Aerospace and the British Shipbuilding Corporation. It was dubbed 'the longest suicide note in history' by the Labour MP Gerald Kaufman. When the Conservatives were returned in a landslide victory with a 144 seat majority in the House of Commons, Mandelson, who was working as a producer at London Weekend Television, must have realised that something needed to change and his experience in broadcasting was to be the way. John Birt had taken over as Programme Director at LWT in 1982 and was bringing in new and more commercial practices to build up the audience figures. It is clear that Mandelson would have begun to appreciate the power and pull of television at this time and conceivably seen a way to help the Labour Party.

Michael Foot resigned and was succeeded by Neil Kinnock who appointed Mandelson his Director of Communications in 1985. He immediately made his mark by running the party's campaign for the Fulham by-election the following year which produced a shock defeat for the Tories returning Labour's Nick Raynsford. It marked a new style in slick campaigning and the prelude to 'New Labour' which would do away with the Red Flag replacing it with the more patriotic Red Rose and seeking to distance itself from overt trade union influence; the miners' strike led by Arthur Scargill had only just ended in March that year.

In 1987 Labour was still worried that it might even be beaten into third place in the general election behind the Social Democratic Party having just lost a by-election to them in Greenwich. In a bold move Mandelson arranged for Hugh Hudson, the film director of Chariots of Fire fame, to direct the party political broadcast. It became known as 'Kinnock – The Movie' and showed him striding across the Great Orme headland in Llandudno, Wales as far removed from the grime of the pits as it was possible to get with his wife, Glenys; the Party was clean, fresh and family friendly it was saying. Labour came second behind the Conservatives which was probably all they were hoping for but the broadcast marked a turning point. Style and presentation mattered – almost above all else. The message had to come across clearly and professionally and it was a strategy every other party adopted from then on – PR and spin was the way ahead.

In March 1990, Mandelson resigned from his post as communications director to fight for a seat in Parliament winning the selection as the Labour candidate for Hartlepool. In April 1992 he was duly elected even though Kinnock and Labour failed to win the national poll. Two other young MPs emerged on the scene at the same time – Tony Blair and Gordon Brown and Mandelson immediately singled them both out as potential leaders, possibly prime ministers.

One journalist quoting an aide who worked with Mandelson in the nineties noted a characteristic that suggested he always needed to please figures in authority which he attributed to Mandelson's sometimes frosty relationship with his father. The aide said "all through that period, you could see that Peter was unconsciously seeking approval. You see it with lots of men whose relationship with their fathers is in some way difficult. They seek authority figures and curry favour. Peter had it almost as a compulsion." And, indeed, there is something of a pattern. Until recently, Mandelson's style had been to identify the most powerful person and then work exclusively, almost slavishly, for them – often at the expense of all other relationships."[138]

By now Margaret Thatcher's position in her own party was under threat as the Poll Tax riots flared up and her stubborn refusal to give way was seen as severely damaging to the party's fortunes. Michael Heseltine challenged her for the leadership but lost out to John Major. Mrs Thatcher's resignation on 28 November 1990 should have been an opportunity for Kinnock who immediately demanded a general election. When it was finally called in 1992 Labour lost again with Rupert Murdoch's *Sun* newspaper claiming in a headline: "It's the *Sun* Wot Won It" after running a front page article on election day saying: "If Kinnock wins today will the last person to leave Britain please turn the lights out." Murdoch later regretted the tone of that campaign but the message was clear – the media could influence elections and by implication should be courted; the subsequent cosying up to the likes of Murdoch by all parties would later prove to be a dangerous strategy.

However Kinnock also realised his time as leader was up after eight and a half years and he resigned on 13 April 1992 making him the longest serving opposition leader in British political history. The Shadow Chancellor, John Smith, took over. However Smith was not a fit man and on 11 May 1994 he died having suffered a massive heart attack after giving a speech at a fund raising dinner in London.

For Mandelson it was time to make a decision: which of his two friends, Blair or Brown, should he back. In the end of course he went for the more telegenic Blair even though Brown was regarded as the more senior member of the party but instinctively Mandelson realised that the television cameras would prefer Blair and his more charismatic style. Betrayal or broken promise, none of that mattered to Mandelson who knew what had to be done to get the party back in government and Blair appointed him campaign director for the 1997 general election.

Labour repositioned itself as a more centrist party and crucially Blair was given a more Presidential role by his highly professional PR machine now joined by the former Daily Mirror journalist, Alastair Campbell; it amounted to a personality contest, the country was either voting for the young, energetic Labour leader or the tired, grey John Major. It chose Blair and handed him a landslide 179 overall majority. Blair with Mandelson at his side was in Downing Street.

But Mandelson had made another enemy, the man now sitting in Number 11 Downing Street, Blair's Chancellor of the Exchequer. The rift with Brown has been the stuff of countless articles and books and even a film: did Mandelson betray Brown? Did Blair renege on his promise? Had there been an agreement hatched at the Granita Restaurant in London where Brown agreed to step aside in the leadership contest following John Smith's death in return for the party following certain polices and an understanding that eventually Blair would himself step aside allowing Brown into Number 10? As it turned out nothing was written down and any deal, such as it was, seemed to have been settled before the Granita meeting when of course both men understood different things had been agreed. The net result in the years that followed was a feud between Blair in the seat of power at Number 10 and his bitter and brooding Chancellor next door.

Mandelson was rewarded with a seat in the Cabinet as Minister without Portfolio to coordinate the government machine and then given added responsibility for the development of the Millennium Dome. This was followed in July 1998 with his appointment as Secretary of State for Trade and Industry as part of Blair's first cabinet reshuffle – he received a standing ovation from the workers at his office and he proved to be a popular minister not least because he was able and willing to take rapid decisions. It seemed to matter not a jot when later Matthew Parris, the former MP and Parliamentary sketch writer revealed on BBC's Newsnight programme that Mandelson was gay. His friend, John Birt, by then Director General of the BBC, banned any further reference to the matter on air. Two years later Mandelson publicly acknowledged his relationship with Reinaldo Avila da Silva when he allowed photographs to be taken of them together.

Peter Mandelson (b.1953)

If anything Mandelson's lack of family may have counted in his favour – politics consumed his time and energy.

However it seems he had also developed a taste for good living and in 1996 had bought a house in fashionable Notting Hill with the help of a loan from the millionaire MP, Geoffrey Robinson, whose financial dealings were being investigated by his department. While Mandelson claimed all along that he had kept out of the discussions he had failed to declare the loan in the Register of MPs' Interests and was forced to resign on 23 December 1998.

One can only imagine how many people felt he had finally had his just desserts but Mandelson had only been out of the cabinet for ten months when Blair called him back to take over from Mo Mowlam as Secretary of State for Northern Ireland.

He proved to be an effective operator in the treacherous waters of Northern Ireland overseeing the establishment of the devolved legislative assembly and reforms to the police force. However it wasn't long before his past association with the Millennium Dome caught up with him. He was accused of using his influence with the Home Office to try and hurry through the passport applications of Srichand 'SP' and Gopichand 'GP' Hinduja, billionaire brothers who were substantial sponsors of the Dome's Faith Zone and who operate a global empire from the top of New Zealand House in London's Haymarket. At the time the family was also under investigation by the Indian government for their alleged involvement in the Bofors Scandal. The Hindujas and the Indian Prime Minister, Rajiv Gandhi, were accused of being involved in kickbacks from Bofors AB during the 1980s and 1990s to win contracts supplying field artillery. The Hindujas were exonerated of any involvement in that scandal but the passport affair cost Mandelson his second cabinet post when he resigned on 24 January 2001, although a subsequent inquiry under Sir Anthony Hammond found that he had not acted improperly.

If his detractors felt his time in politics was over they were to be disappointed. In June that year he was re-elected MP for Hartlepool, seeing off a spoiling attack by rival candidate Arthur Scargill representing what he called Genuine Labour, and declared at the election count that he was "a fighter not a quitter." Nevertheless he was not offered a cabinet post and let it be known that he would like a job in Europe. Both Neil Kinnock and Chris Patten were due to stand down as commissioners and in November 2004 he was offered the post of EU Trade Commissioner. For a time he stepped away from the Westminster political village to concentrate on far wider ranging topics, operating on the world stage and meeting more important international figures. In 1999 he had already been invited to attend the annual conference of the Bilderberg Group (see Chapter 20 – Jósef Retinger) and would address them again in 2009 and 2011. It was described by some commentators as something of an exile to the remote draughty corners of the continent but surely Mandelson would have been astute enough simply to use the opportunity to network with the other Bilderbergers who as we have seen in a previous chapter operate on a different timeframe with a different global agenda.

Some of his networking attracted controversy when *The Sunday Times* reported that he had enjoyed a reception on a yacht owned by the Russian billionaire, Oleg Deripaska, who was a major importer of aluminium into the European Union. The suspicion, strenuously denied by Mandelson, was that Deripaska may have benefitted when Mandelson reduced tariffs on aluminium imports to the EU from 6% to 3%.

Maybe Brussels was simply not to his liking or maybe he saw another opportunity back in London, either way Mandelson made it clear in March 2007 that he did not intend to seek a second term as Commissioner beyond 2009. In any case he would have known that the British political landscape was about to change again and on 27 June Gordon Brown finally succeeded Tony Blair as Labour Leader and at last became Prime Minister.

Brown's political honeymoon was brief and following an initial surge in the polls after he moved into Number 10 Labour's popularity began to slide as the 2008 recession and banking crisis took hold. Brown's stunning reaction when all seemed lost was to reach out to Mandelson announcing on 3 October 2008 that his erstwhile nemesis was returning to the cabinet as business secretary based in the Lords. Mandelson was to be ennobled – Baron Mandelson of Foy – by the very man who must have cursed him every day while he served out his time as Chancellor. However Brown justified his decision by saying the country needed the benefit of Mandelson's unrivalled expertise in dealing with trade and business matters. Mandelson said with a chuckle outside Downing Street that it was 'third time lucky'. *The Sun* said, "The PM took the biggest gamble of his career by reappointing his most bitter foe Mandy to government."[139]

Eric Pickles, the Conservative Party chairman, wondered who was in charge: "It is quite obvious that Peter Mandelson is the real unelected prime minister pulling the strings from No 10. He is Gordon Brown's political life support machine, keeping the plotters at bay. He sadly typifies the Prime Minister's unhealthy reliance on unelected officials."[140]

In June 2009 there was a further cabinet reshuffle and Mandelson became First Secretary of State and Lord President of the Council and, as though he did not have enough titles, it was also announced that the Department for Innovation, Universities and Skills would now be merged and fall under his authority with a newly created title of Secretary of State for Business Innovation and Skills not to mention that he would continue as President of the Board of Trade.

At one point Mandelson sat on 35 of the 43 cabinet committees and sub-committees influencing virtually every aspect of government business and it was too much for some commentators. The satirical magazine *Private Eye* called him "the Prince of Darkness" which it appears was a title he rather enjoyed. He also clearly relished a week in August 2009 when he was in charge of the country while Brown took a holiday. He said, "All this ridiculous song and dance about who is in charge is just a load of nonsense but he is on holiday and if there are small things I can pick up to give him the best holiday that he deserves, I'll certainly do that."[141]

Despite Mandelson's support and intervention Labour lost 91 seats in the 2010 general election, the biggest loss since 1931, and the party was over. On 10 May Brown announced that he would step down as Labour Leader and the next day he formally resigned as Prime Minister to be succeeded by David Cameron at the head of a coalition government with the Liberal Democrats.

The small matter of suddenly being out of office didn't cause Mandelson's elegant progress in life to miss a beat. Barely two months later he published his memoirs, *The Third Man: Life at the Heart of New Labour*, which didn't go down well with some Labour Party leadership contenders. In November he became chairman of Global Counsel LLP a consultancy firm and other offers and directorships were dangled in front of him: would he head up the IMF, join a merchant bank or become Director General of the World Trade Organisation? Whatever outside interests he undoubtedly will pursue in later life he cannot resist giving his opinion about British politics. He is now an elder statesman, even an éminence grise figure with considerable experience and ability and people still want to know what he thinks. It was a mistake he said for Blair to take the country to war with Iraq, in a change of heart he decided Britain's ambition to spend about £50 billion on a high speed rail link

(HS2) between London and Birmingham would be another mistake and he warned his old party that its election chances would be damaged if the public believed that trade unions could "manipulate parliamentary selections" as had been alleged in Falkirk.[142, 143]

For all the critics and the enemies Mandelson may have encountered along his path the plain fact is that he has outlasted and outmanoeuvred them all. His voice is still heard when others, even the two Prime Ministers he helped, have fallen silent. Tony Blair's opinion in the Middle East carries little weight, his name blackened by the Iraqi war and Gordon Brown's very brief time in Downing Street is forgotten.

Whatever posts he fills in the future, Peter Mandelson will always be remembered for turning round the prospects of a political party, redefining the business of electioneering and for setting the standard – high or very low as one's opinion dictates – of spin-doctoring. He was the epitome of the modern day power behind the throne, even choosing the leader and then ensuring that once elected he remained secure. Mandelson was cleverer than the masters he served and has outlasted every one of his contemporaries. He was a manipulator par excellence and possibly even deserved his sobriquet as the Prince of Darkness but he is a survivor and as he himself declared not a quitter. His story is not over yet, his calls will always be taken by the great and possibly even not so good around the world which makes him both interesting and dangerous but Peter Mandelson still has more cards to play.

24

FR GEORG GÄNSWEIN (b. 1956)

Somehow it seems appropriate to move from the so-called Prince of Darkness to a story about the Vicar of Christ and in particular the man who stood faithfully by his side. It is also appropriate in the modern world of internet fame to see how that man was idolised and compared to a movie star and an icon, nicknamed "Bel Giorgio" by the Italian press looking perhaps for something good to say about a church rocked by scandal.

Fr Georg was not a shadow player in the classic sense. He did not negotiate behind the scenes either for or against his master but he was without question Pope Benedict's shadow – at times they even seemed to cast the same shadow – and definitely his protector. If he did not influence Benedict he was obviously a sounding board and no doubt one of the first to hear that he was about to break a 600 year old tradition and retire, making way he hoped for a younger, fitter man having confided in a friend that "God told me to do it". For once it was a real global news story which had not been leaked and genuinely caught everyone by surprise. Fr. Federico Lombardi, head of the Vatican Press Office, said even the Pope's closest aides had no inkling of his decision and were left "incredulous".

According to the Vatican's statistical yearbook, *Annuarium Statisticum Ecclesiae*, the Roman Catholic population is rising – up from 1,196 million to 1,214 million in 2011 or 17.5% of the world's population. It is therefore right to look briefly at the man who stood closest to the leader of so many people and who one day may have aspirations to lead them himself.

Like Benedict XVI, Fr Georg is German, from Riedem am Wald in the Black Forest. He was born on 30 July 1956 the son of a blacksmith, He became a postman, a fan of the pop group Pink Floyd and had a tendency to grow his hair long. There was nothing about his humble background and modern outlook which suggested the religious life that lay ahead. But by the time he was 18 he knew that he wanted to become a priest.

Two years later he entered the International Seminary of Saint Pius X in Switzerland. The seminary, which itself had a reputation for bucking the trend by following what it considered to be the traditional values and teaching of the church, was founded by the French Archbishop Marcel Lefebvre. He fell out with Pope John Paul II over his opposition to changes announced in the Second Vatican Council and defied the Pope in 1988 by consecrating four bishops resulting in their excommunication from the Roman Catholic Church. Fr Georg however was loyal to Rome and was ordained in 1984 aged 28 becoming a curate in his local church.

But he was ambitious and although he was conscientious about his studies he said later that this early period was rather dull: "After half a year I was so fed up I said to myself, now I'm going to the archbishop and ask him to take me back into the diocese because I can't stand it anymore," adding later in the interview, "I'd always studied gladly and easily, but studying canon law I felt to be as dry as work in a quarry where there's no beer – you die of dryness." This was no life for a young man who plays tennis, paid his way through college as a ski instructor and earned his wings with a private pilot's licence.

Having obtained his degree in canon law from Ludwig Maximilian's University of Munich he went to Rome in 1995 and a year later was invited by Cardinal Joseph Ratzinger to join the Congregation for the Doctrine of Faith. He was then made a professor of canon law at the Pontifical University of the Holy Cross, which is run by the ultra conservative Opus Dei, although he is not a member. Fr Georg was following an academic path and working for the man known as Pope John Paul's Rottweiler, therefore very much "on message". Along the way he became fluent in Italian, Spanish and Latin as well as his native German – he was always going to be a communicator. The Congregation for the Doctrine of the Faith used to be known as the Supreme Sacred Congregation of the Roman and Universal Inquisition from where the Holy Inquisition came, so Fr Georg was not going to rock the boat. In fact in 2000 he was elevated to Chaplain of His Holiness by John Paul and became Ratzinger's personal secretary three years later.

Fr Georg Gänswein (b. 1956)

Until 2005 when Ratzinger was elected Pope taking the name Benedict XVI, Fr Georg had remained in the background, handling Ratzinger's daily paperwork as any secretary would do. All that changed on 19 April when he became principal private secretary to the new pope, succeeding Don Stanislaw Dziwisz who had become an increasingly powerful figure preventing only the most essential audiences as John Paul's health failed him. Two things in particular would never be the same for Fr Georg: he was now thrown into the wheeling and dealing of Vatican life with all its intrigues and he was suddenly noticed by the media. Who was this good looking man who was never more than a pace away from the Pope's side? Even *Avvenire*, published by the conservative Italian Episcopal Conference, seemed more interested in his physical appearance than any other credential describing him as "... blond, 1m 80cm tall, athletic body and distinctly good looking man." In no time he acquired his nickname and was compared to the film stars Hugh Grant and George Clooney, while his devoted fans created a personalised website in his name giving his life history, recording his climb to the top in the Vatican hierarchy and a photo album to record his every move. On his own admission he said he had even received love letters from some of his more passionate admirers and had experienced "clerical envy" from his fellow priests.

In 2006 his stardom was only enhanced further when he was made bishop – the vestments seemed to suit him better than any other cleric. In January 2007 the Italian fashion designer, Donatella Versace, launched a collection which she called the 'Clergyman Collection' saying she used Fr Georg as her inspiration, "I was thinking of an austere, severe and ethical man. I find Father Georg's austerity very elegant." A few years later his photograph appeared on the front cover of the Italian edition of *Vanity Fair* magazine and neither Fr Georg nor the Vatican were consulted but stars belong to their public and Fr Georg was a star. Wherever the pope travelled whether by Pope-mobile, train or plane, Fr Georg was at his side smiling beatifically, straightening flapping clothing, handing him his reading glasses or quietly briefing presumably in German about what would be happening next. Benedict by contrast had an image problem – he was regarded as a tough no nonsense preserver of the status quo in church doctrine, his accent was guttural and even his smile looked threatening. Fr Georg was the complete opposite and seemed to provide the user-friendly face of the Vatican harking back to the old charisma of the late John Paul. It was Fr Georg who handed the babies up to Benedict for a Pontifical kiss and even wrote a book about their global travels together called *Benedict XVI – Urbi et Orbi: With the Pope in Rome and travelling the World.*

The question was what did he actually do? He told the writer, Peter Seewald, that the handover from his predecessor had been short: "Fr. Stanislaw handed me an envelope which contained some letters and the key to a safe, a very old German safe; you have a very important and beautiful but also incredibly difficult task ahead of you. All I can say to you is that the Pope must not be crushed by anything or anyone; you will have to work out for yourself how to achieve this." His aim he once said was to be as transparent as glass so as not to obscure the Pope in any way.[144]

Fr Georg gave some insight into his duties by describing the Pope's normal routine: "The Pope's day begins with mass at 7am, followed by morning prayer and a period of contemplation. Afterwards we eat breakfast together, and my day then begins with sorting through the correspondence, which arrives in considerable quantity." He said that he accompanied Benedict to morning audiences, followed by lunch together, a short walk, and a rest, after which he "[presents] to the Pope documents which require his signature, or his study and approval."[145]

In fact it was precisely this paperwork which was to present Fr Georg with his greatest challenge as it directly impacted his office.

The so called Vatileaks Scandal involved the leaking of documents including private correspondence with Pope Benedict uncovering alleged blackmail of homosexual priests, corruption and bribery. The story broke in January 2012 with the broadcast on Italian television of a programme called 'The Untouchables'. Over the following months more private correspondence appeared in the press alleging money laundering scams, power struggles inside the Vatican and even a death threat against the Pope. It came to a head when the journalist, Gianluigi Nuzzi, published a book called *His Holiness: The Secret Papers of Benedict XVI* containing private correspondence from the Pope. According to Nuzzi's account the Vatican was a hotbed of jealousy and infighting. Perhaps some saw it as a chance to fight back against the Germanification of the Vatican, so long the preserve of Italy's finest.

The press went to town not least because of the Vatican's desire to avoid making any comments. One insider broke cover, Cardinal Tarcisio Bertone, the Pope's Secretary of State, who said publicly that the leaks were "carefully aimed, and sometimes also ferocious, destructive and organised." It was assumed he meant they were carefully aimed at him and possibly Fr Georg by others in the Curia (in effect the Pope's Cabinet or court). The Curia it is said preferred other candidates to succeed Benedict such as Angelo Scola, the Cardinal of Milan.

Fr Georg Gänswein (b. 1956)

The suggestion was that there was jealousy if not anger when Bertone, an inexperienced diplomat, had taken over as Secretary of State from Cardinal Angelo Sodano. Bertone had been Ratzinger's number two in the Congregation for the Doctrine of the Faith. It was a battle between the diplomatists and the clerics, the liberals and the traditionalists. Benedict was a traditionalist and said Bertone brought "pastoral care and doctrinal wisdom" to the job. As for Fr Georg, the leaks which included letters signed by him were clearly intended to persuade Benedict to get rid of his personal secretary. If anything it had the opposite effect.

The man accused of leaking the documents in the first place was the pope's own butler, Paolo Gabriele. He admitted the offence and was sentenced by a Vatican Tribunal to 18 months to be served inside the Vatican's police barracks. In the end Benedict personally visited him in his cell in December 2012 to say he had pardoned him for the theft. The conspiracy theorists said Gabriele was a scapegoat and that there was a mole inside the Vatican; if there was so far none has been unearthed.

No hint of scandal or blame for failing to keep control of the papers stuck to Fr Georg even though behind the scenes the knives had long been out for the German mafia said to be trampling all over the preserve of the Vatican old guard. There was also no love lost between those who sought access to the Pope and his gatekeeper, who clearly saw it as his duty to protect his now ailing master. He once told a German paper, *Süddeutsche Zeitung*, that he spent too much time trying to handle endless requests for an audience with the Pope with people saying, "Only a minute ... an exception just this once ... The pope has known me for years, he'd be glad of it." Every refusal made Fr Georg another enemy.

The atmosphere around the Papal apartments must have been poisonous. Fr Georg noticed it at once and candidly told the media, "The Vatican is like a court and so like in any court, rumours and gossip exist here too. But here this is also a conscious shooting of arrows aimed at very specific targets. At first I had to learn to deal with this."

He had to manage the rift which arose between the Italian Prime Minister Silvio Berlusconi and the editor of *Avvenire* which had been outspoken about the premier's apparent liking for teenage girls. It wasn't a scrap the Vatican wanted to get into and Fr Georg manage to keep Benedict out of the argument.

In November 2011 it was reported that a publishing company, Weltbild, owned by the Catholic Church in Germany had 2,500 erotic titles among its publications. Fr Georg was the one who issued a memo – part of the Vatileaks – saying the Holy Father wanted to deal with the matter immediately.[146] This memo combined with a host of letters from priests addressed not to the Pope but to Fr Georg only served to emphasise the power Fr Georg seemed to wield.

It might have been possible for the closest observers of Vatican history to spot that something was about to happen when on 6 January 2013 Fr Georg, now Prefect of the Papal Household, was elevated to Archbishop. Normally pontiffs make these sort of appointments to those in their private office shortly before their deaths as they realise that they are beginning to fade. Benedict was an elderly man, now 86, and had been one of the oldest Pontiffs when he was elected, but his eyesight and hearing were failing him. He may even have confided in Fr Georg that he was finding it hard to cope with the pressures including the sex abuse cases among the clergy which were crowding in around him. Fr Georg would have remembered his predecessor's advice about protecting his charge.

The following month the Vatican announced that Pope Benedict was abdicating, the first pope to do so since Gregory XII in 1415. In a statement he said: "After having repeatedly examined my conscience before God, I have come to the certainty that my strengths, due to an advanced age, are no longer suited to an adequate exercise of the Petrine ministry."

Those with an interest in the shadow men of history wondered what would happen to his right hand man. The answer in part came when the newly elected Pope Francis appeared on the balcony over St Peter's Square to bless his faithful – just in the background behind Francis's right shoulder was the smiling face of Archbishop Gänswein.

As Prefect of the Papal Household he was in a special position not only was it his duty to show the new pope the ropes but he also had the unique responsibility of private secretary to a pope in retirement. He was said to have been in tears when he and Benedict had left the papal apartments for the last time and to have been on hand to help push open the doors for Pope Francis on his arrival.

There has been no-one in history who has fulfilled a similar role acting as the messenger between two popes carrying the wisdom and experience of the Pope-Emeritus to his successor. He has been photographed walking with Benedict in the grounds of his new home at the Mater Ecclesiae monastery in the Vatican saying the rosary but he also has to carry out his duties running the Pontificalis Domus, the Papal Household. That means organising the diary, audiences and papal visits but also sharing the secrets that can only pass between Popes.

Among those secrets are the findings of the Vatican inquiries into the Vatileaks, a secret dossier, two red hardback tomes which are for the Pope's eyes only prepared by the three investigating cardinals Julián Herranz, Josef Tomko, and Salvatore De Giorgi. According to *La Repubblica* the findings identify a powerful "homosexual underground" in the Curia and in the universal Church. It may just have been too much for Benedict.

Fr Georg knows a lot of secrets and he will always protect the men he serves; the coat of arms he adopted on becoming Archbishop shows St George on the right side and Benedict's coat of arms on the left. The question is what should be done with the man? Is he content to serve a quiet life serving Benedict or does he have other and greater ambitions?

The Vatican watchers say there are three choices: one, he gets another post in Rome, two, he is sent back to Germany as head of his own archdiocese or three, he gets a diplomat role as papal nuncio in a prestigious city. Pope Francis might prefer to keep "Don Giorgio" closer to hand possibly even installing him as prefect of one of the nine congregations in the Curia. His critics say his is determined to go all the way – a cardinal's hat will surely follow and then the Pontificate itself may beckon.

In classic style for a shadow player he has served two masters and for a time at least he has managed to serve them both simultaneously. Archbishop Georg Gänswein is an intellectual which is why Pope Benedict appointed him in the first place as well as being a traditionalist. There is no doubt he will continue to serve the man with whom he shares a coat of arms but he is also relatively young in terms of the clerical hierarchy and unless he has made too many enemies he should rise further in the Church establishment.

Pope Francis made it clear that he would make sweeping changes but he would also need a loyal man by his side as even Popes can make mistakes. One of his first appointments was Monsignor Battista Ricca who was supposed to be his point man in the clean-up of the Vatican Bank, more correctly the Institute for Works of Religion. Unfortunately in July 2013 a story broke in *L'Espresso* news magazine alleging that Ricca, a career Vatican diplomat, had had an affair with a Swiss Army Captain during his posting to Montevideo, Uruguay and established an "intolerable ménage" with him.

Problems at the bank are legendary and seemed to keep coming. The greatest scandal was the discovery of Roberto Calvi – God's Banker – hanging from Blackfriars Bridge in London in June 1982. Calvi was chairman of the Banco Ambrosiano whose majority shareholder was the Vatican and it was suggested that the Mafia might have been using the bank for money laundering or that the Masonic Lodge, P2 (Propaganda Due) may been involved. Nothing was ever proved.

No sooner had Francis declared that an independent, no clerical banker, Ernst von Freyberg, would conduct a wide ranging investigation into the bank's activities then a new scandal broke. Nunzio Scarano, a priest working as an accountant in the Vatican, was arrested on charges of money laundering and illegally trying to bring €20 million in cash into Italy from Switzerland on a private jet. Then without explanation the director of the bank, Paolo Cipriani, and his deputy, Massimo Tulli, resigned.[147]

Pope Francis must have known what he was up against or was very quickly brought up to speed by Fr Georg. In June 2013 a transcript of his comments made to a gathering of the Latin American and Caribbean Confederation of Religious Men and Women was leaked to a the Chilean website Reflexión y Liberación (Reflection and Liberation) revealing his understanding and approach to the challenges he faced. First he made it clear to his audience in a frank exchange that he knew that there would have to be a shake-up – "dar vuelta (a) la tortilla" (flip the tortilla). He was also blunt about corruption and homosexuality: "In the Curia, there are also holy people, really, there are holy people. But there also is a stream of corruption, there is that as well, it is true... The 'gay lobby' is mentioned, and it is true, it is there... We need to see what we can do."

At the time of writing Archbishop Georg Gänswein continues in his dual capacity as personal private secretary to a pope in retirement and Prefect of the Papal Household to his successor. Benedict declared that he was now just "a pilgrim" like everyone else and would pursue a life of solitary prayer. The issue for some was would Pope Francis be forever looking over his shoulder or wondering how much information was leaking back to his predecessor. The Vatican spokesman, Fr Federico Lombardi, a fellow Jesuit like Francis, said the prefect's job was technical and was effectively limited to organising the Pope's audiences adding "In this sense it is not a very profound problem."

As we noted at the start of this chapter, there has never been a position at least in the past 600 years as the post held by the Archbishop from Riedem am Wald. No-one has ever served two Popes simultaneously. The Gänswein website will make interesting reading in the months and years ahead.

NOTES

(Endnotes)

1   Illyria was a region in the Western Balkans
2   Desmosthenes (384–322 BC) was a Greek statesman and orator
3   www.livius.org
4   www.livius.org
5   *Secret History* by Procopius of Caesarea b.AD 500
6   Monophysitism declares that divinity and humanity are united in the one person of Jesus Christ
7   Followers who accept the teaching of the Council of Chalcedon regarding the divine and human nature of Jesus Christ.
8   *Women in World History*
9   Before the rise of Genghis Khan the Kereyid were the most powerful of the Mongolian peoples. They converted to Christianity in the 11th century
10 *Secret History of the Mongols* – the oldest surviving Mongolian language work written by an anonymous author after Genghis Khan's death
11 According to *The Secret History of the Mongols* when Tolui's father, Ogodei, fell ill the shamans in the tribe said a member of his family had to be sacrificed to save him. He immediately began to recover when Tolui offered to take the poisoned drink. However it is generally thought he drank himself to death.
12 Bar Hebraeus, Syriac scholar(1226–1286)
13 *Genghis Khan and the making of the modern world*, by Jack Weatherford (Three Rovers Press, 2004)
14 *Daily Life in The Mongol Empire* by George Lane (Hackett Publishing Co., 2009)
15 Nestorian Christians believe that Christ had two loosely-united natures, divine and human it was a doctrine advanced by Nestorius, Patriarch of Constantinople and later condemned as heretical at the First Council of Ephesus in 431.
16 The historian Morris Rossabi described Rashid al-Din as being "arguably the most distinguished figure in Persia during Mongolian rule". His grandfather had been a courtier to Hulagu Khan
17 Sorghaghtani was buried in a Christian church in Gansu
18 *The Mongols* by David Morgan (Blackwell Publishing, 2007)
19 The fifteenth century Muslim historian al-Maqrizi
20 The island was of great significance. Mamluk means 'of the seat' and the seat referred to was the castle on the island.

21 The fifteenth century Muslim historian al-Maqrizi
22 Half sister of Thomas Grey whose sons were tutored by Wolsey
23 Recognising the importance of the Spanish kingdom, Henry VII as part of the Treaty of Medina del Campo in 1498 arranged for his son Arthur Tudor to marry Catherine
24 *The Six Wives of Henry VIII* by Alison Weir (New York: Ballantine Books, 1993)
25 George Cavendish (1494–c.1562) biographer, wrote: *Thomas Wolsey, Late Cardinall, his Lyffe and Deathe*
26 Attributed to various artists including Hans Holbein but probably the work of several painters c.1550
27 www.tudors.org
28 The Old Testament forbade a man from marrying the wife of his brother – Leviticus 20:21
29 *Henry VIII* by Lucy Wooding (Routledge Historical Biographies, 2008)
30 Wilton was a Benedictine convent and held an entire barony from the king, a singular privilege enjoyed by only three others. The convent closed in 1539 with the Dissolution of the Monasteries. The last Abbess, Cecily Bodenham by all accounts didn't put up much of a fight as she was awarded a handsome pension of one hundred pounds a year and a property to retire to gracefully with some of her nuns. One nun recorded in her diary: *Methinks the Abbess hath a faint heart and doth yield up our possessions to the spoiler with a not unwilling haste.*
31 www.tudorplace.com
32 *Notable Mughal and Hindu women in the 16th and 17th centuries A.D*, by Renuka Nath (South Asia Books, 1990)
33 Muslim Rule In India
34 *Mediaeval India under Mohammedan Rule 712-1764* by Stanley Lane-Poole (G.P. Putnam's Sons, 1903)
35 http://www.vimlapatil.com
36 *Queen, Empress, Concubine: Fifty Women Rulers from Cleopatra to Catherine the Great* by Claudia Gold (Quercus, 2008).
37 *Grey Eminence* by Aldous Huxley (Chatto & Windus, 1941)
38 Ibid
39 *Histoire du Cardinal de Richelieu* by Gabriel Hanotaux (Societe de l'histoire nationale, Librairie Plon, 1944–47)
40 *Grey Eminence* by Aldous Huxley (Chatto & Windus, 1941)
41 *Mistresses: A History of the Other Woman*, by Elizabeth Abbott (Clearway, 2011)
42 Religious institutes of the Roman Catholic Church whose patron was the medieval saint, St. Ursula
43 http://www.nationalgallery.org.uk
44 Thomas Carlyle (1795–1881) Scottish historian, essayist and satirical writer
45 http://francishodgson.com
46 On 29 March 1804 the convent of the Capuchin Friars was destroyed to make room for the construction of the 'Rue de la Paix'. The remains of Madame de Pompadour were taken to the catacombs of Paris which are reserved for the Capuchin Friars and were mixed with thousands of other unmarked bones
47 Simone Weil, the French philosopher, wrote that his alleged disloyalty was unfounded because Talleyrand served not every regime but "France behind every regime." (*The Need for Roots*, Routledge, 2001)
48 *Talleyrand* by Duff Cooper (Jonathan Cape, 1932)
49 Ibid
50 This is a combination of two Manchurian tribes: Yeho and Nala
51 *The Last Empress*, by Daniele Vare (Doubleday, 1936)
52 A political and religious revolt which broke out across 17 provinces and cost some 20 million lives

Notes

53 A revolt in the eastern and central provinces of Shandong, Henan, Jiangsu and Anhui.

54 *The Origins of the Boxer Uprising* by Joseph Esherick (University of California Press, 1987)

55 Initially the British contingent was led by Colonel Wahab Lt. Colonel Abud of the Bombay Political Service, later replaced by Fitzmaurice

56 *Aden Under British Rule: 1839-1967* by R.J.Gavin (C. Hurst & Co., 1975)

57 Crypto-Judaism is the secret adherence to Judaism while publicly professing to be of another faith

58 *The Balfour Declaration* by Jonathan Schneer (Bloomsbury, 2010)

59 Ibid

60 Sir William Reginald Hall's autobiography, Churchill Archives Centre, Cambridge. Hall was Director of Naval Intelligence

61 *The Balfour Declaration* by Jonathan Schneer (Bloomsbury, 2010)

62 *The Times* 30ᵗʰ March 1939

63 *Stalin. The Court of the Red Tsar* by Simon Sebag Montefiore (Vintage, 2005)

64 Maria Svanidze was married to Alyosha Svanidze, brother of Stalin's first wife, Kato

65 *Stalin. The Court of the Red Tsar* by Simon Sebag Montefiore (Vintage, 2005)

66 *One Who Survived* by Alexander Barmine (GP Putnam, New York, 1945)

67 'On the Cult of the Individual and Its Consequences' by N.S. Krushchev, speech delivered to 20th congress of the Communist Party, 1956

68 Bukharin was Politburo member who initially supported Stalin but became one of the prominent victims of the so called Moscow Trials of people accused of plotting against Stalin

69 *Stalin. The Court of the Red Tsar* by Simon Sebag Montefiore (Vintage, 2005)

70 Feme or Femegerichte was the name given to a form of vigilantism practiced during the Middle Ages

71 Nationalsozialistiche Deutsche Arbeiterpartei

72 *Leaders of the SS and German Police* by Michael Miller (James Bender Publishing, 2007)

73 Martin Bormann – Jewish Virtual Library

74 *Martin Bormann – The Face of the Third Reich* by Joaquim Fest (Penguin, 1992)

75 *Counselor: A Life at the Edge of History* by Ted Sorensen (Harper Collins, 2008)

76 *Lament for the Death of Eoghan Ruadh O'Neill*, poem by Thomas Davis

77 *The Kennedy Men* by Laurence Learner (William Morrow & Co., 2002)

78 Bay of Pigs Invasion was an unsuccessful attempt by CIA backed brigade to invade Cuba on 17ᵗʰ April 1961.

79 Chris Smith, *New York Magazine* 1ˢᵗ November 2010

80 Ibid

81 Ibid

82 Trafficante was arrested several times but charges were always dropped and he never served any time in prison. He along with other mobsters were implicated in the assassination of President Kennedy but nothing was ever proved. He died of ill health aged 72 in 1987.

83 A U.S. Senate committee chaired by Senator Frank Church which investigated intelligence gathering by the CIA, the FBI and the National Security Agency.

84 *Next to Hughes* by Robert Maheu (Harper Collins, 1993)

85 *Las Vegas Sun*, Ed Koch 6ᵗʰ August 2008

86 Dominions originally referred to any land in possession of the British Empire

87 This affair is said to mark the start of the Cold War

88 *Alaska Highway* by Kenneth Coates (UBC Press, 2011)

89 *Constant Surprise* by Malcolm MacDonald (unpublished autobiography)

90 Ibid

91 Ibid

92 *Straits Times*, 19ᵗʰ August 1955

93 MacDonald opposed Anthony Eden's policy on the Suez Canal and offered his resignation after the attack.

94 Papers released by The US Department of State Office of the Historian
95 The Mau Mau Uprising was a military conflict between the Kikuyu and anti-colonial supporters (dubbed Mau Mau) and the British Army and anti-Mau Mau Kikuyu tribesmen lasting from 1952–1960. It cost the lives of thousands and in 2013 the British Government agreed to pay compensation of £20 million to Kenyans who had been tortured by British Colonial forces.
96 MacDonald Papers, Durham University
97 *Malcolm MacDonald: Bringing an End to Empire* by Clyde Sanger (McGill- Queen's Press, 1995)
98 The Memoirs of Retired General Hossein Fardoust
99 *The Life and Activities of General Hussein Fardoust* has been published by the Islamic Revolution Document Center compiled by Mostafa Javan.
100 *Bearing the Cross* by David Garrow (Morrow, 2004)
101 Ibid
102 *Killing the Dream* by Gerald Posner (New York: Random House, 1998)
103 *The Good Life* by Charles Colson (Tyndale House, 2005)
104 *The Independent* 24th April 2012
105 *Charles Colson – How a Watergate Crook Became America's Greatest Christian Conservative* article by David Plotz
106 *Nixonland: The Rise of a President and the Fracturing of America* by Rick Perlstein (Simon and Schuster 2008)
107 *The Good Life* by Charles Colson (Tyndale House, 2005)
108 *The Ends of Power* by H.R. Haldeman with Joseph DiMona (Dell Publishing, 1978)
109 *Time Magazine* 24th September 1973
110 Transcript: Deep Throat Revealed by Ben Bradlee, *The Washington Post,* 2nd June 2005
111 *Born Again: What Really Happened to the White House Hatchet Man* by Charles Colson (Spire Books, 1977)
112 *Time Magazine* 27th February 1978
113 Ba'athism is a mix of Arab nationalism and Arab socialism.
114 The Non-Aligned Movement was a group of nations not with or against any of the major power blocs, East or West. It was launched in Belgrade in 1961 by India's Prime Minister Jawaharlal Nehru.
115 Frontline
116 Ted Koppel, ABC Nightline 9th June 1992
117 The name was taken from the eighth chapter of the Qur'an Sura Al-Anfal meaning Spoils of War
118 Human Rights Watch
119 Frontline
120 Martin Chulov, *The Guardian* 5th August 2010
121 BBC, David Willey 14th February 2003
122 *USA Today* 3rd May 2003
123 Martin Chulov, *The Guardian* 5th August 2010
124 *Parachuting into Poland, 1944: Memoir of a Secret Mission with Jozef Retinger* by Marek Celt (McFarland & Co Inc, 2013)
125 *Memoirs of an Eminence Grise* by Joseph Ratinger (Sussex University Press,1972)
126 Who was Józef Hieronim Retinger? *by Jan Chciuk-Celt* (internet article, 2013)
127 Who Pulls the Strings? by Jon Ronson, *The Guardian* (2001)
128 Who was Józef Hieronim Retinger? *by Jan Chciuk-Celt* (internet article, 2013)
129 BBC, 10th June 2013
130 *The Balfour Declaration* by Jonathan Schneer (Random House, 2010)
131 James Clarity, *New York Times* 1st September 1994

Notes

132 *The Guardian*, 2009
133 George Mitchell, Washington 22nd January 2009
134 Hamas is an Islamist political group with its own military wing although it claims most of its activity is taken up with providing social services.
135 *The Guardian*, 2009
136 The Iran-Contra affair was a political scandal involving the secret sales of arms to Iran breaking an arms embargo and then using the funds to back the Nicaraguan Contras in breach of another Congressional order.
137 Andrew Rawnsley, *The Guardian* 1st March 2009
138 Edward Docx, *Daily Mail* 1st august 2009
139 George Pascoe-Watson, *The Sun*
140 Murray Wardrop, *Daily Telegraph* 22 Jul 2009
141 BBC, 10th August 2009
142 Patrick Wintour, *The Guardian* 27th June 2013
143 An internal Labour report alleged that the Unite Union was trying to affect the selection of the Labour candidate for Falkirk by signing up Unite members to the local party without their knowledge.
144 *La Stampa*, 17th March 2013
145 Richard Owen, *The Times*, 16th January 2007
146 *Die Welt*, November 2011
147 *Daily Telegraph* 22nd July 2013

WOMAN
ACCEPTABLE EXPLOITATION
FOR PROFIT

SHREELA FLATHER

ISBN 978-184995-002-2 hardback £16.99

'...has the potential of becoming a global movement. I am re-reading the
book and sharing my knowledge with my friends
… *Ladi Dariya, Commonwealth*

This thought-provoking and challenging book is about sex and profits. It
not another call for charitable donations, but a book about investment and
income generation. Shreela Flather cogently and powerfully argues that
women must be central to every initiative, business project and political goal
rather than being merely after-thoughts or decoration.

Woman – Acceptable Exploitation for Profit is a solution for a world in
trouble, a roadmap to greater opportunities, profit, prosperity, health and
happiness for all, regardless of gender.